Peter Johnson

67 + before

77 ... "C 2"

87   praised Brandt

89   Ulbr.

90   reparations

91   D'victor in Wales

150   anti-Nazis

106   unique & barbarous

114   children not responsible

146   todays maj. not guilty

182   pro-Europe

WOTAN, MY ENEMY

And the migration of my parents has not subsided in me.
My blood goes on sloshing between my ribs
Long after the vessel has come to rest.
And the migration of my parents has not subsided in me.

Yehuda Amichai
(*translated from the Hebrew by Barbara and Benjamin Harshav*)

WOTAN, MY ENEMY

Can Britain live with the Germans in the European Union?

Leo Abse

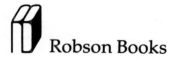

Robson Books

First published in Great Britain in 1994 by Robson Books Ltd,
Bolsover House, 5–6 Clipstone Street, London W1P 7EB

British Library Cataloguing in Publication Data
A catalogue record for this title is available from the British Library

ISBN 0 86051 910 4

Printed in Great Britain by Butler & Tanner Ltd.,
Frome and London.

TO MY CELTIC-SEMITIC CHILDREN, TOBIAS AND BATHSHEBA,
AND TO MARJORIE,
WITH LOVE

Contents

Acknowledgements

Yet again, I wish to acknowledge my debt to the electors of the Eastern Valley of Gwent who, for thirty years, gave me the opportunity to gain the political presumptuousness to write a work such as *Wotan*.

I am indebted to my psychoanalyst brother Dr Wilfred Abse, Emeritus Professor of Psychiatry of the University of Virginia, who read a first draft of Part V of this book and suggested emendations; responsibility for the final content of this section is, of course, mine. I would wish also to thank both Dr Malcolm Pines of The Group-Analytic Practice and Brett Kahr of Regent's College for having drawn my attention to helpful and relevant literature which otherwise would have escaped my attention, and I am grateful to Dr Richard Dove of Greenwich University for his assistance in translating Ernst Toller's *Wotan*.

My amanuensis, Frances Hawkins, has given me unstinting and invaluable assistance in preparing the book for publication. Paul Cavadino assisted me in its format, Jane Mallinson patiently typed the early drafts of some sections, and Jill Duncan, librarian at the Institute of Psycho-Analysis, has been unfailingly helpful. To each of them I give my thanks.

Author's Preface

Suddenly Western Europe is in disarray: we have lost our enemy. The collapse of Soviet Communism has left us bereft. The insistent psychoanalytical view that, tragically, man uses and needs enemies as external stabilisers of his sense of identity and inner control is now painfully corroborated.

During the Cold War we attempted to cast out our demons. Each man, as each nation, has inner good and bad selves, and part of the development from childhood to a mature adulthood is the achievement of an acceptance and an integration of both our selves. But for decades we have cheated. Our wickedness was dumped upon the Soviet Union. We denied our own evil; the evil Empire was elsewhere. In our international politics we used the selfsame psychic defence mechanisms to maintain our poise as is deployed by babes and struggling adolescents; by externalisation we tried to rid ourselves of internal unpleasant and threatening feelings, by projection we attributed our unacceptable thoughts to the enemy, and by displacement we invested our own feared self-destructive hate in the leaders of the Soviet Union. We unloaded our own anguishes upon an enemy whose provocations and military strength enabled us to affect that all our responses were reality-based, uncontaminated by our own pathology.

But now the game is up; the self-deception cannot continue. Western Europe can no longer depend upon the enemy to ensure its cohesion; the uncertainties and turbulence within Yeltsin's Russia, although disquieting, leave the threat of a strong Fascist Russia too remote to bind us together. We know that, fundamentally, lacking any powerful enemy, we are on our own; now we must pass through the rite of passage to more adult political stances, compelled to shift much of our attention away from the lands once behind the Iron Curtain to which we had exported our irresolutions, and embark upon the much more painful exercises of self-scrutiny, and scrutinies of fellow-members of the Community. The glue which the Soviet Union provided to ensure our adhesion dissolves. Our compatibility with our neighbours has therefore to be questioned and tested anew. Whatever partial alliances may be formed, we know that no genuine European Union can come into existence unless Britain can live happily, if at all, with its tentative partners. With many of these partners, like France and Italy, we shall have our quarrels; agricultural issues, airline disputes, steel subsidies, all can set alight old prejudices, but these are, at most, serious vexations. Our concerns, however, over Germany are of such a different order that we are now compelled to ask the question whether Britain can live within the European Community with a Germany no longer clinging to allies out of fear of the Eastern threat.

This essay addresses that question. It does not presume to give a definitive answer, for there can be no apodictic certainty that the marriage, as distinct from the present engagement, will take place or that, if it does, it will not break down. Underneath all the agonising in Britain over our entry into the Community lies a profound distrust and fear of Germany. The anti-German outbursts made by that inimitable Whig Nicholas Ridley, like those made by Tebbit and, in her memoirs, by Thatcher, have expressed more than a personal prejudice. After two world wars precipitated by Germany, and after the German descent into barbarism in this century, large swathes of British opinion look with suspicion at a country with a democracy perceived as parvenu and fragile, and possessed of the largest population and the greatest economic power in the Union; its domination is feared. That suspicion is not the only inhibition which tempers Euro-enthusiasm in Britain, but it is perhaps the most compulsive. Doomsday prophecies of the consequences of an off-shore Britain, and recitals of the overwhelming advantages for a Britain within the Community, leave many unmoved; stubbornly they suspect and continue to fear the Germans. No greater irony can be found in contemporary British politics than the attacks made upon the Maastricht Treaty by those fearful of this German domination; for the main impetus behind Maastricht was born out of Germans' fear of themselves and of continental fears of the consequences of the unification of Germany.

Are those fears, here and abroad, justified? And if they are, wholly or in part, can they be overcome? Almost overwhelmingly the debate so far has focused on the economic and institutional consequences of the proposed liaison; but in a marriage of nations, as of individuals, success is determined not only by financial considerations, nor even by some novel modifications of past habitudes which are the prerequisite of every joint adventure. More is required than is usually yielded by conventional politics: understanding of each other is needed, and hermeneutics unfortunately has increasingly deserted our politics. This book therefore is possessed by the conceit that those of us who wish to see a genuine common European citizenship come into existence, have to explore in depth the psychology of the Germans.

In our private lives we well know, as husbands or wives or as lovers, that intimacy and real attachments mature as, step by step – rarely in a blinding revelation – we gain insights to our partner's anxieties, aspirations, perplexities and dreams; and even as we may strive to unravel their anguish and sometimes add to their happiness, so, in the very process, we may disentangle our own problems, and free ourselves from many of our chains. To attempt to transfer and apply such delicate tasks to international relationships may appear to be a vanity, particularly to a relationship with the most problematic of European nations; but the goal is surely worthy of the effort.

Psychoanalytical findings may considerably help us in our exploration, but I doubt if the German psyche will be revealed to us only by attempting, in too reductionist a manner, to anatomise its manifestations; that is not how we reach out and understand our lovers, and nations will not be understood either if we only apply the scalpel and never the empathy. Such a cold clinical approach to the turbulent *Geist*, which the Germans themselves tell us envelops them, will not by itself necessarily bring us nearer to understanding its influences. A crystal may only be seen when it cracks; but the soul of a nation is not inanimate crystal but, like the individual psyche, is an organic whole which cannot be broken up without a withering of parts. German *Geist* is singularly elusive and can, I believe, escape the grasp of more conventional sociologists and historians. It may perhaps be more likely to be reached by a solitary who, ignoring the misleading signposts of many politicians and scientists, takes a circuitous route.

This essay, therefore, is a deliberately personal one: it is my autobiographical response to the country which more than any other has played the most disruptive role in the lives of my generation. It is necessarily discursive, telling of the German impingement on my boyhood, of my encounters and meetings with expelled *littérateurs* and educationists of the Weimar Republic, of my love affair with a German, of wartime experience in German-speaking lands, of my political involvement in the Commons on the German question, of meeting German politicians and the East German dictator, of the elucidations of German and other psychoanalysts, and of my distaste for the suspect German historians.

The telling of the tale, and the psychoanalytical interpretations which I place on events, will dismay some of those with whom, in rebellion against my party, I went into the lobby more than twenty years ago to vote for Britain's entry into Europe. They may believe such a work as this only adds to the armoury of the Euro-sceptics; but I believe that only when, unblinking, we abandon superficial sightings and peer into the depths of the German psyche shall we understand the Germans, and perhaps encourage them to understand themselves. The alternative is such misunderstanding between Britain and Germany that the European ideal could be shattered.

There are those who will demur. Those who take at their word the declarations of leading German politicians of all the major parties will protest that my attempted exercise is provocative and unnecessary. They are the optimists, full of goodwill, who do not understand the deep disparity in Germany between public acknowledgements of guilt and responsibility for recent events, and individual sentiment; they fail to appreciate, in their Euro-enthusiasm, that for too many in Germany the European idea is something of an alibi, strengthening a wilful amnesia about the past.

Fortunately there are many younger Germans who acknowledge and genuinely feel the burden of the past; these, above all Germans, need friends who do not pretend, in some travesty of the truth, that the past can be resolved in a kind of vague communality. They have need of friends who have a compassion for a people with so rich and so terrifying a history. I hope, therefore, that younger Germans will interpret this essay as an expression, not of hostility, but of friendship.

PART I

Beginnings

Despite the Germans

Despite the Germans, I was born. To my good fortune, some time in 1874, my maternal grandfather, Tobias, still in his teens, quit his birthplace, Simyatich, a small township in the Czar's Russian Poland, and arrived, penniless, in Swansea. With a pedlar's glazier pack on his back and in command of neither Welsh nor English, he walked up and down the Swansea Valley, past the burgeoning tinplate works, sleeping in stables or fields, replacing a broken pane here or there; and thus he survived. God, he believed, was good to him and he prayed regularly in Swansea's Goat Street synagogue which the small Jewish community had built in 1859. German bombs destroyed his synagogue in 1940. Two years later, on 2 November 1942, the Germans also destroyed his Simyatich. There, the sons and daughters of those relatives of mine to whom, as a lad, on my grandfather's directive, I had posted small remittances from the Cardiff GPO, were all murdered.

The 6,000 Jews in the township had been rounded up. There was resistance led by a distant relative of mine, Herschel Shabbas; inevitably it was brutally crushed. The men who survived, together with all the women and children, were put in trucks. The Germans had a simple logistic exercise. The crematorium of Treblinka was but 25 miles away; down to the last child, all were thrown into the gas chambers. Simyatich today is *Judenfrei*; the only Jews there lie in an ancient cemetery behind a grand rusting gate. One eighteenth-century synagogue, now a social centre, survives; it is no place for prayers.

Almost the same martyrdom was suffered by the township of Palanga in Lithuania where my paternal grandfather was born; there, too, all the Jews were extinguished, a task made easier for the Germans by the co-operation of Lithuanian death squads, some of whose members were later to flee to Britain to enjoy hospitality and freedom from prosecution. The 455 Jews living in Palanga were killed in two phases: first the Germans shot all the men, and then several months later they returned to slaughter the women and children. My grandfather, however, escaped the fate of his relatives since he also had come, as a young man, to South Wales, bringing with him as a bride a Jewess from Germany, the grandmother who, partly because of her

3

origin, was to become one of the significant figures within my
determining family constellation.

However, the Germans had not done with me; they made another
attempt to slay me before my birth. In the summer of 1916 my father
was serving with his regiment in northern France; while marching
through the little town of Albert, he collapsed. The doctors, probably
incorrectly, diagnosed a heart attack and he was without delay
hospitalised in Britain. Immediately visited at the hospital by my
mother, my ever sexually vigorous father, despite or because of his
condition, acted true to form: nine months later I was born. On the
day of my conception, 48 hours after my father's seizure, his regiment
was wiped out in the Battle of the Somme. The Germans were too late;
I was on my way.

But still they persisted. On E-deck, in 1942, well below the water-
line, with hundreds of others I was crammed on a troopship in a
convoy going around the Cape, bound for the Middle East. Each day
we went through the charade of boat drill; but we knew that if we were
struck, we would be drowned like trapped rats. The U-boat arrived,
and the blow was struck; it missed me, but hit the neighbouring ship
which went down with perhaps 500 young men. In my war, with my
head down, the Germans never had a second chance. Now I am 77,
and soon, therefore, I shall die my own death. Then it will be my body
that fatally assails me, not the Germans.

But only with my death will I rid myself of the Germans, for the
cadences within the languages spoken in the huge extended family of
my early childhood have meant that Germany, albeit sometimes
benignly, has continued to impinge upon me throughout my days; for
my boyhood, as with every man, remains in my adulthood. And in my
boyhood I had moved between two tribes, the one headed by my
belligerent atheistic grandmother, the other by my Talmudic maternal
grandfather; neither the matriarch nor the patriarch of the clans spoke
fluent English, even as they did not speak confidently the vernacular
Welsh that they had acquired. Each of their Cardiff households,
separated only by a few hundred yards, was in fact a different Babel: in
each, all communication was conducted in a jumble of languages,
never one spoken separately, but all telling of the wanderings of
ancestors, all reflecting temporary sojourns in other lands. There was
only one certain common link, and that was in that marvellous
language of fusion, Yiddish; it is an extraordinary admixture of
Hebrew, variants of the old spoken Latin, German, or Slav tongues,
and of the many dialects absorbed by a peripatetic people for, to

survive economically and politically, the Jews have been so frequently compelled to become a polylingual society. Although the Yiddish that I heard in each of the homes of my grandparents possessed differences that were far more than nuances, still in all the Yiddish spoken the vocabulary and syntax pointed to the cradle of the language: the cities of the Middle Rhine of the tenth century.

In my grandmother's domain, the German emphasis within the language, or added to it in an impromptu fashion, was more marked, for she was born in Königsberg, then in East Prussia and now Kaliningrad within the Russian republic. Her German, however, was impure, for her first language was Masurisch, the tongue now rapidly dying out but then spoken in the region; and it is unlikely that her German was improved by her father, a Lithuanian who came to East Prussia to act as steward on the estate of a German landowner. Since in my grandfather she had married a Jew from Lithuania whose languages were Lithuanian and Yiddish, it is unsurprising that her commitment to Germany lacked the vigour which was possessed by so many indigenous Jews of Germany; in pre-Hitler days their efforts at cultural camouflage, as they declared for what they unwisely believed was their fatherland, are notorious: the East Prussian Jews, xenophobic and ostentatious in their displays of allegiance, treated those whom they dubbed 'Eastern Jews' as alien intruders and, even when such Jews were professional men, some of the Prussian Jews forbade them entry into their homes. My grandmother's fealty to Germany was therefore tempered but, since she did not leave Königsberg until she was 26, all her reading was nevertheless to be in German.

As a little boy I was always fascinated by the unfamiliar script in the romances she was forever reading and I would sometimes see the same novels when I was sent to West Wales for my long summer holidays to join six cousins born to an aunt by marriage who hailed from Danzig; in their home the Low German, of what is now Polish Gdansk, prevailed, with much Welsh and a little English as the subsidiary languages. My pretty, pretentious aunt was ever comparing the style and amenities she had enjoyed in Danzig to those she claimed to endure in Wales, and, in her self-imposed insulation, remained ignorant of the rich cultural heritage of the Swansea valley. Later, as Hitler emerged and Danzig was enveloped, she fell silent, and the German novels were unread, but to me, as a boy, her chatter brought Danzig close. Indeed, I never felt Germany was a distant country. Königsberg and Danzig seemed then nearer to me than London, for no one I knew came from that foreign metropolis. However, I doubt if the

novels my grandmother continued to read until her death were much
more than extravagant escapist tales, for she had more than a touch of
the fantasist in her make-up, a quality she was to pass on to her sons;
when her quiet, controlling, managing husband, who had built up a
moderate fortune, died, she gave her sons full rein – and within a short
time, amidst passionate fratricidal quarrels which I observed and much
enjoyed, the money was squandered on fast cars and fast women, in
that order. When I finished secondary school there was no legacy for
me from my grandmother, other than an unsatisfied curiosity about
German literature. We were not at that time living in poverty but in
indebtedness, a very different, although decidedly debilitating, condition. In my early teens I was familiar not, as were many of my
schoolfriends, with probing public assistance means-testing officials,
but with bailiffs. It resulted in my not going on to university but, at
sixteen, to take up employment.

The kingdom of *Kultur*

Feeling keenly deprived of further education, I thus became an
impossible autodidact; my self-education was utterly unbalanced.
Unceasingly I was reading socialist literature: that became me, given
my age and the disadvantages that I and my South Wales were
experiencing. But almost all my other readings were selections from
German literature and, in particular, from the writers of the Weimar
Republic. I read little of the English classics. By the quirk within my
upbringing, I had been lured into intellectual territory innocent of the
hazards that awaited me. I had entered a Wagnerian land of
'overcoming', where symbol and imagination became the essence of
existence, where the goal was the transcendence of life and reality by
art and imagination, where history itself had become a wholly spiritual
product. I had not arrived in a land content to be merely civilised: this
was a country possessed by more ambitious yearnings. And, young and
foolish, I almost enlisted as a citizen of this state, the kingdom of
Kultur.

There were considerable dangers for an adolescent exposed to *Kultur*,
the impassioned German antithesis to *Zivilisation*. However untutored
and consequently undirected my exploration may have been, it was
sufficient to leave me scorched. I had no English university schooling
based on empiricism, rationalism and utility, on externality, which
could have shielded me against the fascinations of a German idealism

that mocked at the mundane, that claimed to be concerned with essence, not appearance; and I had been brought up within a Welsh idiom saturated with Celtic rhetoric, embellishment and fabulation, tractable to the extravagances of German *Kultur*. I was therefore no stranger to the enticements of myth-making. That so much of the German art and literature of the period lapsed into fantasy and narcissism was unobserved by a youth afflicted with his own adolescent strivings, easily tricked into evading reality by manic denial, as was the habitude of these Germans preaching that the material world could be overcome and transcended. And although I was at the same time reading Marx, that was no antidote. In some ways being thus introduced into the Hegelian dialectic, against which Marx was ambivalently forever struggling, was to entrap me still further. Happily, by nationality and race, I was barred from the illusion that Germany was the principal dynamic representative of the Hegelian world spirit, a metaphysical speculation which contributed so catastrophically to Germany's hubris and precipitated two world wars.

Denn am deutschen Wesen soll die Welt genesen – by the German soul the world will be made free – was doggerel that I found unappealing. And since my unguided survey inevitably led me to the incomparable Nietzsche – a far too heady brew for a raw seventeen-year-old – his piercing irony guaranteed that I would be alerted to some of the absurdities of the claims made for the German *Geist*. But there were other seductive elements within the ethos that found me vulnerable: the search for newness, the contempt for what was seen as the false values and results of bourgeois liberalism, the assaults by the German Dadaists and expressionists on the military, the Junkers and the industrialists, the lampoons and caricatures mocking and condemning the miserable politicians of the Reichstag who had helped to unleash the First World War and betrayed the attempted post-war revolution of the proletariat. All of these proclamations found a resonance in a politically precocious youth, miserable in his factory employment, witnessing in the poverty and desperate grim unemployment of the South Wales of the thirties, the failure of British capitalism, a failure which brought the same deprivations as were being endured by the 7½ million jobless in Germany.

And since so many of the German artists and intellectuals had issued their inspirational millenarian manifestoes supporting the 1919 revolution, and by word, and often by brave deed, had joined in the efforts to establish *Räte Republiken* – socialist republics of workers' and soldiers' councils – in Bremen and Munich, and had also played a notable part in overcoming the *Putsch* designed to wipe out the Weimar Republic, it was not difficult to believe that German *Kultur* was a bulwark against, and not a buttress of, what Thomas Mann was then labelling the 'mystical Philistinism' of 'Aryan radicalism'. Certainly it would have been uncongenial to me to have acknowledged what was the unbelievable fact: that 'mystical Philistinism', despite all the trench war slaughter and the German retreat in the autumn of 1918, had maintained the morale of the German armies even as it was to sustain them right to the bitter conclusion of 1945. It was preferable to assert that the growth of Nazism was an aberration, that the modest naval mutinies at Wilhelmstraven and Kiel, like the uprisings in Bremen and Munich, and the short-lived workers' and soldiers' councils in Brunswick and Düsseldorf, expressed the true spirit of Germany.

Indeed, for many years after Hitler became Germany's Chancellor, when I was sixteen, I continued to resist the obvious: that he was the genuine preferred choice of the German people. The open display of brutality and violence with the police standing by in silence which characterised the 1933 general election is used, as one excuse among many, to explain away a result which gave Hitler the majority in the Reichstag which he sought. But only by yielding to psephological trickery can one suggest that responsibility for the election of the monster does not rest on the majority of Germans. A scrutiny of the five free nationally important elections held between March and November 1932 show an absolute and relative rise in Nazi and Nationalist strength; to seek to use a Nazi decline in strength greater than that suffered by the Social Democrats and Centre in the one election of November is an unconvincing ploy to acquit most Germans of their responsibility. Nor can the final election of March 1933 – which gave a vote to the Nazis and left them the most powerful group, parliamentary or otherwise, to appear on the German scene since the founding of the Republic – be explained away simply in terms of the considerable disadvantages suffered by the Opposition. Almost every fit German, in what was a secret poll, recorded his or her choice: it was an extraordinary 90 per cent poll. Hitler received almost 44 per cent of the vote and with his Nationalist allies, who polled 3 million votes, he was in total command.

Today, contemporary German historians, desperately trying to deny that their fathers and grandfathers had voted power to Hitler, blame the conservative-authoritarian notables who belonged to the entourage of the aged President von Hindenburg for Hitler's rise; every effort is now being made by some German historians and psephologists to establish that this entourage blundered into the belief that the Nazi party would merely provide popular support for an authoritarian rule with Hitler tamed and framed in a conservatively blended coalition. It is a pretty fairy tale, well told, and, if believed, would acquit the German electorate of criminal complicity. In 1933 different but no less ingenious apologias were presented in Britain by older and wiser heads than mine, all corroborating my wish that Hitler did not speak for Germany. And, perversely, holding fast to our dream, two years later, in 1935, we ignored the unequivocal approbation given to the Nazis when, in accordance with the provisions of the Versailles Treaty which had separated the Ruhr territory from Germany, a free plebiscite was held under international supervision to determine whether the inhabitants of the Saar wished to return to Germany, to retain the status quo administered by the League of Nations, or become part of France; in this largely Catholic and heavily industrialised area, 90.9 per cent voted enthusiastically to return to Hitler's Germany.

It certainly would not be in accordance with the reality of the situation in the early years of Nazi power to suggest that, with the collapse of the multi-party system, the German population became an amorphous mass devoid of any capacity to hold independent political and social judgements; that much is clear from the extant Gestapo and district governors' reports of the time. A desire on the part of some to consolidate the Nazi state, institutionalise it, and gain some peace from incessant propaganda and radicalism in a deteriorating economic situation, found some expression in disenchantments which the Gestapo reported to their superiors. But such querulousness – amounting at most to some conscious depoliticisation – that leaked to the outside world, was too often misinterpreted by those of us anxious to preserve our illusions as active opposition to the whole ideology of the regime.

And, because of our desire to acquit Germans of the responsibility for their leadership, we chose to exaggerate to ourselves the extent of the passive resistance of communist and socialist workers, some of whom were bravely dragging their feet and slowing down production in armament factories and mines. There was, too, another opposition group, although one knew little of it at the time: that of courageous aristocrats in the German Foreign Office, men who had military links, particularly with the Abwehr, the counter-intelligence service. They opposed Hitler, not because they did not share many of his expansionist goals, but because they believed his methods repellent, and correctly believed that such methods would lead to German defeat.

They were ready to sacrifice their lives for Germany, but not necessarily for a democratic Germany; these were certainly not the men in our sights when we deluded ourselves that the country's true voice was not to be found in the Nazi party.

Even my awareness of the persecution of the Jews did not shatter my illusion. I saw it in the context of other persecutions which were part of the history of my people, of the expulsion of the Jews for four centuries from Britain, of their expulsion at a few weeks' notice from Spain in the fifteenth century, of the Russian pogroms recited to me by my grandparents who had, as children, experienced them. I believed the story, then peddled, that Nazi anti-Semitism came as an imposition from the top and lacked the populism that prompted the pogroms of mediæval Europe and earlier twentieth-century Russia; that was an interpretation made easier to accept since, apart from the 1938 outburst of *Kristallnacht*, the night of broken glass, action by individuals wishing personally to solve the Jewish 'problem' was prohibited by ordinances carrying severe penalties. I did not then appreciate the cruel refinements, institutionalised by a state determined to appropriate to itself the right to murder, little by little, its Jewish citizens; the Nazi state was jealous of its prerogative to combine ultimate and organisational ability with a system of legalised criminality and criminalised legality.

Not until, as the war came to the end, when as a serviceman, I entered German Europe and witnessed hell, did I grasp that there were no precedents for the Holocaust; to use past persecutions as comparisons is an exercise in trivialisation. Indeed language itself atrophies, its metonymy insufficiently demonstrated, when confronted by this Nazi phenomenon. Thomas Mann in one of his novels has written about the nature of hell:

> That is the secret delight of Hell – the fact that it is not denouncible, that it is secure from language, that it just *is*, but cannot be reported on in the newspaper, cannot become public knowledge, and cannot be brought by any word within the realm of critical judgement.

But in my teens, far from acknowledging the inadequacies of language, it was respect for the words of my literary heroes which, even as they were being scattered to the four corners of the earth, seduced me into the stubborn belief that there was a powerful 'other Germany' and that the exiles would ultimately prove to be the authentic voice of Germany. It was these writers of the early decades of the twentieth century, not

Bach and Beethoven, or Goethe and Schiller, whom I would invoke to validate my faith. I was purblind to the blight that had settled on much of the serious German literature of the period: it was a literature that only exceptionally freed itself from its romantic love affair with tragic destiny, its sick tryst with Thanatos. Subliminally, this element was doubtless for me irresistible: histrionic tragedy is phase-appropriate to adolescence. The young are more in love with death than the old. But more explicitly there were other themes – pacifism, capitalist-induced alienation, the decay of the bourgeoisie, the essential brotherhood of man and, above all, justice – permeating the plays and novels that I was reading with such addiction. What I did not appreciate was that all this literature was minority reading in Germany, that a large proportion of the so-called *Bildungsbürgertum*, the educated élite, pejoratively dubbed it 'modern'. The German middle classes were avid readers but their preference was for nationalist epics, *Völkisch* village tales and historical novels documenting Germany's mighty past, all works which were anticipations of the blood and soil novels which the Nazis were soon to promote so successfully. Nor had I grasped how pervading was the malignant influence of so many of the intellectual right who were continually challenging reason, and preached a bloody irrationalism based on their philosophic belief in the priority of life and action over the processes of adjustment and negotiation.

More oddly, at the time I did not remark that the works which gripped me most were written by Jews. I thought of these men as Germans, a distorted perspective too easily adopted by a young Welsh Jew protected by the happy chance of living in a minority group within another minority group where cultural bastardy was not stigmatised but, rather, was the norm; extravagant and over-determined displays of national allegiances were absent in Wales, and I felt no need to wave Union Jacks, Welsh dragons or Shields of David, no need to choose between a Welsh, a Jewish or a British identity.

That I should have been thinking of the Jews of Germany as Germans was also understandable since that is how, foolishly, many of them thought of themselves. It was ever so. Heine declared that what water was to a fish, Germanness was to him and, to save his fellow-Jews from themselves, he helped to found a society where Jews could be persuaded that the potential of their specific cultural heritage could only be realised within the German *Kultur*. Marx was less solicitous: in his absurd bid to be disencumbered by his Jewish birth, he savaged the kinship he was denying in his tortured anti-Semitic essay on the Jewish question. And even Freud, until his disenchantment, was, in Vienna, a fervent Pan-Germanist; as late as the outbreak of the First World War he was hailing the stiff Austrian attitude towards Serbia and warmly welcoming Germany as an ally. The secular Jews I was reading, although I regarded them as revolutionaries, usually had not dissimilar histories of enthusiastic German patriotism, often displayed in courageous deeds as well as words.

Their ostentatious loyalties did not save them from Hitler burning their books and, if he could, burning them too. Hitler was not deceived. He insisted they were an alien element who could have no place in his *Völkisch* Utopia; he was right. German-Jewish *littérateurs* may have believed they had moved away from the orthodoxies of their fathers but Hitler well understood, as is evident in *Mein Kampf*, that fundamentally they were not enveloped by the German romanticism which was linked to Nazism; their realism, which he dubbed 'materialism', was the antithesis of the 'idealism' he espoused. 'Idealism', he wrote, 'will be the premise of what we designate as human *Kultur*.' It was, he declared, the absence of idealism in the Jew, his individuality, his obnoxious intellectualism, that made him not a nomad but a parasite. 'It is really necessary to confront the master book-keepers of the present material republic by faith in an ideal *Reich*.' And it was those book-keepers that as a youngster I was reading; fancifully I was deluding myself they were the true Germans. Hitler knew otherwise; he was so well-tuned into the unconscious that he knew his enemies better than they knew themselves. The responses that my literary heroes were teasing out from me had little to do with Germany; they had another source. They sprang from our common Jewish heritage.

The starting point: Heine's prescience, Jung's insights

I believe the starting point for an examination of how Britain can live with Germany, sharing a common citizenship within the European Community, must be a scrutiny of Germany's treatment of the Jews. This is not an extravagant ethnocentric approach on my part. Britain is entering into a new relationship with a country, now the strongest economic power in Europe, who so recently, in historical terms, descended into barbarism, a country which slew 1½ million children in cold blood. No Maastricht Treaty, prefaced by splendid aspirations, can cover over that slaughter. We, as individuals and parents, would not readily enter into an association with murderers, and would react

cautiously if our children appeared to be striking up friendships with
their children. That observation, with Germany being the obvious
referent, is not the comment of a primitive hanger and flogger: it is
prompted by my experience as a lawyer in defending and therefore
knowing killers, and by all my work in the Commons which means that
I must accept considerable responsibility for having, in the final stages
of the debates on capital punishment, brought about the end of state
strangulation.

My conclusions from these exposures to the realities of hideous
violences is not that time in itself is a great healer and that the
precaution we would show as parents towards the children of
murderers is misplaced. On the contrary; we must display similar
caution when Britain's future is becoming inextricably enmeshed with
that of Germany. Attempting to monitor and to understand the
relationship between Jew and German is therefore no peripheral
exercise with little relevance to contemporary European politics. Even
as the Crucifixion of the Jew, Jesus Christ, brought with it a message
claimed to be of universal significance, so it may be that the suffocation
of millions of Jews in the German gas chambers brings tidings, ignored
at our peril, for all Europe; if it does, then some little gain at such
terrible expense may be picked out from the charred bones at
Auschwitz.

More than a century and a half ago, long before the victims of the
Holocaust now calling to us from their mass graves to heed the lessons
of their sacrifice, came a warning, so disregarded and mocked, from
one of Germany's greatest poets, the baptised Jew, Heinrich Heine. No
one understood the fearful demonic undercurrents in German history
better than Heine. Yet no one has made more desperate efforts to deny
the incompatibility of the Jewish and German spirit than this baptised
Jew. Living throughout his life in an existentialist crisis, he strove to
resolve his personal identity problem by postulating that a *Wahlver-
wandschaft*, an elective affinity, existed between Jew and German. Like
so many less articulate German Jews, he seemed determined to show
that his Jewish origin made him peculiarly fitted to be a great German
patriot; but he was fated to pine in France in exile, his love affair with
the Germans non-consummated and unrequited. And it was to remain
unrequited in contemporary democratic Germany where a movement
to name the university in his native town, Düsseldorf, after him was
twice defeated by an anti-Semitic Senate and by student plebiscites.
Although certainly no passive acquiescent, in a few respects Heine was
nevertheless a forerunner of those wretched doomed German Jews who,

forever ostentatiously protesting their loyalty to the Reich, trooped in bewilderment, passively, without rebellion, tragically into the gas chambers.

But the real irony of the great ironist's reconciling endeavours is seen in his catalogue of German traits spelt out in his brilliant and tortuous 1835 thesis, *Religion and Philosophy in Germany* where, despite himself, Heine's great jeremiad against the German character stands as a permanent warning to the world.

Heine was aware of the destructive influence of the school of natural philosophy which was enveloping his Germany. He could see the consequences of the provision by Immanuel Kant and his successor Johann Fichte – both still so highly regarded in Germany today – who were providing the intellectual validation of the most archaic mode of thought simmering beneath Germany's public life. Heine did not regard the swagger of Fichte, the patriotic philosopher and rector of Berlin's first university, as mere rodomontade; he saw the poison with which Fichte was infecting the body politic as he proclaimed that the Germans were unique, primal people – *Urvolk*: 'To have character and to be German undoubtedly mean the same . . .' Fichte claimed 'All comparisons between the German and non-German are null and void . . . We are the chosen people. Chosen by God . . . with a moral right to fulfil our destiny by every means of cunning and force.'

Such instruction to Germany by their natural philosophers was seen by Heine soon to become a serious matter of concern for all mankind and caused him to make prophecies of awesome prescience:

> Once the philosophers of nature actively enter into a German revolution the destructive work that will follow will be terrifying. For if the hand of the Kantian strikes firmly and surely, it is because his heart is moved by no traditional reverence. If the Fichtean boldly defies all danger, it is because it has no real existence for him. But the natural philosopher would be terrible indeed because he has allies in the forces of nature, because he will be able to invoke the demonic energies of the old German pantheism, because that ancient love of war we find among the old Germans will once more wake in him and will fight not to destroy or conquer but merely for the sake of fighting. Christianity – and that is its greatest merit – has somewhat mitigated that brutal German love of war, but it could not destroy it. Should that subduing talisman, the cross, be shattered, the frenzied madness

of the ancient warriors, that insane berserk rage of which Nordic bards have spoken and sung so often, will once more burst into flames. The talisman is rotting and the day will come when it will break into miserable fragments. The old stone gods will then arise from long-forgotten ruins and rub the dust of a thousand years from their eyes, and Thor will leap to life with his giant hammer and smash the Gothic cathedrals! When that day comes and you hear the tramping of feet and the clang of arms, beware your neighbours ... do not smile at my advice – the advice of a dreamer who warns you against Kantians, Fichteans and philosophers of nature. Do not smile at the visionary who anticipates the same revolution in the realm of the visible as has taken place in the realm of the spiritual. ... German thunder ... rolls somewhat slowly, but it does come. When you hear its crash, which will be unlike anything before in the history of the world, you will know the German thunder has at last hit the mark. At that uproar the eagles of the air will drop dead, and lions in farthest Africa will draw in their tails and slink away into their royal caves. A play will be performed in Germany which will make the French Revolution look like an innocent idyll. Now ... there are some fellows behaving in a rather frisky fashion, but do not mistake them for the real actors of the play. They're only the little dogs running around in the empty arena, barking and biting each other before the hour strikes and the great army of gladiators enters to begin a life-and-death battle. And that hour will surely strike.

When, one hundred years later, that hour did strike, it was more than half welcome to the German-Swiss psychiatrist Carl Jung who, from his clinical experience was delineating the forces that he claimed enveloped the German masses. Many of his conclusions were congruent with Heine's; but he admired the dynamic that Heine feared. Jung's ignoble role during the 1930s, when he besmirched his reputation by appearing to act as an apologist for Nazi doctrine, has meant that insufficient credence has been given to his insights into the German character; and disgust at his conduct at the time of Jewry's greatest agony has tended to bury the validity of many of his assertions.

But knowing, as Hitler knew, the great divide between German and Jew, Jung declaimed: 'The difference between German and Jewish psychology which actually exists and which has long been known to

sensible people . . . should no longer be glossed over.' He told us: '. . . apart from certain creative individuals, the average Jew is far too conscious and differentiated to go about pregnant with the tensions of unborn futures. The Aryan unconscious has a greater potential than the Jewish; this is the advantage and the disadvantage of the youthfulness that is not yet fully estranged from barbarism.'
For this reason, he instructed his disciples, it was a grave mistake of medical psychology to have indiscriminately applied Jewish categories to the Germanic peoples.

However repellent the value judgements of Jung on the Jew and German 'unconscious', the stress he placed on the fact that the Aryan unconscious is nearer 'barbarism' – in which he saw considerable advantages – should remind us, if his divinations are to be faced, that he was speaking of permanent lineaments possessed by the German people.

In his notorious 1936 essay *Wotan*, he made this explicit: 'The God of the Germans', we are told, 'is Wotan and not the Christian God.' The archetype Wotan 'is a fundamental attribute of the German psyche, the truest expression and unsurpassed personification of a fundamental quality that is particularly characteristic of the Germans'. Economic and political factors, he asserts, do not explain Nazism; that can only be done by noting 'the unfathomable depths of Wotan's character', 'the God of storm and frenzy, the unleasher of passions and the lust of battle . . . the superlative magician and artist in illusion, who is versed in all secrets of an occult nature.'

Jung was acknowledging National Socialism as an expression of one side only of Wotan's disposition, claiming that Nazism was the 'restless violent stormy side of his nature' and that Nazism is simply the precursor to the 'ecstatic and mantic' qualities that will follow. If, however, infuriated by what can be interpreted as a justification for Nazism, we dismiss Jung's identification of the dangerous archetype within the German collective unconscious as a farrago of extravagant mumbo-jumbo, we may be guilty of a grave intellectual error: in many respects his prognostications and hypotheses in the 1930s provide a more convincing explanation of the appalling Nazi phenomenon than do the so evidently shallow and inadequate political and economic theses that have been so frequently proffered as explanations of the eruption of Nazism in a twentieth century Western European state. At a time, as now, when, led by the Prince of Wales and his guru van der Post, Jung's general theories are again becoming fashionable, we cannot selectively dismiss his applications of his theories that we find awkward or distasteful; they may have a greater relevance for our present conduct of our foreign affairs than is dreamed of in Whitehall.

Using Nietzsche's magnifying glass

When the Berlin Wall fell, the demonstrators in Leipzig made their democratic demands, chanting: 'We are the people!' But speedily an undercurrent was to run through the crowds, and another slogan replaced the first. With all its sinister overtones and recalls, the shout went up: *Deutschland – ein Volk!* And it was in response to that call that all economic caution was abandoned and that all the tiptoeing that had accompanied the *Ostpolitik* policies of the Federal Republic was to cease. Kohl, but a few months before while wishing Egon Krenz, the new East German leader, 'success' in the difficult task ahead of him, had assured him that all the Bonn government wanted was 'a calm sensible development'. Now changing tack, Kohl was to say, recalling Bismarck, that this was the moment 'when God passed by', signalling that he was ready to sing the long unsung words of East Germany's own national anthem 'Germany, united Fatherland'. Mendaciously, he soon offered to willingly deceived voters unity of the Germanies at no cost, recklessly challenged the present Polish-German frontiers, and welcomed the ingathering of the descendants of Germans who, from Russia to Romania, hundreds of years ago, had settled in Eastern Europe. The Nazi Nuremberg race laws, with the hideous refinements of the Mischling rules, of first- and second-degree mongrels, were not revived; but nevertheless, though, as I have found, the immigrants often did not speak German, that was no bar: blood, not language, was to be the passport.

The Bundesbank warned of financial dangers and some, like Günter Grass, pleaded for a slower pace and urged only a tentative confederation, but all such warnings were of no avail. The French and Thatcher could sulk, hoisted by their own petard of past lip service to the ideal of a united Germany, but all their misgivings too were brushed aside. Now the slogan, a gory mixture of blood and money, *Ein Volk, Eine Deutschmark!* proved irresistible: ethnocentricity reverberated throughout the soon to be held elections. Oskar Lafontaine, the Social Democrats' candidate against Kohl, was punished by the voters for daring to demur and to tell them that unity could bring in its wake intolerable financial burdens to West Germany, economic catastrophe to the East, and dangerous instability to Europe; the Social Democrats received their lowest electoral score for thirty years. Kohl was confirmed as Chancellor by an enthusiastic electorate.

Thus, yet again, ethnocentricity had acted as the sick dynamic, overruling rationality and ensuring the delusion that, without anguish, the two Germanies could be united overnight. The dream had its source: too many Germans had sought oblivion to wipe out their past, to repress their recollections of their unleashed sadisms, to deny to themselves past complicities; but there is an iron psychic rule that the repressed has a way of returning, and what has been abolished internally, returns from the outside in the form of delusion. In a delusory dream, therefore, the new united Germany was founded even as was Hitler's Reich. Neither we nor the Germans facilitate the mending of old wounds by accepting such denial, rationalisation and forgetting; Kohl's 1990 election tells us again, if we are to reach understanding, not to forget, but to remember; and the subsequent regional election in the Rhineland Palatine, Kohl's home state, underlines the need to remember. In 1991 I witnessed the ugly sight of his conservative electors, shaken by the taxes unification was bringing, angrily wake up from their dream. Showing yet again no insight, they sought to exculpate themselves from responsibility for their own votes cast, in this case, but a few months previously; in the ballot boxes they now projected upon Kohl personally all the blame for the débâcle.

And similarly in 1992 I found dangerous scapegoating rampant among the East Germans. A racially pure, all-embracing Deutschmark had initially dazzled them and they had eagerly delighted in the deceptions of their new leaders; now, dunned by carpet baggers, devastated in a rampant free market, they live on the wrong side of the tracks left behind by the old fortified boundary in what in reality is a federal German occupation zone. And, as with the West Germans, their remembrance span does not bridge a few months; few acknowledge their responsibility for the precipitate reunification of Germany.

Although there still remains some talk of *Vergangenheitsbewältigung*, the coming to terms with one's past, the German electorate of 1990 and 1991, and the mood now prevailing in East Germany, give little encouragement to those who know how long and how profound must be the recall if understanding is to be reached. It is the present shallowness of that recall that can, as the turbulence in British–German relations in 1992 revealed, cause the whole concept of a European Community citizenship to founder. The tensions that have come into existence between Germany and Britain do not spring from one single cause; the Bundesbank's role in driving Britain out from the European Monetary System and forcing a sterling devaluation has certainly been a catalyst, but we mislead ourselves if we believe that if that particular quarrel is resolved, and the balm of royal visits applied, all will be well. If a genuine European Community is to come into existence, we shall need in the years ahead to have a far keener appreciation of the sicknesses within the German culture; and, by recognising them, deepen insights into our own political conduct even as we unremittingly identify their ailments to a German nation reluctant to acknowledge them.

The maladies of the Germans led them to murder some six million Jewish men, women and children; all the various efforts within the Weimar Republic by the Jewish intellectuals of Germany to save themselves, and to save the Germans from their own madness, were made in vain. I believe that in recalling and scrutinising their failure to bridge the gulf between themselves and their fellow-citizens, we and the Germans may gain greater understanding of the pathological elements which have possessed Germany in the past, and which must, if a new Europe is to emerge, be exorcised. Perhaps to gain that needed understanding, our remembrances must not only be in the generality but in the particular; they must be the memories of persons. 'I avail myself,' Nietzsche once wrote, 'of the person as of a strong magnifying glass that allows one to make visible a general but creeping and illusive calamity.' The calamity of which we speak, the phenomenon that shook the world from 1933 to 1945, brings with it such awesome and vertiginous insights into the human soul that one treads warily and with little hope; but a glance at the biography of some of the German-Jewish intellectuals whom I had encountered in my adolescence, and not a few of whom I was to meet, may bring a little illumination.

As Germany, still wrestling with itself, still afflicted with a profound unease, becomes one of the strongest economic powers in the world, we shall need all the light available, if we are not to stumble into a new and final darkness. Looking back at the predicaments of some paradigmatic figures may help us on our way. Four of them, two famous novelists, one revolutionary playwright, and the other an educationalist who, as a less than benign tutor to the Duke of Edinburgh and as a mentor of the Prince of Wales, has brought some of Germany's unresolved dilemmas into the heart of British politics, provide us with chastening case material.

PART II

Contending Souls

The Hebrew *Nefesh* and the German *Geist*

An ensnared novelist: Arnold Zweig

None were more guilty of the charges brought by Hitler against the Jewish intellectuals of the Weimar Republic than the epic novelist Arnold Zweig and the expressionist playwright Ernst Toller. Zweig in the post-war years was to be appointed by Walter Ulbricht, the first dictator of the GDR, to the presidency of the East German Academy of Arts. Toller, the heroic leader of the short-lived 1919 Bavarian Soviet Republic was, after Hitler's accession, to have no future: he was doomed to creative decline and, ultimately, to suicide. Of all the Weimar *littérateurs* whom as a young man I met, none illustrated more dramatically than these two men the chasm, perhaps tragically unbridgeable, between German and Jew.

Arnold Zweig's eight-volume cycle of war novels illuminating the effect on German society of the First World War includes the most powerful indictment of German militarism ever written. His *Der Streit um den Sergeanten Grischa* (*The Case of Sergeant Grischa*) is perhaps the greatest war novel of this century. The tale of the escape of a simple Russian soldier from a German prisoner-of-war camp is enthralling in itself, dwarfing as it does the torrent of trivial escape stories that sprang from the Second World War; but this is no mere well-told yarn. The good Russian soldier's vain struggle to regain his liberty is a paradigm: the redeeming role of an individual challenging the seemingly inexorable might of the military machine is to be found in the failure, not the success, of his defiance. Nothing succeeds like this Russian soldier's defeat. This is a wondrous parable telling how inner freedom can be gained as the reward of a commitment to an external struggle against the abuses of power. The story spelt out is of an unselfish man's inner resource, as well as of his resourcefulness. It is written by a Jew who knows he belongs to a people whose strength is attributable to surviving millennia of defeats and not to banal triumphs.

But above all it deserved Hitler's stigma of it being a Jewish work, not because of its pacifism or because of its realism unmitigated by any vulgar, tawdry sentimentality, but because of its passionate insistence

23

that justice alone, not power or even love, can keep a society from
regressing into barbarism. Not by chance the most significant of the
subsidiary protagonists in the novel is an Orthodox Jew, a lawyer
serving as an officer in the legal department of the German army;
from his Torah learning, with its morality and ethics based not on love,
as are the Gospels, but on justice, he fights desperately to save the
recaptured sergeant from execution. It proves to be a vain fight; the
obsessional traits leading to the substitution of military orders for
conscience defeat him. This conclusion of the book is an awesome
premonition of Eichmann and his henchmen, and of the ruthless
German contempt for the non-Germanic peoples of Eastern Europe
which, some twenty years after the novel was written, led to the slaying
of millions of Poles and Russians.

Arnold Zweig, however, managed to escape from Hitler's clutches to
Palestine, and it was there, while serving in the RAF in the Middle East,
that I first met him. On each yearned-for leave, I would quit the desert, or
the filth and degrading poverty of Egypt's delta and the bitch city of
Cairo, to go to the villa built on Mount Carmel just before the war by
my maternal grandfather who, having lived most of his life in Wales,
went to die in his Holy Land. I discovered Zweig was living nearby
and, with some trepidation, called on him, literally to pay my respects.
He was a lonely, alienated man, troubled by his own failing eyesight
and even more by the narrowness of vision of Zionists who resented his
heavily qualified approval of their over-confident enthusiasms.

I was to endure later in my life similar resentments, for they are
easily provoked. In 1973 I felt the full force of them when I went to
Israel with David Frost to have a televised dialogue with a local
audience: my tempered criticism of the needless shooting down of a
civilian Libyan plane aroused the Israeli press to fury. And when, in
1982 the Zionist leaders of the British-Jewish Establishment, from the
safety of the heights of Hampstead, were cheering on Israeli generals
marching into Beirut, they became apoplectic as I denounced on the
BBC the folly of the invasion, and called upon the young Israeli
soldiers to lay down their arms rather than submit to their immoral
orders. I have always expressed the view, to the vexation of the rabid
right-wing Zionists, that the establishment of the state of Israel was
Jewry's greatest defeat. For 2,000 years, with incredible fortitude, the
Jews withstood Christian and pagan cruelty, stubbornly maintaining
their messianic belief in the redemption of all mankind; but in the end,
after the final Holocaust, in order to survive they were compelled to
capitulate to the mean concept of a nation-state. I take no joy in their

enforced retreat from their cosmopolitanism. Nor did Arnold Zweig, and his impatience with the religious Hebrew language fanatics of Palestine who resented his continued writing and speaking in German had, shortly before I met him, led to ugly political scenes. In Tel Aviv, as in the fastness of North Wales, it is often necessary to recall that in Babel diversity of language was a curse, and not a blessing, imposed upon mankind for the sin of excessive pride.

Arnold Zweig, to my good fortune, was pleased to have me accompany him in his slow walks across the anemone-covered Mount Carmel, then free from its present over-development, and would tell me of the pre-Hitler German literary world of Musil, Mann, Wasserman, Brecht, Georg Kaiser, Toller – all of whose tortuous quests then had for me an almost sinister fascination; and we would speak of Nietzsche, whose genius still captivates me, and Zweig would cast a singular illumination upon the prophet; and in return, no doubt, as a young man I gave him my faith in the post-war Britain and made temporarily a little less bitter his disenchantment and displacement. My political precocity opened a window to him upon the current British democratic scene, relieving the claustrophobia he felt, de-Europeanised, in wartime Palestine.

Zweig's exposure to religious nationalist sentiments was an early intimation of the intolerant mood that hitherto has always threatened to engulf Israel. Since the destruction of the second Temple in the first century, Judaism had happily lacked any connection between religion and state; it was the Jews' good fortune that their religion was deprived of political power at so early a stage in their history, for from this serendipity sprang the emphases of the rabbinical tradition that Judaism did not hold an exclusive passport to salvation. Living within a dangerous diaspora, the Jews were taught by the best tutor of religious tolerance – the experience that you cannot survive without it. Now, with religious fundamentalists seeking power over the state of Israel, the traditional fortunate disjunction between religion and power is challenged; it is fortunate that the change of government in Israel in 1992 has checked the fundamentalists. Arnold Zweig, however, suffered its very early encroachments; it was not surprising that he yielded to the opportunist GDR invitation to return in honour to Germany when, during the Cold War, on his way from Palestine to London to attend a peace conference, he found himself stranded in Prague, banned because of his political views from entering Britain. The GDR had a propagandist triumph in offering status and a haven to the world-famous novelist, and Zweig found himself in a new home back in East Berlin.

It was therefore in East Berlin that, fifteen years later, I again met Zweig. Shortly after entering the Commons I had decided to yield to the blandishments of Will Owen, the MP who was later to be acquitted of espionage, to join a small party of Labour MPs invited to meet Ulbricht, the dictator of the GDR. Gaitskell, then the leader of the parliamentary party, a Little Englander and Cold War warrior, absurdly preaching non-recognition of the East German republic, publicly condemned the visit; it was not the first or the last time I found myself in conflict with him, for I mistrusted his dogmatic political judgements and, unlike many of my colleagues, I was impervious to his charm. On my arrival in East Germany the usual preliminary rounds of talks with ministers and officials began and the inevitable offers to show us all followed. I declined a tour of yet more factories and housing estates and, sensing resistance, I almost demanded that I should see Arnold Zweig. I affected I knew he was at that time in East Berlin, although, in truth, I had no idea of his exact whereabouts.

There were good reasons why I was eager to see him in East Berlin. It was shortly after my last meeting with him that I had been arrested by the military authorities in Cairo and put into detention because of my political activities within the RAF; only a parliamentary row and ultimately a debate freed me, but my experience, slight as it was in comparison with the agonies endured by Sergeant Grischa in his isolated struggle against German militarism, meant that the novel had acquired singular significance for me in the post-war years. Certainly when, in 1989, so many years after my arrest, the BBC broadcast a three-part televised faction-drama telling of the events in Cairo which led to my arrest, I felt embarrassed by the depiction of my political naïveté when I was a young serviceman, but I felt too a nostalgia for the purity of motivation which had informed me and which, alas, was gradually to become tarnished by thirty years' exposure to the cynicism of the Commons. In the late winter of 1958, when I sought out Zweig, I wanted to discover how this creator of a pure character, within a saga that is so memorable an indictment of institutionalised injustice, was, as an honoured writer, surviving in one of the most rigid of communist countries.

Zweig and his artist wife received me warmly at their home and, unencumbered by the clinging official interpreter whom I dismissed, soon appeared to be speaking to me with his former frankness; but ere long his fervent apologia for the German republic and his catalogue of its achievements became over-determined, and I told him so. I sensed the unease of his wife as I commenced to press Zweig, questioning him about the relationship of the author and the State in the GDR. Rumours about recent trials had come to the West but I did not know any of the details that were only to emerge decades later. In fact, unknown to me, but only a year before our meeting, the show trial of Walter Janka, the director of the GDR's most important publishing house, had taken place; he had been arrested in the wake of the Hungarian uprising on a trumped-up charge of plotting to overthrow the Ulbricht government, and was sentenced to five years' imprisonment. I do not know whether Zweig was present at his trial but certainly a whole array of the state's cultural élite attended, including Anna Seghers, Helene Weigel, Brecht's widow and director of the Berliner Ensemble, and the expressionist poet Johannes Becher who had become the GDR's Minister of Culture. In any event it would have been impossible for Zweig, as the man who had so recently been head of the German Academy of Arts and a member of the East German parliament, not to have known the whole sickening story. It was a grim irony that the man who had reached his artistic apogee in a novel centring on an unjust trial, like other leading authors in the GDR, made no protest against a Stalinist act of repression so deliberately aimed at unnerving their literary world. Doubtless Zweig's defence of his position would have been that later proffered by others: that they were, as far as possible in the circumstances, public defenders of the state's humanistic ideals against a party which had abandoned them in all but rhetoric. But Janka's condemnation, published 25 years later, after he came out of gaol, of what he regarded as their moral failure was well-deserved. 'Silence,' he wrote, 'can sometimes be as bad as lies, for silence can be taken as consent.'

The content of the defence that, 45 years ago, Zweig put to me of the GDR, the State claiming to be the *Leseland DDR*, the land of reading, was an anticipation of the dispiriting debate now raging in united Germany, where the writers of former East Germany assert that they are being subjected to a witch-hunt by arrogant *Wesses* intellectuals sitting in moral judgement upon a past they have not experienced. The literary history of the GDR has become the focus of an acrid post-unification controversy about the role of East Germany's writers under the dictatorship, and the allegation is made that their readiness to work within the system contributed to its strengthening.

Christa Wolf, East Germany's leading writer and, as such, the main symbol of its literary production, has found that the very style of her works, which have enjoyed near cult status in Italy and France, is

labelled as cowardice. One of West Germany's main literary critics has
accused her, and those influenced by her finely wrought literary
artifices, of indulging in the 'Christa Wolf Sound, a limp melody of the
noncommittal cast in finely formulated language, the typically blurred
relation between the real world, which shimmers as a distant
presentiment, and the poetical world of her texts'. Such intemperate
criticism is suspect, and has led Anne McElvoy, the often sharp *Times*
correspondent then in Berlin, to conclude that the controversy 'shields
a much more thorny problem – that of the relative ease with which
Germans adapted to living with dictatorship twice in one century, and
the retrospective urge to find individuals to blame for this phenomenon'. Ludke, West Germany's most distinguished literary editor, in an
East and West German writers' symposium in London in 1992, told us
that the whole world of German literature seems to be wearing itself
out over the Stasi past of some of its representatives, and that as part of
this process, Wolf was being proffered as a 'sacrificial lamb'; and, he
pertinently added: 'It is worth noting that this development has drawn
attention once again to the post-war period, with its suppression of past
memory in the West, and in the East the anti-fascism which was
exploited to the very end in under-pinning the legitimacy of the State.'

Certainly the West German intellectuals would be better employed
in scrutinising the guilt of their parents rather than sitting in
judgement on the culpability of East Germany's writers; the predicaments of those writers were real and, if the authors displayed little
nobility, not a few of them survived without losing their essential
integrity.

But at the time, and now, I find it hard to extend such extenuation
to Zweig. His work revealed his profound understanding that social
justice is a sham if it is unaccompanied by scrupulous care that justice
should be available to the most aberrant and the most simple of
citizens. I therefore found his equivocations particularly discomfiting,
and to avoid my continuing embarrassment which I sensed was shared
by his wife, I deliberately moved the conversation to talk of Freud for
whom I knew, from our encounters in Haifa, Zweig had unstinted
admiration. I was certain that Zweig would never permit any ideology
to temper his hero-worship of Freud. He had dedicated his treatise on
anti-Semitism to Sigmund Freud and a Freudian analysis had, he
asserted, freed him from his personal neurosis and released his own
creativity; and his gratitude was boundless. A filial relationship was
established between Freud and Zweig and for many years, until
Freud's death, they conducted a constant correspondence.

The doubts, however, behind his earlier defensive assertiveness became even clearer as he showed me the letters of Freud which were in his possession, for I could not resist teasing him as he told me of his intention to write a book containing his letters with Freud and a commentary on his relations with the founder of psychoanalysis. My raillery that it would be impossible to publish such a book in a Communist state agitated him. He well knew that Freud had asserted that the Communist, as the fascist, state would not tolerate the insights of psychoanalysis, and his dogmatic and loud assertion to me that such a book would and must be published in the German Democratic Republic I regarded as a vain rehearsal for the violent arguments in which the issue would eventually be embroiled. Zweig did have the courage in 1963 to write a novel where he was able to make a tribute to Freud, but the book and letters of which he spoke to me remained unpublished, and, defeated, the head of the Cultural Front ultimately had to communicate privately with Ernst Freud in London asking him to edit his grandfather's letters; and ironically, on Zweig's deathbed, they were published in the West Germany that Zweig despised and, later, in 1970 in Britain.

Yet I learned more of the German Republic on that visit from Zweig's artist wife than from him. As I entered the house I saw a bowl of anemones and, commenting on their loveliness, I said to her that these were perhaps all that the Crusaders had usefully brought back to Europe from Palestine, for I could sense her nostalgia for Mount Carmel. When I was leaving, she quietly drew me aside and asked me not to mention that I had seen those flowers in her home; she had obtained them from West Berlin and this was then against the law. After the spirited defence of the State that had been given to me by her husband this was indeed a chastening leave-taking.

I left believing Zweig was entrapped. He would have been wiser to have taken advice given to him by his hero in 1932 when he had sought to engage Freud in an acknowledgement that they shared a common Germanness although 'it's a Germanness of the past'. Freud would have none of it. In one of the letters in Zweig's possession was Freud's withering reply. 'When you tell me about your thoughts, I can relieve you of the illusion that one has to be German. Should we not leave this god-forsaken nation to themselves?'

Ten years after my meeting with Zweig, when he reached his eightieth birthday, he was the centre of elaborate celebrations in the East German Republic. Pompous newspaper stories told how representatives of the state and of the ruling party assembled in order to congratulate him. Over fifty delegations of cultural and political organisations were enumerated, and he was hailed as the Grand Old Man of socialist literature and a favourite of the people. In the following year when he died he was accorded a State funeral and honoured by lengthy laudatory obituaries throughout the East German press. It was a long-postponed funeral, for the Germans, many years before his death, had long since killed the Jewish writer of *Sergeant Grischa*.

Toller: the forgotten man

In 1985 Klaus von Dohnanyi, Lord Mayor of Hamburg, a brave son of a brave father who was executed as one of the participants in the July 1944 plot to assassinate Hitler, opening a visiting international conference, declared:

> We Germans are no doubt a people in trouble, fearful of being left behind, of not being loved, of not being recognised. It can hardly be a coincidence that the three great innovators, Marx, Freud and Einstein, all spoke German as their mother tongue. But then it is also no coincidence that they were all driven out of the country by us, and regarded English as the language of liberation. Whoever says our Bach, our Beethoven, must also say our Hitler.

But not all distinguished Jewish exiles found liberation in the English language; for Ernst Toller, Germany's foremost playwright in the Weimar Republic, the loss of his opportunities to communicate in German sealed his fate as an artist, and in England and in Hollywood he lost his way.

Toller, a legendary figure throughout Europe in the 1920s and 1930s, is now a forgotten man. Few of the significant Weimar writers have received much attention in post-war Germany, and those regarded as left-wing have been particularly avoided. The notorious amnesia of so many Germans, which excludes remembrance of their participation in Hitler's barbaric regime, also operates against those Weimar writers who, if now acknowledged, would tell of their slaying or exile; only now, so belatedly, is there a possibility of Toller's works being republished in Germany. The covert hostility to Toller in post-war West Germany was matched by the ambivalence shown in the former GDR. It was embarrassing to that regime to bring out of the shadows an anti-Nazi socialist hero who so determinedly throughout his life distanced himself from the dogmatism and rigidity of the German communist party.

Only once in post-war West Germany was homage paid to him: that was in 1968 during the short-lived student uprising when he was depicted in a play touching on events in the Munich of 1919. But that flicker of remembrance was soon quenched. It was not in Germany but in Britain in 1990 that at last he found his biographer, but the work of the Englishman, Richard Dove, who meticulously and objectively told of Toller's extraordinary life was little noticed by young literary editors with insufficient historical sense. When Toller was in exile, Hitler made strenuous efforts to kill him off; at first it seemed that the Führer posthumously had found colluders ready to continue his efforts to extinguish him. Fortunately, belatedly, a paperback of Dove's biography has now been published.

It has been said that Toller's conduct in his early life would not have raised the expectation that he was to become a famous pacifist dramatist, and still less that he would become a revolutionary international socialist, head of the Red Army in the Bavarian Soviet Republic. Yet, as with all of us, the formative period of his life is to be found in his early years; the initial artificial extravagance with which he denied his Jewish heritage, and the consequent intemperate affirmation of his unswerving German patriotism, was inevitably to lead to a shattering disenchantment when, in the trenches, he experienced the terrible consequences of the jingoism which he had so fervently expounded.

The small town where Toller was born in 1893, although peopled by Germans and a dwindling population of Jews, lay within the eastern province of Polsen. It was almost wholly Polish; in this outpost of the German empire, the Germans who had originally annexed the area despised the conquered Poles and, within their island and possessed by the nationalist sentiment of colonists, were fierce patriots; the Jews, German-speaking descendants of the original traders who had come with the German conquerors, identified themselves with the German minority. But Toller's parents evidently had their reservations; they preserved a cherished and Orthodox Jewish family life, and Toller's pious mother maintained all the traditional rituals, ensuring that their son in his earliest years attended a Jewish school; the ethical values he was taught there were permanently embossed upon his character and, although he was soon to make desperate efforts to escape the destiny of his birth and to grow into a good German citizen of the *Kaiserreich*, assiduously cultivating its aggressive nationalism, he was engaged in an uneven struggle.

His determination to be German was not in itself a personal idiosyncrasy; other Jewish communities in France, Poland and Czechoslovakia were always perplexed by the Reich's Jews whom they labelled 'Germanisers'. Their desire to be assimilated was so powerful that they often strove to renounce within the timespan of a single generation all that had previously characterised them: a ritual and a community, a language and a culture. They saw their 'emancipation' as a child of the 'German Enlightenment', and on its altar their ancient faith was sacrificed; their traditions became an embarrassment to them and, determined to slough them off, the German Jews made a contribution to Germany in the sciences and philosophy, the arts and the humanities, which in sheer size and importance remains without parallel in any other country. They wished to assume that the secularisation spirit of enlightened tolerance which had opened up German society to them was to be a permanent feature of the German state, and they were blind to the dangers that were always lurking beneath the surface.

When Toller, in his teens, enthusiastically embraced the chauvinism embedded within the Prussian educational system of his secondary school he was, therefore, taking up a well-defined option: he responded to the anti-Semitism which the colonial Germans expressed against Jews in his home town by outdoing them in displays of approval of the German ethos of heroic militarism, and by a manic denial of his origins. At eighteen he was writing a poem claiming a parthenogenic birth:

> I died
> Gave birth
> Died
> Gave birth
> Was mother to myself.

The ablation of parents, the denials of a biological past and an insistence on being self-made with no umbilical link to a mother's womb, is a phenomenon not unknown to psychoanalysis; doubtless with Toller an explanation of the ætiology of this attempt to obliterate his parents would reveal unresolved oedipal rivalries, but the prevailing values of German Jews, hell-bent on assimilation, enabled him to act out those buried personal conflicts in a manner exceedingly acceptable to his own self-esteem.

With his Jewish past thus erased, loudly singing 'Deutschland, Deutschland über Alles', the twenty-year-old left for student days in Grenoble; there he kept the company of his compatriots, behaving as a representative of a higher culture able to treat the French with disdain. He wrote: 'I am living in France and have never left Germany.' As soon as war broke out he rushed to the colours, bursting with patriotic pride, ready to defend his fatherland, totally accepting the mendacious government propaganda that Germany was a victim of aggression, that the French had dropped bombs on Nuremberg and that Cossacks had crossed the border into East Prussia. When he went on active service, his first demonstration of his pride in his uniform was to write to the authorities in his home town requesting that his name be removed from the local list of members of the Jewish community. He was indeed the best of Germans; this was the man who but a few years later was to be convicted of high treason.

With Toller, it was not a question of rhetoric: his insistence that he should not remain in his base posting and that he should be sent to the front line was typical of the conduct of so many young German Jews bent on rescinding their separate identity. The number of Jews who died fighting for Kaiser and country was proportionately greater than any other racial group in the Reich, including the 'pure' Germans; it was the last desperate attempt at assimilation.

At the front, as a machine gunner, Toller is on record for his courage; but that period of his life, when he was in one of the bloodiest sections in the trenches proved to be traumatic. Gradually, as the months wore on and the killing fields were choked with dead, the self-questioning began, and it was to end with his whole system of beliefs being turned upside down. The bellicose patriot became a pacifist; hatred of the enemy was replaced by an affirmation of the brotherhood of man; the nationalist became an internationalist. The poems he wrote changed and acquired the messianic quality that literary critics were later to note as the strength and weakness of his later creative work: he had returned to his home in Zion and, in secular terms, was forever after to preach the revolution that would redeem mankind and establish the New Jerusalem on earth.

His new-found zeal found active expression even before he was fully discharged from the army; he became heavily involved in an anti-war strike, where he discovered his oratorical skills were able to move hitherto docile workers into militant action. His mentor, who was co-ordinating the strike, was Kurt Eisner, soon to become prime minister of the Bavarian Soviet Republic, who led the independent socialist party in Munich. Eisner was yet another of Germany's secular Jews who tortuously sought to coalesce their ancient collectivist tradition with German philosophy; to more pragmatic British socialists, the efforts, as in Eisner's case, sometimes seemed bizarre. He belonged to the group influenced by Hermann Cohen, Germany's leading neo-Kantian scholar whose intellectual antics somehow led him, by regarding the State as the embodiment of ethical consciousness, to insist upon the compatibility of Kant's system of ethics with the objectives of democratic socialism. Eisner developed the theme but it was his charisma, purity and idealism that made him the dominant political figure of Bavaria.

Inevitably Eisner's tenure did not last long: in accordance with German custom, as a Jew taking a leading political role, he was assassinated by a Nationalist. The more a Jew seeks through politics to make his contribution to the German weal, the more likely is he to get his unjust deserts. Rosa Luxemburg, founder of the German Communist party, born Polish-speaking, at home in Russia, educated at a Swiss university, but typically over-determined in her choice to be a German intellectual and politician, was soon slaughtered. Hugo Hasse, the brave lawyer and parliamentary leader of the Socialists in the Reichstag, was brutally murdered by Nationalist thugs. Walther Rathenau, an industrialist, immersed in German philosophy, official organiser of the war economy and, later, foreign secretary, was rewarded for his work by the assassin's bullet. Gregor Gysi, who in the final days of the GDR, almost single-handed transformed the bankrupt Communist Party of East Germany into a party of democratic socialism, after the displays of anti-Semitism against him in the 1990 elections, should be well aware that murder is one of the occupational hazards of a Jew leading a political party in a German parliament.

It was the slaying of Eisner that catapulted Toller into the group leading the revolutionary council which for a short time took control of Bavaria in 1919. The announcement had been made that it was to be 'a revolution, perhaps the first time in the history of the world, to combine the idea, the ideals and the reality'. Most of the leaders were writers and Jews but the unmistakable German idiom in which they announced their revolution clung to the millenarianism which sprang from so different a tradition. But they did not merely make a call to arms; they acted on it and it led to Toller, still only 26, becoming the field commander of a Red Army mobilised to defend the revolution.

To have a pacifist as the commander was to lead to many droll and bitter consequences: one was that Hitler's life was spared. Hitler, then an obscure figure in the grubby right-wing groups of Munich, fantasised in *Mein Kampf* that single-handed he drove off the three men who came to arrest him. It is much more probable that he was saved by Toller's intervention; during Toller's short command he insisted, to the fury of the Communists within the leadership, that they were 'not making a Russian or Berlin revolution of bloodshed, but a Bavarian revolution of love'; he released members of the counter-revolutionary forces who had been taken prisoner, stopped Communist plans to shoot captured officers of the regular army, sought to prevent arbitrary arrests and attempted to stop the taking and shooting of hostages belonging to proto-Nazi groups. He was, some years later, to say: 'Hitler hates me because he was once in my power. I could have had him killed, for Bavaria was in my power. I should have had no mercy.'

No such mercy was extended by the army and counter-revolutionaries when the utopian Bavarian Republic was crushed: most of the leaders were executed. A few, although sentenced to death, escaped. One of them was the intriguing Ret Marut who, under the name of B. Traven, later became an internationally known novelist whose *The Treasure of the Sierra Madre* was to be translated into a score of languages and made into a renowned film. Toller himself narrowly avoided being murdered when taken into custody but was sentenced to five years' imprisonment. Much later he was offered his freedom but he refused unless every one of his surviving comrades were also released; that request, denied to him, meant that he chose to remain in prison to the last day of his sentence.

The years of his imprisonment did not destroy him; indeed, they were the most creative period of his life, for Toller had a considerable capacity for self-dramatisation. He belonged to those romantics whom some American psychoanalysts have described as men who cultivate autobiographical lives: some of these often live all their lives with their biographers in mind. Such romancers I have often found in public life; they are the politicians who, like Tony Benn, never desist from keeping diaries and, too impatient to await their own death, publish them prematurely. They are determined to write and shape their own obituaries, wishing even posthumously to practise their deceits. I have found no less shallow romancers among some men in prison; when circumstances caused me to meet and interview in their cells a number of spies, I found they sometimes distanced themselves from their terrible predicament by metamorphosis, by becoming characters in a shabby novelette. They fictionalised their lives in prison even as they had played out their infidelities outside, before their capture: they retained their intactness only by dramatising their roles and, since most them were half-educated, they would address me in stilted literary language, acting a part in a debased Dostoevsky story. They of course lacked the imagination to be more than second-rate heroes and their histrionics did not enhance but only trivialised the real tragedy of their position.

With Toller it was otherwise: every year he was in prison he wrote a play, so transmuting the personal consequences of his defeat and incarceration that the characters in his plays achieved an almost universal significance. Sometimes, as in his *Masse Mensch* (*Masses and Men*), he employed a deliberate anonymity in such a form that the characters he was depicting became concrete and recognisable, but only as Everyman. While he was in his cell, with parole refused to enable him to supervise rehearsals, the production of his plays literally caused riots in almost every city in which they were performed. Right-wing Nationalists and Nazis would buy tickets by the hundreds: the actors' voices would be drowned by 'Deutschland, Deutschland über Alles' and songs of hate; and if that did not halt the staging, producers and actors were forced to desist under threat of murder.

None of his plays aroused more anger than his *Hinkemann*, a biting allegory of the human condition, told as a story of an unemployed ex-soldier emasculated by a bullet wound and abandoned to his fate in the post-war world of ruthless German capitalism. All the specious 'heroic' values of the German right are subverted; and the puritanical hard left were no less offended by the frankness and the inherent pessimism of a play that insisted 'tragic man' would find his fate mitigated but not ended by a socialist society.

However, there was one play above all that literary historians turn to with surprise, for, in their pedestrian approach, they unwisely do not expect a poet playwright to be an exemplar of political foresight: such was Toller in his *Wotan Unchanged*, a comedy he completed in 1923, before Hitler became known through his failed Munich *Putsch* and a decade before Jung was identifying what he claimed was the ever-present archetype of Wotan in the German soul. Toller was clearly not boxed in by mechanical Marxist formulae which influenced but did not dominate his thinking; he had the sensibility to appreciate that there were dangerous unconscious forces at work, and, by using mockery and parody, he made an attempt to destroy by laughter the revival of Teutonic mythology.

The prologue, set in Valhalla, debunks the Teutonic deity. Wotan appears as a circus turn, dressed in a wild-cat skin, knotted diagonally across his bare chest and wearing a bard's helmet, with absurdly mighty horns dangling from his side. Astride a fire-breathing black stallion, swinging a lasso, he is meant to attract laughter; but Toller has him, amidst the laughter, turning upon the audience to remind them of the casualties of the 1914–1918 war, and then giving the audience a chill warning: 'Mark, oh audience, don't laugh too soon! Once you laughed too late and paid for your blindness with your living bodies. Don't laugh too soon, but laugh at the right time.' And when the play proper begins, the main character is named Wilhelm Dietrich Wotan, an uncanny anticipation of Hitler and of his early career. In later productions of the play, by which time Hitler had emerged, Wotan was made up to look like Hitler: the dramatist's warnings were indeed an example of what Trotsky once explicated under the rubric that history limps behind art.

It was not surprising, when the end came and Toller was forced to flee Germany, that Hitler still pursued him as the playwright became a wandering Jew moving from one European capital to another. German newspapers distributed abroad would record all of Toller's movements, always accompanied by a distorted photograph of this handsome man, showing him resembling an anthropoid ape; Toller felt, and was made to feel, under constant threat, forever in receipt of menacing phone calls, and there was a time, when he was in London, that he was placed under police protection. He was undeterred, and for a little while, using his legendary political and artistic reputation as he sought to mobilise liberal opinion in Europe and the United States against the Nazis and their excesses, he became a symbol of German opposition in exile. He had some initial success, not least at a famous international Pen Club congress presided over by H. G. Wells in 1933 at Dubrovnik, where, despite the anger of the German, Austrian, Dutch and Swiss delegates, the writers of the world decided to quit their traditional policy of political neutrality. In a moving and eloquent address he persuaded the majority of the delegates, and no doubt himself, that 'millions of Germans' could no longer speak freely and that it was he and the other exiles who must now speak for them. Thus, explicitly, he evoked for the first time the 'other Germany' which he claimed he was representing; it was a noble conceit of little substance, but it was to become the solace and unifying theme of exile literature.

When Toller first came to Britain he was lionised by London's literary world, and this homage and his hyperactive life as a committee man organising protests against Nazi Germany, buoyed him up; but as hopes receded of reversing the tide, so he would fall into a trough. Only those of us who lived through the period can tell of how, despite our demonstrations, marches and meetings, despair began to engulf all of us as the 1930s advanced. We could not move an apathetic wider public who passively accepted the appeasement policy of a government that smugly believed it could turn Germany against the Soviet Union, and leave Britain untouched. It was during such a time, when defeatism was so hard to ward off, that I, then all of seventeen, met Toller.

By chance I had discovered from a small note at the tail end of a column in the Cardiff evening paper that on the following evening a 'Mr. E. Toller, a German poet' would be giving a talk at a meeting of an obscure church dramatic society in a room in a down-at-heel inn in a township some twelve miles from Cardiff; the auspices were as unlikely as the venue. The little town, Pontypridd, was then an unkempt pile full of empty, boarded shops and peeling buildings, a dispirited half-hearted market centre reflecting all the wretched poverty of the mining valleys. At the top end of the nearby Rhondda Valley, brave spirits in the Labour and Communist Parties tried to maintain hope in the face of the appalling unemployment but it was beyond their limited resources to reach this dejected plot.

I told some of my friends belonging to our small Cardiff socialist youth club of the odd coming of one of our heroes, and it was arranged that we would attend, taking the decrepit bus serving the township. I had well-founded misgivings, however, and I went ahead. A little early, I arrived at the meeting-place: the dark brown room, dirty, dank and cold, was littered with used cigarette packets and matches, and a dozen or so wooden chairs, some broken, were piled up against one wall. I stood alone there, as desolate as my surroundings.

A decade before, Toller in Germany would have received so different a welcome. While he was in prison, he had devised *Massenspiele*, mass spectacles for performance at trade union festivals, enacted episodes in working-class history; they required active collaboration by large casts with the participation of audiences of thousands. His first production in Leipzig was performed by a cast of 900 workers to an audience of 50,000; his last, in 1924, had a cast of over 1,000. All these celebrations of socialist heritage, and all these dramatic rallies calling for peace and international brotherhood were, of course, unknown to the little vicar who, a few minutes after my arrival, joined me in that unwelcoming room. His main concern was that some members of his small dramatics society, then preoccupied with rehearsing what he regarded as an uproarious farce, would turn up to listen to some unknown German poet; he evidently felt that the British Drama League in London, to whom his society was affiliated, had let him down by sending such an unsuitable figure.

My friends arrived and we swept the floor, laid out the ramshackle chairs, and soon a handful of members of the dramatics society appeared; the leading lady, a solicitor's wife, came with a bevy of bank clerks and, while waiting, they bantered together repeating some of the excruciating dialogue of their latest church-hall production. When Toller arrived, his disparate audience was less than a dozen.

Toller's striking physical presence imposed itself upon all who met him; but those who have attempted to describe him are curiously contradictory, as if they were so dazzled that their vision became distorted. Christopher Isherwood remembered 'looking into the famous burning dark eyes which every photograph has failed to produce'. Yet his perceptive journalist friend Robert Payne has described Toller's eyes as 'smoky-grey'. When the police put out a WANTED! notice throughout Germany in 1919, he was stated to have a 'piercing gaze and large brown eyes'. Now, some sixty years since I saw him, I recall only the impact, not the fact, of the man: that his eyes were arresting; that although he was of medium height, perhaps because of his big head and mop of black wavy hair, I remember him as tall; that, I most hesitantly assert, while speaking he would wave his singularly delicate and tender hands. All this emphasises that this indeed was a man larger than his parts.

I do not remember any of the content of his lecture. I remember only my humiliation that in Wales he should have been treated in so curmudgeonly a fashion. In adolescence we can lack a carapace, and I was taking on myself responsibility for the whole shambles. Shortly after Toller began speaking, a dance band struck up in another room in the inn: a dance was about to start in the adjacent small hall. I left to plead with the bandleader to desist; I succeeded only in obtaining the compromise that, as the dance had to commence, slow foxtrots and waltzes only would be played for half an hour, and to such muted accompaniment Toller concluded his talk. I saw the minister mumble something to him about expenses and then, having made some perfunctory goodbyes, abandon him. I plucked up courage and went up to Toller, stammering out apologies for the small audience and the surroundings.

It may have been some balm for him on such a disconsolate occasion that an enthusiastic youngster, familiar with his work, was treating him as an inspirational leader. To my delight, he asked me to

join him for a meal. We could not have gone to a restaurant, for none
such was then available in Pontypridd; no doubt we ate at a *bracchi*, as
the valley's little Italian coffee shops were called, named after one of
the original immigrant families. Nothing more than tinned spaghetti on
toast would have been available, hardly a cheering meal for a man who
was a bon viveur. He laughed a little at my concern for his bad
treatment and to reassure me reminded me of his real deprivations in
the years of imprisonment and spoke of how commitment can be
insulated from austere or uncomprehending surroundings. But before I
left, despite his encouraging words, I sensed depression was enveloping
him.

That melancholy evening was but a small portent of the frustrations
and defeats he was fated to endure. While in London, supported by
psychotherapy given to him by the psychoanalyst Dr Hilde Maas, he
kept afloat, but as he continued to swim against a cruel tide, his
stamina petered out, and he was to be drowned in a sea of sorrows. A
contract in Hollywood brought no success: he could survive in a prison,
but never in a gilded cage. And in Spain all his quixotic efforts to
organise the delivery of food to both sides in the Civil War ended in
fiasco. He suffered and battled against repeated nervous breakdowns,
his letters telling of his fears of depersonalisation. He was disintegrating, becoming uncertain of his identity. He was suffering fatally from a
sickness endemic among the Jews of Germany but unknown to the
Jews of Russia and Poland: he was dying of the disease of Exile.

He was vulnerable to the virus, for his secular millenarianism,
though springing from his early Jewish upbringing, was of quite a
different order from that espoused by the Jews, both religious and
secular, of the Pale. For them Exile, *Galut*, was a necessary condition,
merely a precursor until the Redeemer came unto Zion. No matter how
many centuries their families had lived in Poland, Russia or Lithuania,
they always considered themselves to be in a temporary abode. One
day the Messiah would come to collect them, and they would quit their
lodgings with no regret. Meantime, although they might have to wait
thousands of years, they would not be deceived; if anyone arrived, as
occurred from time to time, and declaimed himself the Messiah, the
wise rabbis always dubbed him a pretentious impostor. No matter how
long the dalliance, they would not fall in love with the towns or
countries that encompassed their ghettoes; they had no territorial
attachments and they would not give their true fealty to mere princes
or czars. Their fidelity was to the Book, to the Torah. And when the
liberalisation movement, the *Haskalah*, spread among them, those who

emancipated themselves from anachronistic dogma found secular alternatives in Zionism, Socialism, Communism and a host of other gospels; one, however, was excluded: patriotism. Despite the pain of their estrangement from the faith of their fathers, they would not yield to the notion that they could find relief by donning the vestments of their reluctant hosts. Their Yiddish tag tells us all: 'Being born in a stable does not mean one is a horse'. They scoffed at the patriotic Jews in Germany who affected to be Germans and whose prime loyalty was to the Kaiser. Even as Toller was growing up, millions of Jews quit the pogrom-ridden lands of Russia, Poland, Lithuania and the Ukraine, most to go to the United States or some, as my grandfathers did, to Britain, in what was the greatest migration in the history of the diaspora. And when they left their birthplace, they did not look back.

But Toller, as a Jew of Germany, was afflicted with searing nostalgia. When, in his wanderings, he wrote a partial autobiography, he entitled it *I Was a German*. His predicament forced him to acknowledge he was no longer a German, but never to disavow his belief, specious though it was, of his original identity. Even as he was continuing to insist it was the German language and culture that had shaped him, leaving Germany had left him bewildered, unable to survive on the stony soil of exile. In anguish he cried out:

> Am I therefore an alien in Germany? Is blood the only valid test? Doesn't the country I grew up in mean anything? Or the air I breathed, the language I spoke, the spirit which formed me? If I were asked, 'Where are your German and where are your Jewish roots?' I should not know what to say.

Rootless, he could not live on. He had told a friend that if he was suddenly found dead never to believe he had committed suicide, and that it would have been the work of Nazi agents. In 1939 he was discovered dead in his shabby hotel in Manhattan, hanging by the cord of his dressing-gown. Whether his death was by his own hand, or by Hitler's minions, there is no doubt about the real slayer. Toller had dared to defy and laugh at Wotan; but it was Wotan who had the terrible last laugh.

Wasserman: ecumenical yearnings

Although they may have been living in Germany for forty decades, still the Jews felt themselves rejected by the national organism as a foreign body; the spectrum of responses by the Jews of the Weimar Republic to their predicament would, however, be incomplete without considering some paradigmatic figures, lacking the political radicalism of Zweig and Toller, who made efforts to overcome the existential dilemmas that afflicted them. Jakob Wasserman, one of the Republic's most widely read novelists, and the egregious Kurt Hahn, educator of the Duke of Edinburgh, are two representative figures who, in their several and different ways, tell us of the more conservative and majority responses of Germany Jewry.

Wasserman was among the first of the German novelists I read; nearly all his novels were translated and, at thirteen years of age, I recall reading his *Der Fall Maurizius* throughout one whole night entranced by his depiction of the struggles of the adolescent who was the main character of that story. Many of his novels ran to three editions in Britain, and in Germany they were best-sellers. Literary critics may today regard him as a middle-brow writing for unexacting readers; the quality of his work may be judged by our Arnold Bennett's repeated assertion that Wasserman was the biggest of modern German novelists, a comment that perhaps sprang from Bennett's literary values and the nature of his own readership. But there were others, whose judgements would perhaps command greater respect, who praised unstintingly this baroque storyteller. As he poured out an immense cycle of earnest novels, of novellas, polemics and confessions, Thomas Mann paid tribute to his 'magnificent mixture of virtuosity and seriousness'. Wasserman was a writer bent on subtly portraying what he called 'the indolence of the heart', and, in this pursuit, always his temperament as a reconciler was revealed. His tales often reflected his dilemma, as he persistently sought to earn his parents' approval even as he battled against their insensitive demands that he enter a commercial career.

In 1921 his ecumenical impulse took another turn. It may be that his success had fed delusions of grandeur, for he set out, with deliberation, to become the 'bridge' between German and Jew. To the surprise of his wide German readership, he revealed in his *Mein Weg als Deutscher und Jude* his torment at the ambiguity he felt as a Jew, despite his family having lived for centuries in Germany. To a Welsh Jew the anguish found in that work is bewildering; it reveals a tension between a reluctant host group and a longstanding and apparently integrated immigrant community that has no parallel anywhere else in Europe.

Wasserman, although he makes no acknowledgement to Heine, hoped to construct his 'bridge', even as the young Heine did, on the

basis of an elective affinity between German and Jew. His concern for
the Germans took precedence over his pain: he took the stance of a
grieving, self-sacrificing, rejected lover. 'Does one not feel,' he asked,
'the greatest sorrow for those that one loves most deeply, even though
that love be wholly unrequited?' Undaunted by the task, he sought to
find the congruences between Jew and German, but even as he spelled
them out, he could not successfully smudge the divisive force of the
deities they separately acknowledged; he turned to metaphor and
dream in this desperate effort to attain the consummation he so
ardently desired. He wrote:

> A non-German cannot possibly imagine the heartbreaking
> position of the German Jew. German Jew – you must place full
> emphasis on both words. You must understand him as the final
> product of a lengthy evolutionary process. His twofold love and
> his struggle on two fronts drive him close to the brink of despair.
> The German and the Jew: I once dreamt an allegorical dream . . .
> I placed the surfaces of two mirrors together; and I felt as though
> the human images contained and preserved in the two mirrors
> must needs fight one another tooth and nail . . . Let me endeavour
> to interpret my metaphor of the mirrors.
>
> That a similarity of destiny and character exists here is evident.
> In both we see centuries of dismemberment and decentralisation.
> A foreign yoke, and a messianic hope for victory over all foes, and
> for unification. Indeed in this connection a special German God
> was invented who figures in every patriotic hymn as the Jewish
> God figures in prayers. With both we find misunderstanding on
> the part of the outside world, ill-will, jealousy and suspicion: in
> both a heterogeneous configuration within the nation, dissension
> among the tribes. And we find irreconcilable contrasts of
> individual traits: practical activity and dreaminess; the gift of
> speculation in both the higher and the lower senses; the impulse
> to learn, to acquire knowledge and serve it; a superabundance of
> formulae and a lack of form; a detached spiritual life that
> imperceptibly leads to hubris, to arrogance and unteachable
> stubbornness. In both, finally, we find the dogma of election.

There was nobility in Wasserman's attempt to span the divide but the
eloquence of his plea did not leave him fully convinced. He felt
compelled to conclude: 'Contact has resulted in abrasions, and the
abrasions have become bleeding festering wounds. In the weaker body,

wounds that will never heal.' His misgivings were tragically well-
founded: twelve years later the Germans gave Hitler power, and the
wounds became fatal. Wasserman's 'bridge' was never built; instead, a
yawning chasm opened into which millions of Jewish men, women and
children were mercilessly hurled to their death. Wasserman, after 1933,
fell into total despair; beset with domestic worries, the political
situation added to his corrosive torture. He could write no more; he
was driven to an early grave.

Hahn: the apostate

Wasserman asked what was the Jew to do to cope with German anti-
Semitism; he warned that it was no answer for the Jews 'to return to
rigid adherence to their ancestral form for that spelled out petrifica-
tion'. But he was even more derisive of another option: 'Apostasy is
automatically excluded for anyone with self-respect. Secret assimilation
is effective only for those fit for assimilation; that is, for the weakest of
individuals.'

Such a discreditable option was the one chosen by Kurt Hahn,
headmaster to princes, including our Duke of Edinburgh, first at Salem
in Germany and later at Gordonstoun.

Hahn was born of wealthy Jewish parents; he accepted his
inheritance but was determined to reject his lineage. He set himself the
task of being the educator of the children of the German aristocracy so
that, as Christian gentlemen, with the values he would inculcate, they
would become the leaders and virtuous warriors of Germany. To be a
suitable exemplar he embarked upon an unauthentic life of sly
renunciation: he would stifle his homo-erotic inclinations and he would
erase his genesis. He deluded himself that by an act of will he could
sustain these denials. Freud's law of the return of the repressed, and
Hitler's racial laws, ensured that he failed. But his determination to
model himself, and the schools he founded, upon the ideals of
fantasised pure and desexualised Teutonic knights of yore, was,
nevertheless, an extraordinary mimetic exercise, flattering to his
patrons and congenial to the parents of his pupils.

By making a synonym of sex and dishonour, the celibate headmaster
imposed a regime upon his schools which could enable him to keep his
own virginity intact; to the point of near madness, he attempted to
outlaw puberty among his pubescent pupils. Thomas Mann's younger
son, the historian Golo Mann, a past student and a devoted admirer of
Hahn, has recounted a little of the school life at Salem:

He saw puberty as an unavoidable disease that one should try to ignore, to overcome by keeping busy with healthy pleasures and strenuous activity and, if need by, by cold showers . . . One of the first battle cries I heard when I arrived at Salem was 'Sticky! Sticky!' The expression came of course originally from the headmaster and his staff. It was 'sticky' when one boy put his hand on another's shoulder, when two boys rode on the same bicycle, when there was not enough space between boys during the evening 'lying down' period, and so on. Any dirty word, any obscene joke, even when we were among ourselves, was avoided as a matter of course; the atmosphere required that.

Self-control was the watchword. Mann tells us:

After a few months a pupil was given the right to keep his own 'training log', noting for each day or week the goals he had met: the morning run, a certain number of high jumps, jumping ropes, cross-country running, no more than three glasses of water a day, no between-meal snacking, and so on. If one slipped up, one had to record a 'minus'.

Touching was not only a minus quality if disobeyed between boys; the 'no-touching' ukase was applied in the few coeducational schools with which Hahn was to be associated. Here, of course, chivalry was all: the boys were taught to be knights in shining armour, ever ready to defend the honour of their maiden colleagues. Flesh and blood relationships thus banned from his schools, Hahn created the ethos within which he, undiscovered, could live his camouflage life.

The sickly chivalry that Hahn espoused was not only intended to govern human relationships; such delicacy was also to be applied in warfare. While the Jew Toller was writing his pacifist plays from prison, the ersatz German and zealous Christian was calling a different tune at Salem, one much more agreeable to his patriotic sponsors. Unlike Toller, he had experienced a good war, exempt from military service 'because of weak health', he had been assigned to a section of the German foreign office to study the English newspapers and to prepare reports on how to estimate and to lower morale in Britain, a task which Mann says he performed 'brilliantly'. Thus equipped, in the post-First World War years, he pontificated to his pupils, telling them that they should always remember the virtues of war. These virtues could be practised in the 'second war' which he would welcome as a means of restoring Germany's previous frontiers; his only proviso was that it should be fought out against an isolated France, and not against Britain since, evidently, his studies of British morale and a year he had enjoyed amongst public school types up at Oxford, persuaded him that it would be inopportune to engage Britain. But in the war he visualised, one could mobilise the virtues of the good soldier – comradeship, courage, Samaritan impulses and, above all, willingness to sacrifice.

Faute de mieux, no war available, this was the virtue that his charges were exhorted to pursue in peacetime. 'One might even say,' Mann has written, 'this was the underlying concept of the school.' Hahn was following the well-trodden path laid down by that most grand of Jewish converts, Paul of Tarsus. His fascination with the Passion was morbid: repeatedly within his schools and, more publicly, he would declare that sacrifice and Samaritan service were the source of the 'revelation'. And this puny Paul, if he lacked the language of the belligerent disciple, certainly did not lag behind in his mentor's histrionics; for this was no gentle, self-effacing saviour. He revelled almost embarrassingly in theatrical presentations of his views, always in his writings italicising any word that he felt would sensuously engage his reader. Boys should not be trained for rescue, but for *dramatic* rescue. Young people should undertake not labours of love, like helping to preserve the treasures of 'mother nature', but *epic* labours of love.

He was obsessed with these rescue fantasies, ever conjuring up situations where, ready to sacrifice all, the hero would emerge. In his schools, games for fun were dethroned; training for rescue took their place, rescues from distressed ships at sea, rescues of fallen mountaineers, rescues from drowning: life was achieved only by risking, or indeed suffering, death.

The source of such exotic rescue fantasies, which were so imperfectly sublimated in Hahn's school curricula, has long since been marked out by psychoanalysts. Thoughts of parental sexual relationships, both on account of jealousy and on account of the repression of incestuous cravings, can be exceedingly distasteful to the child who likes to imagine that the loved parent enters into such a relation unwillingly and under compulsion. This is a fantasy which has found expression in many legends, of which that of St George is the most widely known, in which a distressed and beautiful maiden is delivered by a young knight or hero from the clutches of a tyrant giant or monster. Hahn, by the training he provided, enmeshed his pupils within this fantasy; it was not a difficult task to tease out resonances from youngsters during the period when the primal oedipal strivings of their childhood were reactivated as, with puberty arriving, their sexuality began to assail them. This technique of character formation left some traits permanently embossed upon them. It is difficult not to feel unease when the Prince of Wales, the most famous of pupils brought up within the ethos Hahn was to bequeath to Gordonstoun, courts death by leaving defined ski slopes or, in disobedience to his medical advice, persisted in playing dangerous games of polo which can result, as in June 1993, in most painful injury; this is a type of risk-taking that the curriculum of Salem, and, later, of Gordonstoun, would not have discouraged.

For Hahn, his school at Salem was certainly a cunning device: through pedagogy, in a socially approved manner, the hero acted out his unresolved Oedipal problems and killed off the Jewish dragon-father and all the traditions of his accursed procreator. More, too weak-kneed to live without a father, he seduced another man who was a true German aristocrat, the former German Chancellor, Prince Max of Baden, who endowed Salem and gave it the status which Hahn required if he were to fulfil his ambitions of becoming the *éminence grise* to an élitist Aryan government. Of all the Jews who made a bid for total assimilation, not one exceeded Hahn in his efforts to become a German.

He almost succeeded, for he was acting out his personal dilemmas within an extraordinarily receptive culture. The two tenets central to the curriculum of his schools, sacrifice and heroic safeguard of mother nature, belonged to the intellectual temper of Germany. Graf Hermann Keyserling, the philosophically minded East Prussian aristocrat, in 1933, when seeking to explain the electoral success of Hitler, succinctly identified Germany's self-sacrifice syndrome and made a tragically accurate prognosis of where Hitler was leading the nation:

> Hitler is emphatically the suicidal type, one who, in seeking death, embodies a fundamental trait of the German nation, which has always been in love with death, and for whom *Nibelungennot* is a constantly recurring fundamental experience. Only in this situation do the Germans feel entirely German: they admire and desire death without a purpose, self-sacrifice. And they sense that through Hitler they are once more being led towards grandiose destruction, towards another *Nibelungennot*; that is what fascinates them about him. He is fulfilling their deepest longing. The French or the English want victory, the Germans always only want to die.

Indeed, the works of the conservative writers of Hahn's generation, as of the previous generation, powerfully setting out the noble tradition of

Geist and of literature's national responsibility, were pervaded with
sacrificial themes and were replete with appeals to *Götterdämmerung*-like
destruction. And such attitudinising was not confined to more
traditional writers. Franz Werfel, another converted Jew, whose novels
were among the most widely read of Germanic writers in pre-war
Europe, in his 1945 Hollywood exile repented the follies of his youthful
membership of the expressionist avant garde, and admitted he too was
guilty of luring Germany into the abyss. He overstated his priority but
not his responsibility when he said of himself and his talented
colleagues: 'We not inconsiderable men were the first to bring the fuel
to the hellfire in which mankind is now roasting.' The fact is, as the
late Professor J. P. Stern authoritatively pronounced: 'There is no
major German writer who does not comment on and often contribute
to the catastrophe-mindedness of the age and its bitter delight in its
apocalyptic visions.'

Golo Mann, with self-declared embarrassment, diffidently acknowledges, when paying homage to his headmaster, that congruences
existed between Hitler and Hahn; but he avoids stressing how both
these skilled manipulators used the prevailing German ethos to mask
their personal travails. Both men sought to displace their masochistic
passions, their yearnings for self-abasement, by calling for a society
governed by heroic self-sacrifice, a call which prompted such ready
response in Germany. Although one may note greater fastidiousness at
Salem, the ambience of Hahn's schools is repugnantly similar to that
enveloping Hitler's *Table Talk*. In that book there is scarcely a page
which does not bear the stamp of the self-sacrificing syndrome: 'So if
somebody tells us, "The future too will demand sacrifices", then we
say, "Yes, indeed it will."' But sometimes in the company of his
gangster table companions at his Wolfsschanze at Berchtesgaden,
Hitler drops his guard and reveals his lust for death which alone,
unlike any woman, can provide him with the desired consummation:
'All in all it is surely best for someone who has no heir for his house to
be burnt in it, with all its contents, as though on a magnificent funeral
pyre.'

But the conjunction between the Nazi gospels and Hahn's teachings
is not only to be found in the sacrificial motif; that is only one theme
which emerges from a larger orchestration. The Nazi 'intellectuals' had
provided a 'religion' as an answer to Christianity, which they found too
full of Levantine accretions to be acceptable. They inflated still further
the Wotan cult which had been part of the *Völkisch* ideology of the last
years of the Wilhelminian era; and they taught that the true god of the

Germans is Wotan, the Usurper, *der Ergrieter*, a god of rebirth and decline, a dispenser of the blessing of sin. This was the German god who, long before semitic Christianity, brought his people all the strong virtues – nobility and truly manly piety, belief in fate and, of course, capacity for sacrifice. So many of the virtues that Hahn, in more anæmic fashion, was idealising in his school were part of the pagan doctrines of these Nazis; indeed, they sprang from the same ultimate source, for Wotan had emerged from the mists of a pagan mythology of blood and soil, *Blut und Boden*.

The nineteenth-century German Romantic movement, characterised by man's aspiration to be as one with nature, had prepared the way for much of the farrago of nonsense peddled by the Nazis; and the same influence showed at Salem as Hahn initiated his malleable pupils into the wondrous benefits of communion with nature. The unconscious motivations, however, of all these various inheritors of this romantic tradition lacked innocence; they were of similar quality, although more deeply pathological, as those possessed by not a few of the over-zealous protectors of nature, and of those who fiercely oppose them, whom I encountered when I involved myself in the nascent 'green' movements of the 1970s. At that time I sought in vain to persuade my party to take environmental issues into mainstream politics. I led to Trafalgar Square the first national march of 10,000 young and apolitical protesters against the dangers of civil nuclear energy, and addressed the assembly from the plinth; and followed this by succeeding in initiating in 1978 for the first time a series of debates in the Commons on the hazards of the developing nuclear energy programme and the follies of using Windscale as a reprocessing centre for the nuclear waste of the whole world. It was during this political interlude in my life that I became keenly aware of how in ecological politics there is a background of underlying emotions, music to which political prot-agonists are often supplying only banal librettos.

But professed nature-lovers of Hahn's stamp, whatever the words they may use, are so often out of tune; they lack the ear the genuine committed environmentalist possesses. That environmentalist is often one who, as a child, learned to decathect its love for the mother and spread it over the face of the world until its objects came to safeguard the child's sense of the goodness of life; as an adult such a child, in gratitude, will protect nature. Hahn's relationship with mother nature lacked such tranquillity. He appears as battling for nature and against her, forever staging within his schools happenings where nature could be rescued or overcome; his ambivalences to his mother and his

resentments against his father were never worked through. He acted
them out often in theatrical presentations in which his pupils
enthusiastically participated; it was a technique that was akin to
Hitler's staging of demonstrations. It is difficult to believe that, but for
one circumstance, Hahn would have found it impossible to accommodate himself to the German Nazi regime.

But when in 1933 the shadow fell, not all his royal connections could
save him from the blood of his mother who had betrayed him by being
both Polish and Jewish. To the end, he had still hoped Hitler would
save him, and, anticipating our odious contemporary revisionist
historians, he had continued to exculpate Hitler and throw all the
responsibility for the excesses on his subordinates. Persecuted, hobbled
in his activity with sadistic subtlety, banished with a right of travel in a
limited area, forbidden to communicate with his former pupils or their
parents, his property in Baden and Hermannsberg confiscated, his
life's work, his money all gone – still he declaimed his German
patriotism: 'One must love one's fatherland,' he affirmed, 'even when it
does not love one back. In fact that is the essence of patriotism.' If he
had been taken to a death camp, he is the Jew who, singing
'Deutschland, Deutschland über Alles', would have marched cour-
ageously into the gas chambers. In the event, after his imprisonment
for some weeks, the international royal network went to work: Ramsay
MacDonald, the renegade Labour leader who had become Prime
Minister and never could resist the aristocratic embrace, intervened
and Hahn was released to come to Britain where, with the help of the
house of Windsor, he founded Gordonstoun.

He drew some bizarre lessons from his experience: still incorrigible,
as late as 1965, he was lecturing Britain on how the world could be
saved from 'the progressive inhumanity of society' by rescue operations. On one occasion he bemused at least some of his listeners as he
explained that these inhumanities could be overcome by 'healing
forces' which could be set in motion 'like the Surf Savers of Australia
and the National Ski Patrols in the United States of America'. He
added to his examples those who go to the aid of mountaineers in the
Caucasus and, of course, the four rescue services he had now
established at Gordonstoun. 'I will always remember how on stormy
nights our watches were on duty in our coastguard tower, looking into
the darkness lest a vessel in distress burns an inefficient flare.' For these
boys waiting expectantly for disaster he had devised a pledge: 'I
promise to serve Hopeman Village and this district, through them my
King and Country, and Christ through all.' Now, predictably baptised

and received into the Church of England, he sought the Archbishop of York's approval for the wording of the pledge; the good William Temple evidently found the proselyte zeal too much for him and despairingly responded to the Jew: 'Can't you leave Christ out?'

Undaunted by the declines he saw advancing at an 'alarming' rate, he once explained to a large audience that he was not pessimistic. The 'healing forces' would overcome, as was clear to him from a recent Royal College of Surgeons convention which had been addressed by his admired pupil, the Duke of Edinburgh. The Royal College had, he explained, found its members alarmed by deaths from exposure occurring during adventurous pursuits and had manfully responded to the challenge. He excitedly declared he was now inspired 'by the wish of the surgeons to instruct laymen in the rediscovered expired-air method of resuscitation, then originally introduced by the prophet Elijah, and in the closed cardiac massage developed in the USA'. It was within such a framework that he introduced the concept of 'active citizenship' a generation before it became the figleaf to cover up the depredations of Thatcherism. However, it was in his moulding of the royal pupils of Gordonstoun, the Duke of Edinburgh and the Prince of Wales, that we find this apostate's more significant contribution to British politics.

The future consort

The future Queen's consort, Philip Schlewsig-Holstein-Sonerburg-Glucksburg, to give him his full name, was in his element in a school governed by Hahn's carefully constructed *Weltanschauung*. Prince Philip had originally been under Hahn in Germany and then, when thirteen, had rejoined Hahn after the schoolmaster had left Salem and established Gordonstoun. There would have been little in Philip's background to make him feel alienated from the ethos of Gordonstoun for, although there was a time when hostile journalists, provoked by his arrogance, dubbed him 'Philip the Greek', they were wide of the mark and would have been more accurate if they had indulged their xenophobia by describing him as 'Philip the German'. In fact, beyond by chance being born in Corfu, he has no genuine ethnic link with Greece. When he came to Gordonstoun he was entering a culture familiar to him because his earlier conditioning had been within a German idiom.

His maternal grandfather, Prince Louis of Battenberg, always

thought of his Schloss Heiligenburg in the heart of Hesse-Darmstadt as
his home, and it was there that the marriage of Princess Alice of
Battenberg, Philip's mother, was celebrated; Philip was born into a
family that found Germany especially congenial, and all his four
sisters, given the family ambience, not surprisingly married German
princelings, three of whom were to become high-ranking officers in the
German army and one of whom, Prince Georg of Hanover, was
eventually to become headmaster of Salem.

As a boy, Philip's mother and father were continually sending him
on rounds of visits to the castles of his German relatives, and the lad
especially enjoyed his sojourns at the Grand Duke of Hesse's summer
villa in Panka where the dark forests came down to the Baltic Sea, and
where he made great friends with Baltic fishermen. His visits to
Germany, where he could relate to his many cousins, must have been
especially welcome, for he received little attention from his feckless
father and had little communication with his mother who was
congenitally deaf; although she had been taught to lipread, and would
have, in a fashion, been able to speak English and German to her son,
she seems rarely to have done so. The handicaps of this introverted and
deeply religious woman, whose final instructions were to ensure that
her remains were taken to Jerusalem, were considerable. She bravely
sheltered a religious Jewish woman, with whom she had established
some relationship, in the royal palace in Athens during the Nazi
occupation of Greece; but more usually, she seems to have maintained
a distance from the real world, as from her son, and spent the latter
portion of her life at a Christian sisterhood centre. Philip's father,
Prince Andrew of Greece, certainly did not provide him with
compensatory emotional support. Exiled from Greece largely as a
consequence of his royal family, contrary to the wishes of the Greek
people, supporting Germany against the Allies in the First World War,
the Prince spent his time with his birds on the Riviera. Neither parent
felt much responsibility for raising their only son.

When Philip came under Hahn's tutelage, the now separated parents
were shadowy figures; nevertheless they had attuned their son to the
mode of the German aristocracy; it is an aristocracy which he still
gathers around him when he visits Germany. During the Queen's 1992
state visit the British ambassador was instructed to arrange for the
British Residence in Berlin to organise a dinner with the Duke's
relations, who still cling to their regal titles from the days of Imperial
Germany's profusion of minor royal houses. As a lad, Philip's life with
such cousins indeed prepared him well to receive Hahn's instruction.

At Gordonstoun Philip blossomed. He became 'Guardian', head boy, of the school, and Hahn would have gained vicarious satisfactions by placing the strikingly handsome adolescent of Nordic appearance in the costume plays that were much encouraged in the school. But the recognition given to Philip may not have been due entirely to Hahn's favouritism, although it is well-recorded how, back in Salem, the son of the former German Chancellor, Prince Max, Hahn's patron, was accorded special privileges. More probably Philip gained his prestigious position in the school on merit, comfortably adapting to the headmaster's regime and endowed with an intelligence that does not fall below his arrogance, as anyone who has had the slightest exchange with the Duke can testify. In his adult life the impress of Hahn can often be observed but not always so benignly as in his capable and enthusiastic presidency of the World Wide Fund for Nature, or in his Duke of Edinburgh Award Scheme – instigated by Hahn, which claims to encourage 'adventure and personal achievement' and which, perhaps, does no harm and does a little good; but there are other commitments which cause concern and remind us that from the time of our Hanoverian Kings, the importation of German princes into Britain has sometimes been less than successful.

The Duke's revelatory comments – for example, when, in a visit to the East, he described his Chinese hosts as 'slitty-eyed' – speak of a racial élitism which would be unthinkable to the Queen whose selfless commitment to her Commonwealth has brought her the especial admiration of black African leaders. Perhaps I am over-sensitive to the racialist overtones which can be introjected into debates on the need for population control, another of the Duke's hobbyhorses, for I became acutely aware of these hazards when, in 1967, I successfully sponsored the first family planning bill, and, later, helped to put through a Vasectomy Act, giving publicly funded, assisted facilities free to those wishing to choose another contraceptive technique. Then, not for the first time, I realised how in politics one can often choose one's enemies but can rarely choose one's allies. I spoke of planned parenthood and personal choice; but there were other protagonists in the debates who spoke of birth control, with the emphasis on control. They described unplanned children as 'mistakes', and labelled women using no regular contraceptive technique as being at risk, as if pregnancy was a disease. I sought to distance myself from these determined Malthusians, never forgetting that Malthus's notorious essay on population was initially based on a reactionary polemic against the anarchist egalitarian William Godwin and the early Welsh Co-Operator, Robert Owen, who were among my boyhood heroes. I particularly suspect of possessing

racial prejudices those with preoccupations on the growth of
population amongst people of a different colour from themselves; too
often they are masking their élitism behind a show of concern for the
welfare of people whom they regard as both threatening and inferior.
The Duke's views find their source in Hahn's. Hahn, as with Malthus
who shared his mother with seven other children, came from what he
regarded as an overcrowded family world; with three other brothers on
the scene, his desperate unconscious fantasy of denying his mother's
copulations by postulating that she was an unwilling partner who
needed rescuing, found further expression in a philosophy which
included a hostility to the fecundity which, he believed, led to world
over-population and the despoilation of 'mother earth'.

Some of Hahn's emotionally prompted extravagances on population
issues lace the Duke of Edinburgh's warnings on the dangers of
population and one sometimes feels he is talking about controlled
culling rather than family planning. He dogmatically asserts that 'these
islands are already overcrowded' and joins those who are as
apocalyptic in their assessments of the consequences of over-population
in Britain as in the 1930s and 40s population fanatics, like Quintin
Hogg (now Lord Hailsham) in the Conservative party, had been of the
consequences of under-population. It is perhaps a sociological riddle
why earlier in this century the castration anxieties of many politicians
were warded off by urging more and more conceptions; and yet, later
in the century, elderly politicians and publicists refuse to acknowledge
their own fear of the threat of impotence, and then, using the well-worn
psychological mechanism of projection preceded by denial, deal with
their acute anxieties by demanding the symbolic castration of all others
through State population control policies.

Flawed gurus

Hahn's influence over the royal family was not limited to the Duke of
Edinburgh. Philip, usually an absent father whose interest in the early
years of Charles was minimal, finding he had a sensitive child whom he
regarded as sickly, brutally intervened in his education and, to make a
man of him, insisted Charles should be sent to Gordonstoun. By that
time, Hahn had formally retired, but he never relinquished his firm
connections with the school. Many of the teachers who taught Charles
had been appointed by him, and the ethos of the school, with its
emphases on 'rescue operations', on the value of sacrifice, and distaste

for any overt expression of sexuality, remained firmly in place. The headmaster, Robert Chew, appointed by Hahn to be his successor, had been at Gordonstoun since its inception and was well-schooled in Hahn's injunction that the institution should aspire 'to kindle on the threshold of puberty non-poisonous passions which act as guardians during the dangerous years'. Chew prohibited any association by the pupils with neighbouring girls' schools, and ensured that the maids who worked in the kitchens were imported from the Gaelic-speaking Outer Hebrides and kept strictly segregated from the boys. He maintained Hahn's techniques of dealing with any expression of sexuality, including 'solitary vice', by nourishing in the pupils a deep sense of guilt, rather than by a master's chastisement; pupils should discipline themselves and feel 'dishonour' if they broke the code; miscreants would be sent on 'silent walks' to reflect on their dishonourable wrong-doing. Whatever Charles's smouldering resentment against such a regime, and against his father for having submitted him to the ordeal, outwardly he conformed and followed his father's example and, in due course, was cited as Guardian of Gordonstoun.

Nowadays his public pronouncements reveal a highly intelligent man whom Britain will be fortunate to have as king; but too often his courageous interventions are marred by distortions attributable to his early training. When the Prince boldly intervened in the educational debate, echoes of Hahn's doctrines resounded throughout the celebrated Shakespeare speech; indeed, the content of the rallying call was initially prompted by the able Eric Anderson, now Headmaster of Eton, the English master approved of and appointed by Hahn before Charles's pupillage at Gordonstoun. Anderson's informed zeal would have satisfied Hahn's notorious need for dramatic presentation; such theatre, Golo Mann has told us, was a significant feature of Salem where pupils were trained in choreographed drills: 'festive competitions and performances in uniform that seemed intended for an audience even if none existed'. Hahn brought high camp to Gordonstoun and delightedly concurred in the dressing-up of young noblemen in the costumes of British kings and princes of yore, even as he had incited his German pupils to model themselves on mediæval Teutonic knights. Charles played the role of Exeter in *Henry V* and took the lead in *Macbeth*; Anderson, no sycophant, has said he has never seen the part played as well. Such performances, when attended by Hahn, of the good-looking, costumed aristocratic adolescents would have brought to him thrills prompted not only by his absurd snobbery but also by his imperfectly buried homo-erotic yearnings. When Hahn was Head-master, his excitements had infected the adolescent pupils he was forever manipulating; they were to continue to impinge upon those who later were to be enveloped in the ethos of the school he founded. The intemperate enthusiasm for Shakespeare displayed by Charles has some of its sources in the conceits and camp of Hahn.

When the inadequacies of our educational system are so self-evident, and where there is such a simplistic and regrettable polarisation in the education debate between traditionalists and supporters of the child-centred approach, it is unfortunate that so weighty a contribution as that made by the Prince of Wales should be viewed with so much suspicion; but the resentments of the wretchedly paid comprehensive school-teachers, so often besieged in overcrowded, run-down and under-funded schools, are bound to flare up when presented with a lecture laying down such emphasis on a literary tradition remote from the lives of their often socially disadvantaged pupils, and moreover given by a man whose children will buy their Shakespeare at Eton.

These days it is fashionable to indulge in idealisations of the old grammar school system; as a former pupil of an appallingly down-at-heel secondary school, where valiant teachers fought to maintain the morale of pupils profoundly conscious of their second-class stigma which designated them inferior to the pupils of the well-endowed, fee-paying grammar school a few hundred yards away, I am impatient of the current nostalgia for the old divisive system. And I am unrepentant that, a few years before I entered Parliament, as a councillor I led my party to an electoral victory in Cardiff that enabled the city to end the eleven-plus examination and initiate abolition of the tripartite education system which I, unlike too many of my classmates, had only just managed to survive. Excellence is one matter, élitism is another. Marking out special preserves for educational instruction is the hallmark of those resentful of the ballot box, as Hahn was and as the Prince of Wales's guru, Laurens van der Post, remains. Recently van der Post again expressed his hostility to universal enfranchisement: 'Democracy is increasingly becoming more archaic, because it ultimately becomes more and more dependent on number. The number of votes cast and not the quality of the votes cast. And this is a great political danger.' It will be a greater political danger if, within our constitution, we found we had a king hostile to the principle that every man and woman has the right to vote. It is, I believe, because the Prince of Wales when laying down his views on the moral purpose and values of a modern educational system has so clearly been over-influenced by the ideas of Hahn and van der Post that his intervention has received a less positive response than it deserves.

Too often as the Prince, meticulously fulfilling his duties, takes up a didactic stance, we hear Hahn speaking to us from the grave. In the summer of 1991 the Prince chose to address the Royal College of Psychiatrists. It was the instruction Charles had obtained from a school governed by a Hahn regime that caused him to tell the psychiatrists: 'Suffering, if handled sensitively, can be transmuted in a positively redeeming process'; and this masochistic theme continued unabated throughout his address as he invited his audience to see that illness has value and meaning; that the restrictions imposed by sickness can lead to the stricken man 'rediscovering the divine elements in his being'. While such Hahn sentiments, expressed in the vocabulary of Jung, to whom the Prince often acknowledges his indebtedness, may bring responses from some troubled souls, there will be many who found the Prince of Wales's comments, placed in the context of the importance of doctors being able 'to communicate clearly and skilfully' and to assist in needed 'spiritual healing', as droll, for his lecture took place at a time when the press were already bewailing the Prince's lack of communication with his own wife. The separate bedrooms, the failure to be together on significant family dates, the prolonged silences observed between the royal couple on public occasions, had already become the common fare of the gossip columns and they reflected not merely prurience but a genuine concern that a future king and queen should be failing to act as exemplars of the values of family life now so disturbingly under threat. Now that the divorce of the couple has become inevitable, it is a concern that has increased.

The Prince has the handicap of belonging to a family that is divorce-prone; his sister and brother have both suffered marriage breakdowns. Doubtless a royal family is subject to extra external pressures which do not burden most families; but my experience as a divorce legislator and lawyer has long since taught me that when siblings, without exception, all find difficulty in adjusting to married life, diagnosis of their condition requires a hard look at their upbringing; and the destabler which leaves them with their problems is usually to be found in their relationship with one or both of their parents.

The philosophising of Prince Charles tells us of the destabilising forces in his life which he valiantly, but not always successfully, endeavours to overcome. His philosophising is often essentially non-corporeal, often abstract and disembodied. Freud believed Jung was avoiding facing the full implications of the Oedipal struggle, of the

incestuous desires of the infant and his wish to overcome and become
the father; the father, however, when perceived as tough and
tyrannical, can be too intimidating and the boy can consequently
retreat from adult sexuality and attempt to make a detour. His
identification with his father becomes an artifice, not authentic as in
the identification of a boy who has worked through his Oedipal
predicaments. By a process of mimesis the over-fearful boy can, in
short, adopt his father's ideas but not his aggressive manhood. There
are indications that Charles unconsciously sometimes adopts such a
survival strategy. Oedipal strivings are the lot of all of us in our earliest
years but the domineering Duke of Edinburgh would have singularly
added to Charles's predicaments. Throughout his childhood Charles
was to endure endless provocations, none more wounding than when
Philip summarily dismissed Charles's surrogate mother, the protective
Nanny Lightbody; she was the only woman who had provided Charles,
until he was eight, with an escape from the emotional quarantine
which he endured in the royal household.

No one who has met the Duke of Edinburgh and Prince Charles,
however briefly, cannot but note the contrast between the unpleasant
assertiveness of the father and the sensitive, painstaking and
sympathetic son always insistent that he is well-briefed on his
programmes and on all those his duty requires him to meet. Princes,
however, like all of us, cannot escape the influence of those who begat
them and those who educate them; in his progenitor and in his
educator, Prince Charles has been less than privileged. It certainly can
have been no help, given the nature of the relationship with his father,
to have been placed in a school where his problems were bound to be
compounded, not resolved; for he was in a school where Hahn's writ
ran; a school with a mentor who had fabricated his own personality
and, by the ablation of his Jewish descent and thus the very existence
of his parents, manically denied his own unresolved Oedipal problems.

High Brows, Low Loins

With a father whose communications with him as a youngster were
largely confined to written notes, Charles, understandably, has a
penchant for seeking guidance from older men; his father had utterly
failed him. But it is unfortunate that in his search for father surrogates
he has chosen mentors who comfortably respond to his own yearnings;
men like Hahn with an antagonism to sex, or Jung, whose break with

Freud stemmed from his resistances to the whole concept of the sexual libido, are dangerous heroes to emulate. *Pour trouver la vérité, il faut travailler contre soi-même*: and if the Prince is in search of truth he would surely be wise to strive against, not indulge, his temperament. If he cooled his enthusiasm for Jungian psychotherapy, however beneficial it may be to some, and submitted to some classical Freudian psycho-analytically orientated psychotherapy, he could perhaps escape from the shadow of his father and of his father's hero; he would undoubtedly receive some analytical shock, and such an undertaking would certainly not lead him to discover 'the divine element in his being' but, to the greater satisfaction of the nation, it could perhaps have helped him to find his way to his wife's bedroom.

He married a woman who is the victimised child of a disturbed and broken family and such a child, to survive, can become extraordinarily manipulative. The Princess of Wales's other talents may be meagre but she has exploited her manipulative capacities to the full, engaging the sympathies of the public as she adds to Charles's predicaments and casts him unfairly as the sole villain of the piece. She has described herself, with little exaggeration, as 'thick as two planks'; but she is certainly not lacking in either mischievousness or a talent for role-playing and, encouraged by a doubtful entourage, she displays too many signs of the wilful mother who abandoned her and of the egregious stepmother whom I knew as Lady Dartmouth; Diana's compulsive attention-seeking as an adult tells of a child whose early narcissistic needs were never met by a self-regarding mother and stepmother. Her maternal models ensure she is ready to play any part, including the unlikely one of Mother Diana-cum-Teresa, to ensure that she retains the glitter, prestige and money of a princess. It says much for the restraint of Prince Charles that despite many provocations, including the well-publicised, studied photograph of the 'lonely' little girl in front of the Taj Mahal, that he retains his dignity.

The obtuseness of the palace advisers, wishing to feel assured that heirs would be guaranteed, and more concerned about breeding than emotional stability, never discouraged this marriage; but the deed having long since been done, it would have been only a more emotionally mature husband than Charles who could have ever been able to heal the scars of Diana's childhood which, judging by her relapses into bulimia and reported suicide attempts, are deep and many. Thanks, however, to early malign influences, one of which was Hahn's credo, despite Charles's considerable intelligence, his emotional life has suffered its own arrests.

The fundamental difficulty appears to be that teachers administering and governed by Hahn's credos, were lamentable surrogate fathers for Charles: to the image of the dominating real father, already felt to be threatening – and that, at least unconsciously, is felt by the boy as threatening to an expression of sexuality – came the school which outlawed sex, declaring it 'sticky', filthy. Hahn's displaced rescue fantasies imperfectly concealed his unconscious imaginings that his mother only under compulsion had submitted to his father, that he had rescued his mother, and that she remained pure and unsullied; the chivalric ethos Hahn bequeathed to his schools was almost a guarantee that the pupils would believe that women were near angels and that if they departed from this ideal, they were prostitutes.

Perhaps some dissociation of sexual attraction from tenderness, esteem, regard, admiration and other components of a fully developed love, is an inescapable feature of the sex drive in the human male; the fusion of desire and tenderness, of lust and concern, is certainly not always capable of achievement in human relations. But even a dichotomy that is not as complete as that expressed by unfortunate men who think sex is so degrading that they can only copulate with prostitutes, or those they can regard of lower social station or inferior morality, can be self-destructive; obviously the phenomenon can cause havoc in a monogamous society.

The pedagogical influence of characters like Hahn on pupils, already in difficulties because of unresolved Oedipal problems, can lead them to become adults who equate sex with dirt, and who can only really enjoy it when, in effect, they are revelling in mud. It is an affliction which may sometimes be particularly observed in those who seek to escape from their dilemmas into expositions that are over-intellectualised and are excessively replete with ideational content. As Aldous Huxley once remarked, 'High brows, low loins'. The intolerable intrusion into Charles's private life which brought the Tampax tapes into public view would suggest that the prince, in a mild form, may suffer from the syndrome; but few men with claims to intellectuality could claim to be totally exempt from the syndrome. Indeed, in Charles's case, to considerable public benefit, he shields himself against such internalised fractures by constantly affirming that there must be what he repeatedly describes as 'holistic', whole, integral approaches to our external national problems. We should therefore refrain from odious moralistic cant and, rather, direct our anger at those who have added to the burdens he has to bear; in my opinion, no single person bears more responsibility for his personal problems than Kurt Hahn.

The irony is that the very dilemmas to which Hahn's doctrines have contributed may yet be resolved as Prince Charles uses but transcends the pedagogue's indoctrination. The Prince's pungent and persistent expressions of ecological concern would have greater, and needed, impact if they were not discounted by doubts prompted by his penchant for communing with nature and with his 'retreats', often for weeks. Hahn would no doubt have approved of his interest in the mystical pretensions of van der Post and Jung, but it has led to an image of him, fostered by the tabloids, of a man who talks to flowers; and in other circles his official sojourns among ambassadors has led, as I have found, to many within the diplomatic world speaking of him as a 'nutter'. But Charles has considerable courage; aware of the misgivings, in the spring of 1991 he vigorously counter-attacked those who 'labelled him as an alarmist and crank', and he has continued unremittingly to focus attention upon needed environmental priorities. He has not been helped by a petulant Diana whose public display of sulks in South Korea in 1992 sabotaged his efforts to draw attention to the important waste-cycling programme he was, for the world's instruction, helping to set up in South East Asia.

Fortunately the Prince has stamina; in Mexico in 1993, undistracted by a silly wife, he skilfully drove home to international business leaders his message, and extracted from them the promise of a wide range of environmental projects. His aides made it clear to the media that he saw his future as a leader of a world crusade to rescue the environment: in doing so he may well also rescue himself. One witnesses the transformation into a splendid reality of the infantile rescue fantasies of Hahn. There is a nobility in these endeavours to break loose from the coils of an unfortunate marriage and live constructively as a solitary. It is to be hoped that he will be able to maintain the dynamic of his laudable environmental efforts while sloughing off the apocalyptic intellectual mush which, through Hahn's sick ethos, comes to him from German *Kultur*.

A long sixty minutes

Once, in South Wales, I involuntarily met Hahn. He had come to establish the Atlantic College in a castle on a piece of coast not far from my constituency. There, carefully selected sixth-form boys from various countries, all potential university material, were to have a strong dose of Hahn's character and leadership training. Four rescue services were to be operated on the ten miles of dangerous coast that were to be entrusted to them, and they were especially charged to be on duty at weekends during the 'drowning season'. The ingenious biology master had devised a special crane that could be operated on the cliffs; and the headmaster, a retired admiral, had, Hahn affirmed, 'a mission in life to encourage in the art of life-saving that meticulous care which is generally devoted to the art of war'. Hahn had been invited to a television studio to explain the objectives of this college.

By chance, I too had been invited to be interviewed in a section of the same programme as Hahn; happily we were not appearing together. The programme was being boxed in advance and, some technical hitches arising, both of us were required to wait together in a guest room, alone most of the time, for an hour; it was a long sixty minutes.

He had, before my arrival, already been made aware of the nature of my contribution to the programme. Nowadays one hears frequently of pre-Wolfenden and post-Wolfenden attitudes, as if the report was the watershed in attitudes to homosexuality. In fact it took almost a decade of campaigning after the report before, after many attempts, I succeeded in 1967 in persuading Parliament to accept my bill ending the criminality of homosexuality between consenting adults; this little television interview was one of many centring on my campaign. The subject matter could hardly have been more uncongenial to a repressed homosexual; the manner in which he spoke a few cold words to me as we were introduced made me immediately conscious of the extraordinary strangulation of emotional response which afflicted the wretched man. When the interviewer came into the room for a few minutes, in front of Hahn, I provocatively suggested that on the programme I should be asked what prompted me to be so concerned about homosexuals, so that I could explain to viewers that, as a Jew, I was naturally concerned about the fate of all other persecuted minorities; and Hahn, as I intended, flinched.

Our enforced rendezvous continued uncomfortably; the fascination which he so successfully exercised on many did not extend to me. I coldly asked him about his Atlantic College project, and he responded icily. Impatient with his schemes, I recall asking him ironically why he was going to such trouble placing his pupils in a castle, and setting up such an elaborate organisation. Could not his character-building exercise perhaps be better achieved by seconding his young sprigs to the mines in my constituency? There, sometimes in grim conditions, my miners daily faced hazards and only too often were involved in rescue operations. I conceded that perhaps this contributed to the strength of character and the sense of community which, above all my other constituents, I admired in the colliers. He, of course, knew I was mocking him. Not surprisingly, the programme completed, he speedily made his goodbyes and fled from me. But it was not from me he was fleeing; it was, as ever, from himself. And so he continued to flee until, in the end, he returned to his native land to be buried, as he wished, in his beloved German soil.

Why Heine, Zweig, Toller, Wasserman and Hahn failed

In 1854 Heine wrote: 'The character of the Jewish people has a great affinity with the Germans.' Certainly there was one indisputable affinity: both peoples, as Jakob Wasserman stressed, clung to 'the dogma of election'. The one believed themselves to be the Master Race, the other the Chosen People. Out of the Teutonic Valhalla, Germans, as Jung insisted, had selected Wotan as their god. The Hebrews, bringing to the resentful world the monotheistic religion, permitted the nameless god to be referred to as Yahweh or Elohim, but never to be anthropomorphised; and, scorning polytheism, declared all other gods to be trash. It was their provocations, coming down through æons of time, that nullified all the efforts of Zweig, Toller, Wasserman and Hahn, as of all the Jews of Germany, to become members of the German nation. For Wotan, the principal god of the Teutonic peoples, and regarded as such by the ancestors of the Germans for centuries after the birth of the Jewish Christ, had never in Germany been extirpated by Christianity. In the 1930s Wotan and Yahweh clashed in the heavens and, on the ground, for a terrible time, as Yahweh appeared to be overcome, the German god all but annihilated Yahweh's chosen people.

The myths that govern the politics of a nation determine events far more than do party· manifestos. The myth of Siegfried, direct descendant of Sigi the son of Wotan, pervaded Nazi propaganda. Siegfried was Hitler's model of German youth joined in love and honourable marriage with pure German Brünnhilde. Only the sorcery of an inferior race could bring these two noble creatures into dishonour. Siegfried was stabbed in the back. Brünnhilde was led astray by magic. The Versailles Treaty and the 'stabbed in the back' theory of how Germany lost the Great War were echoes of the portrayals in Wagner's operas of the German psyche; but neither

Wagner nor Hitler invented Siegfried. He had a potency and a history among the Germanic tribes long pre-dating their encounter with the Christ story.

When a scrutiny is made of a nation's decision-making, only those who have had no immersion in politics would shrug off the dominance of myths. Those academics who, fearing to plunge into deeper waters, attribute the genocide perpetrated by the Germans to a political strategy, or as a symptom of lower-middle-class malaise, or a product of declining capitalism, are dangerously naïve. That a people could become a nation of child murderers on a scale that leaves Pharaoh and Herod mere petty criminals is not to be explained as a secular socio-economic phenomenon: the explanation of the deliberate slaying of more than a million Jewish children cannot be located within a rational secular grid. The eruption of barbarism has another source, and Jung, a German-Swiss, able to hear the heartbeat of his people, and to feel so nicely the pulse of his race, found his answer as he used his singular capacity to empathise with Wotan.

He appraised 'the formidable phenomenon of National Socialism on which the whole world gazes with astonished eyes' as an expression of 'an Aryan unconscious', one quite different from that possessed by Jews. The Jews were fatigued members of

> . . . a race with a three thousand year old civilisation . . . The still youthful Germanic peoples are fully capable of creating new cultural forms that still lie dormant in the darkness of the unconscious in every individual – seeds bursting with energy and capable of multi-expansion. The Jew who is something of a nomad has never yet created a cultural form of his own. . . . [These nomads are] badly at a loss for that quality in man which roots him to the earth and draws new strength from below. This chthonic quality is to be found in dangerous concentration in the German peoples. . . . The Jew has too little of this quality – where has he his owner under foot?

He was not alone in these mantic efforts to divine the origins of German Nazism. In Vienna Freud, from whom he had long since been estranged, was, unknown to him, simultaneously also coming to extraordinary phylogenetic conclusions as he searched for the sick dynamic behind Nazi anti-Semitism. For the Jew Freud knew his people were being assailed by a fierce hatred with no precedent even in the long history of persecutions that they had endured. Arnold Zweig showed me in Berlin the letters from Freud where, for the first time, in

1934, he revealed he now had a draft of the work which ultimately was to be published in English as *Moses and Monotheism*. In those letters Freud made explicit his motivation for writing that book. He had written to Zweig: 'Faced with the new persecutions, one asks oneself again how the Jews have come to be what they are and why they should have attracted this undying hatred.' Jung was attempting to discover what moved the Germans, and revelled in the vigour and *élan* which he believed Wotan had brought to them. By contrast, Freud was concerned to discover how the Jews 'have come to be what they are' and why they were hated. Like Jung, he was dismissive of those offering answers in a current socio-political or economic mode:

> The deeper motives for hatred of the Jews are rooted in the remotest past ages [he concluded]. They operate from the unconscious of the peoples. . . . I venture to assert that jealousy of the people which declared itself the first-born favourite child of God the Father has not yet been surmounted among the other peoples . . . it is as though they had thought there was truth in the claim.

It was the grounds upon which the Jew laid claim to be the favourite that was especially infuriating to the German: the Jew said he was so blessed because he had undertaken to bring monotheism to the world, and that explanation inflamed the wounds the German had suffered when Christianity was imposed upon him. Freud affirmed:

> We must not forget that all those people who excel today in their hatred of Jews became Christians only in late historic times, often driven to it by bloody coercion. It might be said that they are all 'misbaptised'. They have been left, under a thin veneer of Christianity, what their ancestors were, who worshipped the barbarous polytheism. They have not got over a grudge against the new religion which was imposed upon them; but they have displaced the grudge on to the source from which Christianity reached them.

It may well be that the fierce denunciations of Martin Luther, the man who was the first great national prophet of Germany and the forger of the German language itself, sprang from his anxieties that the hold of Christianity upon the Germans was slight, and could be overthrown; that it was, as Freud described it, 'simply a veneer'; and the blame for this condition Luther projected upon the Jews who were thwarting the fulfilment of his mission to save his 'beloved German

nation' who, but for the despoiling Jews, could become mankind's
redeemers.

The fault of the Jews was that they would not yield up their ascetic
monotheism, refusing to respond to Luther's attempt to convert them
to a religion which in their view was a cultural regression taking over
symbolic pagan rituals and finding room in its creed to introduce many
of the divine figures of polytheism only lightly veiled, albeit in a
subordinate position. Jews, by their stubbornness, Luther held, were
holding Christendom hostage since Christ could not return in the
Second Coming until they should be converted; their rigid attitudes,
contemptuously dismissing Christianity as a blasphemous compromise
with polytheism, put the German peoples at risk, tempting them to
revert to full polytheism if Christianity was not able to guarantee them
the certainty of Christ's return. The frustrated Luther, whose doctrines
remain engraved upon twentieth-century Germany, found the remedy
to end the doubts: it was to eliminate the Jews totally. 'I cannot
convert the Jews. Our Lord Jesus Christ did not succeed in doing so;
but I can close their mouths so that there will be nothing for them to
do but to lie upon the ground', he told his congregation in 1539. Four
years later he was being even more explicit: '. . . they are our masters
and we their servants . . . we are at fault in not slaying them.'

Four centuries later, Hitler repaired the omission. Those who fail to
acknowledge this extraordinary continuity in German history, who
base their political stances towards present-day Germany on an over-
valuation of the importance of symbolic dates like 1918–19 and 1933
and would have us believe that the Third Reich was an aberration,
totally out of kilter with Germany's past and present, are engaged in
dangerous self-deception. Both anti-Semitism and the tug of polytheism
have endured for centuries in Germany. No one has more eloquently
expressed the continued resentment the Germans feel at being deprived
of Wotan and all the gods of the Teutonic pantheon than the other
great German prophet, Nietzsche. He spelled out the German sense of
loss, asserting that in polytheism lay the freedom of the human spirit,
its creative multiplicity. The doctrine of a single deity, whom men
cannot play off against other gods and thus win open spaces for their
own aims, is 'the most monstrous of all human errors' (*die
ungeheuerlichste aller menschlichen Verirrungen*).

Given his goals, Nietzsche's attempt to reclaim polytheism was not an
ignoble aspiration. But such an articulate revolt against the monotheistic god was useful material for the Nazi intellectuals like Alfred
Rosenberg and Wilhelm Hauer who perverted his doctrines, and

provided their party with a religious doctrine alienated from Judaeo-Christianity; they proffered a gospel of a superior Aryan-Germanic tradition which must be maintained and extended by the 'master race'. They applied to the German Reich the same concept of consubstantiality which Christians apply to the Church when they refer to the mystical body of Christ. To be an Aryan was to feel the galvanising current flowing through the whole body of the nation. And there was nothing metaphorical about their concepts: the German nation was literally to be a single body made up of identical cells. The issue was to create a *blutgemeinschaft*, a community of blood. Hitler in *Mein Kampf* expressly declared that it was the absence of 'unity of blood' which had robbed the German Reich of 'world domination'. Not surprisingly, his deputy Hess said: 'National Socialism is nothing but applied biology.' And to such 'scientific' instruction, the German people responded.

The exclusivity preached and accepted by the Germans, giving them the moral sanction to annihilate Jew or Slav, is uncomfortably close to that practised by latter-day fundamentalist Judaism with its taboo against intermarriage, a prohibition against exogamy unknown to its founders; such concepts of exclusivity, peddled by fundamentalists and right-wing Israeli politicians, exacerbate, even though they do not create, the problems of a region, which, as the Iran-Iraq war, the civil wars of Lebanon and the struggle between Iran and the Gulf States revealed, have only little relevance to the creation of the state of Israel.

The resolution, however, of the dilemma of a people burdened with a traditional claim that it is chosen to redeem all mankind even while it remains separate, is essentially a domestic problem for Jewry. The resolution of the German question is of another order and, in the light of Germany's conduct in this century, it is an imperative for all Europe, and in particular for Britain. A people possessed with a sense of mission, believing destiny has favoured them to be a redemptive élite, as their philosophers taught the Germans long before Hitler's arrival, will not be easily exorcised of their delusions of grandeur; but if Britain is to wrestle successfully with the German question, if it is to contribute to the creation of a European Germany and prevent the formation of a German Europe, then its foreign policies must be emancipated from its own pretensions; and they are many.

We should recall there was a time when England, like Germany in the twentieth century, believed itself to be an 'elected' nation. In John Foxe's sixteenth century polemic Protestant tract, *The Book of Martyrs*, England is specifically designated as an 'elect' nation under a godly queen singled out by God as an instrument of divine providence:

Elizabeth ordered the work to be placed alongside the Bible in every church in the land. Our pretensions have since diminished, but have by no means vanished; in recent decades our prime ministers have deliberately corroborated the nation's grandiose self-image. Alec Douglas-Home's East of Suez defence policy was matched by Harold Wilson's daydream that our frontier was on the Himalayas. Wilson's 1964 proclamation 'We are a world power, and a world influence, or we are nothing' was echoed in the Conservative's 1987 election slogan: 'Britain is great again', while Thatcher trumpeted to the electorate that 'this is no ordinary country'. At the Conservative Party conference in 1992, Major's grudging acknowledgement of Britain's changing position, expressed in his commitment to the Maastricht Treaty, was yet again camouflaged under tired, moth-eaten, patriotic garb leaving the conference delegates free to sing 'Land of Hope and Glory' and retain their inner fantasy that still the sun never sets upon the empire.

The task of freeing Britain from its imperialist past is certainly incomplete; but the task of Germany emancipating itself from its horrific, more immediate past has barely begun. And those of us who want one Europe, free from the domination of any single nation-state, know that, brutal as we must be in casting aside our continuing imperial pretensions, no less merciless must we be when we address Germany's deep-seated yearnings. Panglossian opinion suggesting that thereby ghosts are being evoked long since laid to rest, that we now have a democratic Germany, and that we should simply be nice to the Germans and forgive and forget, do a disservice to the Germans and ourselves.

Repeatedly during 1990 and early 1991, I was being told by German politicians and academics that my apprehensions were outmoded, that no one of any significance any longer indulged in Bismarckian – or worse – delusions, that Western Germany was regionalist and cosmopolitan, and that the real difficulty was that German politicians were so provincial that they would not even peer over the *Länder* borders to see the Brandenburg gate. In June 1991, however, these comforting self-assurances vanished. In Bonn the demonstrating crowds, demanding the town remain Germany's modest capital, held aloft banners declaiming: 'We want no Fourth Reich'; but the Bundestag determined otherwise and the old grandiosity reasserted itself, as, despite the huge economic cost, irrationally, Berlin was declared the capital. The Bundestag had responded to Chancellor Kohl's irresistible appeal when, unveiling his ambition, and all the symptoms of German sickness, he euphorically declared Berlin would become the 'fulcrum of a United States of Europe encompassing the European Community, Scandinavia and Eastern Europe'.

We cannot, out of misguided goodwill, ignore either the deeper implications of the establishment of Berlin as the capital, or of Germany's precipitate reunification; nor can we ignore the sinister implications of the race riots flaring up throughout Germany, and treat them as of marginal significance. Above all, we should remember that the European Community was essentially a creature of the Cold War and that, now the external Soviet threat has vanished, Germany's moorings within the Community are no longer securely anchored. If we are to ward off further bouts of the German sickness afflicting Europe, we need to achieve a genuine understanding of its nature; and that requires applying hermeneutic, rather than tired conventional political diagnostic skills; reassuring ourselves that our treatment, by way of nineteenth-century political and diplomatic responses, is appropriate, and pronouncing optimistic prognoses is to deny the total failure such an approach to the German phenomenon has provided in the past. Jung and Freud knew understanding required the daring to probe the German soul; we need to follow their examples. The Germans have never ceased to declaim the overwhelming significance of the German *Geist*; we would be wise to take them at their word.

PART III

Denying the Past

An *affaire* in Africa

In the middle of the war, in improbable circumstances, in the heart of Africa, I had my fateful meeting with the handsome young German woman, Greta. The man responsible for bringing us together was a group captain, a regular serviceman who, for a while, was my commanding officer; he was possessed of extraordinary charm and even more astonishing resourcefulness. Somehow taking advantage of the confusions of Rommel's advance, and his friendship with Air Marshal Tedder, he managed to move himself and some of those of us attached to his unit out of the Middle East war theatre to an isolated spot, almost on the Equator, in the interior of East Africa. Our bewilderment at suddenly finding ourselves perched on the Kenya highlands ended only when we discovered what had brought us to so remote a location; the group captain's mistress owned the nearby farm, and he was indeed well provided for.

We, however, were not so fortunate; we had not an available young white woman within hundreds of miles. There is a presumptuous myth prevalent amongst the young that sex began in the sixties; how their fathers and grandfathers, as lusty young men, behaved during the long war years, they are too prudish to scrutinise. In fact, most of them conducted themselves healthily, when the opportunity arose, as they should have. And when a handful of us took a break to visit the pygmies near the Congo border and Ruwenzori, the Mountains of the Moon, in Uganda, a blissful serendipity appeared to fall upon us: we found the attractive Greta, quite alone, within the vicinity, making the same exploration.

The competition for the Nordic beauty was intense, but my eager comrades, despite many cunning assaults, were soon repulsed. I had hesitated, alerted by her diffident comment, clearly regretted as soon as made, that it was difficult to consort with members of the Force that was bombing her homelands; my colleagues insensitively interpreted the remark as coquettish teasing, not an expression of anguish. Greta was in fact a most serious and torn religious young woman who had reached her position as a teacher to Africans in a North Uganda Protestant mission station only after much travail.

73

Born into a conservative Junker family, many of these conflicts arose
from her past commitments to Germany's Evangelical Church whose
leaders had found little difficulty in accommodating themselves to the
Nazi state, for they had always regretted the departure of the Kaiser
and the subsequent end of the traditional authoritarian state which had
upheld the links between Church and state embedded in Reformation
theology. This established Church, dominated by pro-Nazi clergymen,
had always been hostile to the Weimar Republic, which it regarded as
the carrier of godlessness and Marxism; some of its more radical
elements were openly supportive of *Völkisch* nationalism of the Nazi
variety, and these German Christians had as their slogan: 'The
swastika on our breasts and the Cross in our hearts'. With such a
helpful established Evangelical Church, the Nazis were prepared to
accommodate its demands, in 1935, to chasten the open practitioners of
the Wotan cult who engaged in public conversions to paganism. The
Nazis, now firmly in power, saw no need for Wotan worship to be
institutionalised in any alternative church; the Evangelicals, soaked in
Lutheran anti-Semitic doctrine, were sufficiently primed.

From their pulpits they preached Martin Luther's doctrines of
hatred against the Jews, frequently reciting extracts from Luther's
poisonous pamphlets. He had ironically written:

> Cursed *goy* that I am, I cannot understand how they manage to be
> so skilful, unless I think that when Judas Iscariot hanged himself,
> his guts burst and emptied. Perhaps the Jews sent their servants
> with plates of silver and pots of gold to gather up Judas's piss with
> the other treasures, and then they ate and drank his offal and
> thereby acquired eyes so piercing that they discovered in the
> Scriptures commentaries that neither Matthew nor Isaiah himself
> found there, not to mention the rest of us cursed *goyim*.

With such sermonising in the churches, the Nazis could rest content.

There was, however, one group within the Evangelical Church
which was unable to reconcile Nazism with the theological principles of
Reformation Christianity, and its members found it unacceptable that
the secular Führer should take precedence over Jesus Christ; their
reservations were often limited, and not all of them were prepared to go
as far as opposing persecution of Jews who had been converted to
Christianity, but they felt compelled to demur to the main ethos of
their Church. They formed a small independent church, the Lutheran
Confessing Church, and some hundreds of their pastors suffered
harassment from the Nazis and were subject to periods, usually short,

of incarceration. Greta, in her adolescence, had evidently come under
the influence of some of the pastors of this secessionist group and,
finding her predicaments becoming intolerable, with their aid had
managed to leave Germany before war broke out.

Greta and I, when we met, were both in our early twenties, but the
attempts we had made to still our earlier adolescent turbulence within
ideological and intellectual rationalisations had taken place in
strangely different milieus. The Christianity which, as a Jewish boy, I
knew began with my participating with my schoolmates in the local
Chapel's jolly Whitsun treats; my schoolfriends bore the first names of
the Jewish prophets, and patronyms like Levi were frequent. In
Cardiff, in the northern part of the city where I lived, unlike in the
predominantly Roman Catholic southern part, the local preachers and
Nonconformist Sunday schools laid great emphasis on the Old
Testament and I consequently was regarded as a privileged member of
the 'People of the Book'. And, a little later, when I joined in agitations
with young socialists, my comrades, in the Welsh manner, found their
political faith far more in Methodism than in Marxism; nowhere more
than in Nonconformist Wales, where the memories of the battle for the
disestablishment of the Church still remained, was there a greater
distaste for a linkage between Church and State. Discovering the
allegiances Christians gave in Germany to nation and State, which
were those belonging to Greta, was for me a voyage into strange
territories.

And no less disorientating for me was the realisation that
Schopenhauer's plea for an Aryan Christianity, one de-Judaised, had
received warm and continuing response from many German Christians; the pessimistic philosopher had equated Judaism with a soul-
corroding optimism which had seized hold of European man and must
be overthrown if mankind was to find true redemption and liberty. In
Christian Wales, belonging to the same people as Jesus and his
disciples confirmed an advantage upon me; now I was learning that
Germany had fostered a different brand of Christianity, one determinedly separating itself from its Jewish parent, and resentful of
anyone who belonged to the circumcised tribes, for he may tell that
Jesus belonged to the House of David.

There were, too, other bewilderments between Greta and myself.
The fatalisms integral to Greta's overvalued attachments to honour
were quite alien to me. From her I was to receive intimations of the
mind-set of the men who, a few years later, were to attempt to
assassinate Hitler: because of their class and culture, to which Greta

belonged, they despised the vulgarity of the upstart corporal and, although knowing they would not succeed, were ready to make a bid to kill him. For the sake of their personal honour, as well as for the honour of Germany, they deemed it necessary to sacrifice their own lives. As Berthold Stauffenberg, one of the main participants in the assassination plot of July 1944, put it: 'The most terrible thing is knowing that it cannot succeed and that we must still do it for our country and our children.' Such notions of honour would not appeal to a Jew who belonged to a people who suffered enough martyrdoms without seeking them out; and Welshmen, who always fundamentally retain their realism amidst all their romantic rhetoric, would regard such displays of honour as plain daft. Yet the self-same conceptions of honour were those held by this young German woman.

It was inevitably, therefore, an overlong wooing: there was talk – too much talk – and so much philosophising. She had constructed a tough carapace to shield her from the hostilities of the insecure, crabbed wives of white settlers, fearing the reactions of their husbands to an apparently accessible pretty young woman, and she had to endure continuous clumsy enquiries from security investigators suspicious of this footloose, intelligent German girl in British territory. In response to her isolation, and no doubt for less creditable motives, I wrote a few articles for the Forces' journals circulating throughout East Africa questioning the views of the influential civil servant Robert Vansittart, later Lord Vansittart, whose widely publicised attacks on Germany were being popularly interpreted as asserting that the only good Germans were dead ones. Vansittart's pre-war assessments of the Nazi threat to Britain had proved to be as accurate as they were uncongenial to his then political masters who had believed they could accommodate Hitler, and then unleash him against Bolshevik Russia. For his pains, Vansittart was demoted to the Lords; but not before he persisted in his sweeping condemnations of the Germans. But I could not accept that the German social history with which I had a little familiarity had been totally erased, that the Germany which had taken the initiative in tackling oppressive social conditions at an earlier stage of the industrial era had vanished. Could the world's most powerful socialist movement of the last third of the nineteenth century, one which imposed a notable compromise in social legislation on the conservative forces under Bismarck, have left no impress?

At that time, however, I had not grasped the full significance of the heritage of the German socialist movement. I did not understand that its cradle, the much acclaimed German cultural revolution of the early nineteenth century, could not be neatly fitted into the formula that would have us accept that revolution was a perennially progressive liberal or left-wing phenomenon, and that 'race' was to be regarded as an irrational aberration of right-wing thinking devoid of revolutionary content. The thinking of the German Social Democratic movement in fact never fully emerged from the mists of the German philosophy which would instruct us that the Western liberal idea of revolution, as expressed in the French Revolutions of 1789 and 1848, were but superficial manifestations of the revolutionary spirit; that the true metapolitical meaning of the revolutionary process was revealed by Kant and Fichte and their heirs, a process of quasi-religious profundity, which would lead to the German race blazing a path to freedom; and that freedom was not the prosaic freedom sought by Western liberalism but one of a different order, a transcendental redemptive freedom which the Germans alone could bring to mankind. Such maniacal pretensions, pursued with a revolutionary fervour, were to lead to the racial obscenities of Wagner and, of course, to envelop Hitler's National Socialist party; but the theoreticians of the German socialist movement, and not least Marx himself, were also badly seared by the inflammatory legacy of German revolutionary nationalism. Insufficiently aware as a young man of this background, I was jejune enough to equate German Social Democrats and Communists with those wearing the same party labels in the Welsh Labour movement.

My contributions to the Forces' press, therefore, were inevitably naïve; they sought to sustain my old belief in the existence of the 'other' Germany, and by thus corroborating my own illusions reinforced them, and was to make my subsequent rude awakening to the realities a harsher shock. After such gestures and long treks to visit Greta's remote mission station within the diocese of the Upper Sudan, ultimately the citadel fell. It was too late: ratiocination had drained passion. Our *affaire* continued for a while but was saved from foundering by my being posted away; fortunately we left each other unharmed, with her self-esteem unwounded, and I went on my way a wiser young man, tutored a little in the convolutions of the German psyche, but still stubbornly refusing to acknowledge the awesome convulsions of which it was capable.

The blank walls of Vienna

That over-delayed acknowledgement I made a few years later, as the war drew to its close; the reactions of those who had sight of the victims of the barbarity of the concentration camps were various. Mine was rage, ungovernable rage against all those responsible; and it is a rage that has never stilled and will, I hope, be with me unto my death. If time, forgiveness, or mitigation, ever allow it to be diminished, then the brutes who perpetrated the killings will have triumphed: conceding extenuation, mankind will have diminished itself. All this anger in the last phase of my military service was focused on the Austrians; and I could not have found more deserving recipients than in Hitler's native land.

With the war ended, the Russians having reluctantly permitted the Allies a small presence in Vienna, I found myself, after a short sojourn in Carinthia, among the first to arrive in that city; and in the eight months that elapsed before my demobilisation, my own detestation and contempt for all but a few of the Führer's fellow-countrymen almost self-destructively overwhelmed me. The Austrians had originally incited Hitler to take them into his embrace; it was immediately after his visit to the town where he had spent his schooldays, Linz, where he had been ecstatically received, that he marched to Vienna for his notorious tumultuous welcome. Austria was to remain the most fanatical of the Germanic regions: there were more members of the Nazi party in proportion to the population in Austria than there ever were in Germany; in the Viennese, all the worst characteristics of Germany were deeply and ineradicably etched. It followed that from the moment of the Anschluss there was a viciousness and open brutality against Austrian Jews even more savage than that which had been displayed up to that time in Germany.

The Viennese, long before I had arrived, had made their city *Judenfrei* but their belief in their Aryan superiority was now finding new expression in their hostility to the small number of foreigners who in the mêlée following upon the German collapse, had tried to take refuge in Vienna. One of these outsiders was Lucy, a young woman to whom, to this day, I remain indebted. She had been born to a Byelorussian father and a Polish mother; trapped in the territories where the battles of the Eastern front had raged, she had lost her husband, her baby and her parents. She, alone of her family, survived, and succeeded by her command of languages, her fair appearance, and indomitable courage, to avoid being drafted into the slave camps, and to secure employment on the German international telephone exchange.

She was working in France when the Allies landed and, determined to avoid another searing experience as armies clashed, abandoned her post and made her way to Vienna, correctly anticipating that by the time that city was taken, the disasters and excesses accompanying advancing armies would have petered out. By my second meeting with Lucy, we both knew what was unspoken: that we would become lovers; but there were constraints. All the norms of human relationships – always tenuous in Vienna – had collapsed; hunger and defeat took their toll in a city where a cloying romanticism had, in any event, long been used to excuse promiscuity and infidelity. Now, with most of Vienna's men either still prisoners in Russia or slain on the Eastern front, there were seven women to every man. The servicemen could frolic, chatting up a Frau or Fräulein in the morning, who would then fall in love with him in the afternoon, before going to his bed that night. Only the most gullible did not understand that these shallow personal relationships were wholly manipulative and exploitative: the currency was food, cigarettes and gifts – not love. The young British soldiers and airmen gathered their rosebuds as they might, and often much else; it was fortunate penicillin was just beginning to be available to the Forces; and the Fräulein, the minor calamity discovered, would invariably tell the tale how she had been raped by a Russian before she had found her only true British lover-boy.

In such a meretricious world, to establish, untainted by sanctimonious attitudes towards others, an authenticity in affection and desire between a young man and woman needed delicacy; the suspicion that material dependency, not emotional inter-dependency was the prompter, could be invasive and not easily repulsed in the Vienna of 1945–6. But the black market which engulfed the city came to our rescue. The British occupied zone of Austria was contiguous with Italy and I had access to a small RAF van, and sufficient petrol; I knew my Italy, and a few forays there enabled me to provide Lucy with 'capital'. Within a few weeks, she had insisted upon repaying me for the goods I had bought, and I was able to end my smuggling activities. Nimble, elemental and, unlike the Viennese, adapted to survive in the most hostile of environments, with her unusual linguistic abilities, she was soon on her feet, moving skilfully through the world now known to millions because of its depiction in the film *The Third Man*. The most adept of the *fartopchiki* of those days, the Russian political commissars to whom she introduced me, were, I observed, in awe of her trading and commercial skills. Now she was free, full of laughter and unabated sentimentality, and we lived together giving each other, despite the outside corruption and squalor, much happiness and sufficient pain, the prerequisites for any real relationship.

She mocked my earnestness, teased me about my continuing political idealism which, understandably, given her experience, she found silly, but she was too tactful to dismiss it explicitly; yet despite the treatment she had received at the hands of Germans and Austrians, she continually sought to dampen my ever-mounting anger against the Viennese. There were particular reasons why my rage was constantly being refuelled. I was one of the few Jews in the small British force in the city, and I found I was being deluged with requests from Jews in London who had quit Vienna in time but whose relatives had been left behind. These exiles desperately wanted to know the exact fate of their parents, brothers or sisters, and would direct me to Austrians who, they thought, had been close friends and whom they believed would be able to give some information.

Everywhere I met a blank wall; if I was received by these erstwhile friends, I would hear much of their present plight but they blotted out any recollections, and feigned they had no knowledge of when or where or how these Jewish friends had disappeared: they had vanished mysteriously, as far as they were concerned, even if they had been living in the next apartment. Some of these friends were crooks, fearful that valuables that had been entrusted to them by their neighbours would be reclaimed; but most were engaged in a frantic effort to de-realise the Nazi past, to empty it of reality. My intrusive enquiries were insensitive; they were activating recollections which, if they surfaced, could overwhelm them, compelling them to acknowledge both guilt and their humiliation at their country's defeat. In a sense Lucy was right when she tried to persuade me that they had no alternative but to behave so appallingly: so great had been their identification with Hitler and his regime that this almost psychotic denial of the immediate past was their only method of avoiding depersonalisation, of total disintegration.

Lucy was five years younger than me, but her understanding of the dilemma of the Viennese was greater than mine; where she was wrong was in believing that in time they would be able to face both their past and that of the Reich. Forty years on, in 1986, during Austria's presidential campaign, I was present in Vienna again to witness their continuing denials, and felt the same ugly hate which possessed them when they welcomed Hitler and persecuted the Jews. Enthusiastically they voted for the lying Kurt Waldheim. When during a broadcast I shared with Waldheim's daughter, she assured me and the listeners I was wrong to accuse her father of war crimes and that some of her, and her father's, best friends were Jews – then I was made painfully aware of how little had changed in Vienna since 1946. And when, in 1991, the

Austrian prime minister so tardily at last asked his people to acknowledge their responsibility for the Nazi atrocities, it was impossible not to fear that the 'apology' was for foreign consumption; it came at a time when Austria wished to be respectable enough to gain entry into the European Community. Even this fear of Austria being treated as a pariah did not stop 100,000 people, in Vienna alone, in 1993 signing an extreme right-wing national petition calling for changes which, if implemented, would have resulted in the most racially discriminatory legislation anywhere in Western Europe.

Still so many of the Austrians cannot accept the loss of their favourite son: the flagrant manner in which they continued to refuse to stigmatise their past reveals what is so often camouflaged in present-day Germany. I became increasingly infuriated in 1946 because I realised the Viennese had not, could not, give up their Führer, for they had encapsulated him; the death of Adolf Hitler could not take place. To him they had abdicated all responsibility; he was their collective ideal, possessed of omnipotence, and they had taken him into their very core. Hitler had entered their souls, and to acknowledge the humiliation of his defeat would have been soul-death for them. Rather than concede the defeat, they denied the battle; but secretly they nursed their revenge, for they saw themselves as victims not aggressors and, whining to me about their discomforts, they had no feelings of sympathy for the Jews whom I was seeking; the only object deserving of sympathy usually turned out to be themselves. It comes as no surprise to me that historical research has now suggested that although the Austrians made up less than 10 per cent of the population of Hitler's Reich, they were involved in half the crimes associated with the Holocaust.

Demolished bridges

It is not only Austrians or, as I have observed, so many Germans, who have sought to avoid intolerable emotions by breaking all affective bridges linking them to the immediate past: the same phenomenon can be seen in the Americans. The massive USA intervention in the Gulf war cannot be understood without an appreciation of the failure of America to handle emotionally their defeat in Vietnam. Opposition to that war was expressed by a small minority and, in the subsequent inquest, an organised force of direct survivors, as Vietnam veterans, for a short while infused the public perception with the follies of the war with a special authority. But the rapidity with which Vietnam disappeared in the USA from public discussion, and the way in which its highly significant relationship to the entire Watergate scandal, leading to Nixon's downfall, was all but ignored in the various disclosures, reveals the morbidity of America's response to the defeat.

During the Vietnam war, criticising the British support for the USA, I once told the Commons:

> In the end, the USA, spitting in the face of history, is bound to lose the war after terrible losses of young American lives. We, in our great maturity as a country, should not incite or condone actions which allow this war to continue. Psychologists say that defeat is analogous to death; and the great American people appear to have a flaw which expresses itself in gardens of rest, morticians and embalmers – a whole funeral industry. They appear to find great difficulty – like the Pharaohs – in accepting the fact of death and hence, perhaps, difficulty in accepting defeat.

When the end came, the Americans failed to mourn the death embedded in their defeat; they would not confront their psychological experience of having colluded, albeit for most at a distance, in the killings. They could not acknowledge their guilt for the hideous destruction they had wreaked: they buried it, remaining in a state of psychic numbness, locked in a silent but explosive conflict. But the explosion had to come, the vengeful feelings, never worked through, had to be released. Saddam acted as the detonator. The tens of thousands of retreating Iraqi conscripts mowed down by the USA bombers, the sufferings of the Kurds, the destruction of Kuwait, was the ironic price the USA demanded for having, in vain, destroyed Cambodia and murdered hundreds of thousands of Vietnamese: the Americans at last had their revenge and rejoiced in their 'victory' parades.

All this has been perpetrated by a country always exhilarated by its commitment to democratic ideals; if such a failure can occur within a traditionally open society, how much more likely is some long-delayed outburst to come from a state which has suffered unavenged catastrophic defeat and which lacks a democratic tradition. Democracy, and its structure, was imposed upon Germany by Allied decree; contemporary Germany has not emerged out of a political process possessed of natural organic growth. In many ways a democratic Germany is a disjunction in its history. That was how the German people viewed their past in 1933 on the 'Day of Potsdam' when

President Hindenburg and Chancellor Hitler, the 'old' and the 'new' images of Germany, joined hands before the tomb of Frederick the Great: the seal was symbolically set upon the most glorious German tradition, and the Weimar Republic was rubbished as a treacherous interlude.

It would therefore be folly to overlook how tenuous are the roots of present-day democracy in Germany; so many living in West Germany today, rejecting any inner involvement in their own behaviour, or that of their parents, under the Nazi regime, eschew identifying with any political institutions and they identify themselves only with Germany's economic system, not its democracy. This autistic behaviour is their defence against the self-devaluation which otherwise could crush them if they faced up to their personal responsibility for their nation's immediate past. But it is a dangerous strategy to employ to protect their own self-esteem; it was the one used when, at the end of the war, a nation so unreservedly committed to Hitler did an astonishing and lightning shift in mood. It assumed a different self-image, that of a peaceful industrious people concerned only to achieve wealth more and more rapidly.

And now, more recently, I have met in East Germany too many of those aptly named after the bird we call the wryneck and which the Germans call *Wendehals*, literally 'turnthroat'; these turncoats, once zealous Communist Party bosses and *apparatchiks*, are now the enthusiastic company directors of the privatised companies. The most repulsive example of this instantaneous switch of allegiances was within the organisation which claimed, above all others, to be loyal to the old GDR, the NVA, the state's defence forces. Led by a man ostentatiously anti-Nato and always flamboyantly pro-Soviet, with underlings who for years had been engaged in anti-Western indoctrination of their troops, the NVA accepted the new dispensation without demur: no immolations of tanks, no scuttling of ships. Without even a short interlude between one allegiance and another, as took place when, in the West in the 1950s, ex-Wehrmacht officers clamoured to be allowed to join the Nato-supervised Bundeswehr, the NVA, with no twinge of conscience, actively co-operated in its own dissolution.

The magic of relics

Such collective switches of behaviour, prompted by denial not acknowledgement of the past, can, however, be based on shifting sands.

It warns us how quickly everything can be changed in Germany. The sound of Thor's distant thunder can be heard too often for comfort in today's Germany, and I already heard it as I saw, almost immediately after reunification, cars from Traubants to Mercedes sporting stickers alongside the 'D' for Deutschland, that proclaimed 'PR' for Preussen. Winston Churchill in 1945 described Prussia as the 'root of all evil' and acquiesced in its dismemberment, leaving Russia and Poland with most of its territory and the rump split between a divided Germany; but the yearnings persist, and were fanned in August 1991 when, despite protests from many sections of German opinion, Kohl, knowing he had a majority on his side, ostentatiously attended at Potsdam the ceremonial reburial of Prussia's warrior king, Frederick the Great. Pomp and military ceremony marked the occasion; hundreds of thousands came to applaud, and millions viewed on television the removal of the relics. German apologists, seeking to contain the outrage felt by some at home and by many abroad, defended the militarist conqueror by pointing to his liberality in giving refuge to Voltaire and allowing the entry of Jews and Huguenots into his ever-expanding kingdom – provided, of course, they were prepared to fight in Frederick's wars. One doubts if those thoughts, however, were in the forefront of the multitude attending the reburial. It was an occasion undoubtedly relished by the wealthy Prussian families who, to the discomfiture of a Polish government now committed to allowing free sale of land, are presently offering attractive Deutschmarks to buy back their former estates; this, it must be conceded, is a less brutal technique of acquisition than that practised by their ancestors, the Teutonic knights who massacred the original inhabitants of Prussia and confiscated their lands.

Under pressure, Kohl became increasingly prolix in his defence of his attendance, claiming his postgraduate history studies had taught him that Frederick's reign marked 'the beginnings of a rule by law that pointed the way to the future'. But the heated dialogues on the issue were not simply disputations between those presenting different extrapolations based on the events of Frederick's reign; nor can the episode be dismissed as obtuseness and an insensitivity to international opinion and, in particular, to Germany's near neighbours. Golo Mann described the reburial ceremony as 'tasteless'; but it certainly was not merely a matter of taste. The heat the issue engendered did not spring from the passions aroused by many of the intellectual arguments of the protagonists; it came, quite simply, from bones. And bones, in societies not governed by rationalism but by magic, superstition or faith, can have a wondrous potency. The sinister significance of this battle of these relics is contemporary Germany's continued facility to quit the twentieth century and glide effortlessly back into the mediæval eras.

In other times, when God's will was believed to be made visible through miracles, saints' bones were the intermediaries. Battles were fought over relics, for their possession was priceless, and God was a living power, physically present in the bones contained within the sumptuous reliquaries of the shrines of mediæval Europe. Abbeys and churches vied to possess the most famous bones, often making elaborately conceived plans to steal them from one another; for the relics were the lure of the great pilgrimages, the source of funds which contributed to the building of the great cathedrals. The pilgrims reaching the reliquary of the great, expected miracles to result, with the sick and dying eagerly searching for a magic cure. The removal of Frederick's bones to Potsdam sprang from one near-miracle, the unanticipated reunification of Germany, resulting from an astonishing series of events. When the pilgrimages to Potsdam begin, as they surely will, what further miracles can be expected by the pilgrims?

The bones of the expansionist military king, unlike the saints' bones, are certainly not perceived as intermediaries between man and a Semitic God; but are they not intermediaries with the Germanic gods? What 'miracle' now will they exude to ensure that Frederick's kingdom is restored, and the lands of Prussia yet again contain the 'lost territories'? When, at the stroke of midnight on 17 August 1991, the bones of Frederick were placed within the vaults of the glittering reliquary of Sans Souci, who but the unimaginative would doubt that in the heavens the Valkyries were joyously riding high?

Kohl's declaration that he went to Sans Souci only in his individual, and not in his representative, capacity was indeed a mendacious affectation. He well knew the unspoken message he was sending out to the nation, for Potsdam's jewel has historical memories for all Germans which go beyond its connection with the Hohenzollern dynasty. It was there during another August, in 1945, that the victorious Allies decided that enough was enough, and that the boundaries of East-Central Europe had to be redrawn; with considerable sagacity they ruled that, although it meant a cruel compulsory transfer of perhaps some ten million ethnic Germans from the eastern territories, that was an essential precondition for a stable peace. Kohl, like millions of Germans, has never accepted the justice of that decision. To this day, the conservative newspapers *Frankfurter Allgemeine Zeitung* and *Die Welt*, refer to eastern Germany as *Mitteldeutschland* on the grounds that what was historically called *Ostdeutschland* – Upper and Lower Silesia and Pomerania – is now in Poland. In 1985 Kohl received a rapturous welcome as he demonstrated his resentments by attending the convention of the Association of German Expellees from Silesia, an association dedicated to undo the Potsdam decisions. While he was speaking publicly, endorsing the German state boundaries of 1937 which, of course, include about one-third of Poland, the banners were unfolded in the auditorium reading: 'Silesia stays German!' And as the Berlin wall fell, in his euphoria, Kohl again blurted out his covetousness for the eastern territories.

Kohl's attendance at Sans Souci was no act of passive homage: he was there to show his followers he was ready to stir Frederick's bones into action. With such encouragement given to those seeking to glorify an imperial past, it is unsurprising that by September 1993 the town of Koblenz, in another conscious effort to revive memories of the same order, erected a copy of the original statue of Kaiser Wilhelm I, founder of the Second German Reich, which had been destroyed by Allied bombs. As if to ensure that France was aware of the implication, the statue faces downriver, looking towards France, and its unveiling took place on the anniversary of Germany's humiliating defeat of the French in the Battle of Sedan in 1870.

Kohl may encourage his countrymen to remember Germany's triumphal past, but he most certainly discourages his nation to dwell on the immediate past. For that he disclaims all responsibility, since he was blessed by 'the fortuitous grace of his late birth'; and so he talks about 'this generation not being affected by the Nazi past'. He claims that he and his generation were 'liberated' by the Allies and, upon such a claim, with singular insouciance, he based his right to join the Queen, Presidents Clinton and Mitterand, and five other Allied heads of state at ceremonies to be held this year commemorating the 1944 Normandy landings; veterans of the Second World War regarded the claim as outrageous, and, under pressure, John Major was forced to tell Kohl to desist.

Kohl's responses to Germany's recent past are indeed widely different from those of Chancellor Brandt, who fell upon his knees in tears before the Auschwitz concentration camp memorial, an act that at the time seemed to provide an ineradicable counterweight to the unspeakable conduct of the Germans in Eastern Europe. Now I have to grit my teeth as I have repeatedly heard Germans who dismissed Brandt's plea for forgiveness as the maudlin gesture of a man who had had too good a lunch, and who, even after his noble death, continue to

refer snidely to his drinking habits. Brandt was acknowledging the
horrors visited not only upon the Jews but on the entire resident
population of occupied Eastern Europe by the Germans.

What made the Allies believe that expulsions were necessary was not
simply a need to assuage the violent hatred displayed by Czechs and
Poles to the Germans still in their midst at the end of the war; it was
because they had concluded that in the light of the history of German
minorities in Eastern Europe between the wars there was no
alternative. The many millions of ethnic Germans who found
themselves living in newly created states, such as Poland and
Czechoslovakia, at the end of the First World War, became saboteurs,
not citizens, of the lands in which they lived. They were willingly used
as tools to destabilise these two states and provide Hitler with an
excuse to take over the Sudeten territory and to invade both countries.
If the expulsions had not taken place, there would have been no
political stability or durable peace, and the Allies' hard-won victory
would have been in vain.

Kohl, to ensure that his compatriots and a forgetful world blot out
these facts, cunningly deploys necromancy, an art in which he is a
distinguished practitioner. He conjures up a glorious past from the
bones of Frederick, but he can also manipulate other skeletons to erase
memories. On the occasion, in 1985, of the fortieth anniversary of
Germany's unconditional surrender, the opportunist turned it into a
celebration of the Western Alliance, a moment when a line would be
drawn and no distinction would henceforth be made between German
murderers and their victims. He personally induced Reagan to come to
the Bomberg military cemetery where, alongside ordinary soldiers,
there lay numerous bodies of Himmler's Waffen-SS men; and the
oafish Reagan under Kohl's spell, like a ventriloquist's dummy, told
the world what Kohl wished it to hear: 'All those young men are
victims of Nazism also . . . they were victims as surely as the victims in
the concentration camp.' He refused even to 'balance' the visit by
going to a concentration camp, saying the Germans 'have a guilt
feeling that's been imposed on them, and I just think it unnecessary'.
The Germans were given the exoneration which Kohl believes is their
right, an exoneration which he ceaselessly demands. Sometimes his
relentless pursuit provokes a backlash as in November 1993, when he
endeavoured to have placed on Berlin's first national war memorial an
inscription to 'The victims of war and tyranny'. This smudging of the
roles of perpetrators and victims provoked widespread protests and,
ultimately, reluctantly, Kohl yielded to the protesting organisations so
that a long inscription was added: 'To millions of murdered Jews, to

murdered gypsies and those who were killed for their religious beliefs, for their homosexuality or becasue they were physically or mentally handicapped'. Kohl was thus, unusually, outmanoeuvred; but those who too readily dismiss Kohl as an unintelligent blunderer are wide of the mark. The current recession and the failed promises made at the time of reunification may yet mean that Kohl will become Germany's scapegoat; and the German media forecast that we now have a *Kanzledämmerung*, a 'twilight' of the Chancellor may, in 1994, be proved correct. But in the meantime he is a chancellor who is indeed the voice of today's Germany.

Consorting with the wicked

Observing Kohl's stances, and talking to his political supporters, repeatedly takes me back to the confrontation I endured 35 years ago with the East German dictator Walter Ulbricht: for Kohl and his like are men whom the dictator would have had no difficulty in fitting into the demonology which, as political philosophy, he had attempted at our meeting to impose upon me. The meeting had been instigated by the egregious MP Will Owen, a spy who later resigned from the House after being charged with espionage and then acquitted by a credulous jury. Shortly after I had entered the Commons, Owen, around the tearoom table, had heard me provoking one of the praetorian guards of Hugh Gaitskell, then the rigid leader of the Labour Party, by knocking the official party line of approval of the government's policy of total non-recognition of the GDR. Owen rightly assumed that I might be responsive to an invitation to meet both Wilhelm Pieck, the East German president, and Ulbricht. I had no illusions about Owen's murky roles, nor indeed of the GDR; but I went with a few other colleagues to East Berlin with the intention of discussing with Ulbricht the proposals he had then been canvassing: that there could be a peaceful co-existence in central Europe with the two states living together within a confederation, with Berlin as a demilitarised city, and with both states disengaging from the East and West blocs, declaring their neutrality and becoming free of nuclear weapons on their soil.

Even as this meeting with Ulbricht was taking place, Hugh Gaitskell, who knew of my intentions and, furious that any maverick should be appearing to subvert the official policy, publicly condemned the dialogue; the British press, taking their cue from Gaitskell, declared myself and my colleagues to be Communist dupes.

The accusation was that we were consorting with the wicked; it was, of course, confusing. It is simpler to have a vision of the world in terms of black and white, of gods and devils. It is tough to acknowledge our darker drives, examine them and so subject them to the more rational control which can at least partially be exerted upon them when admitted to consciousness. It is easier to repudiate our aggression and project it upon others; but that is the method that leads to us having no more hope of effectively dealing with the aggression of others than of coping with our own. Ulbricht and his crew certainly needed containing, and it was important they knew the boundaries we set; but it was no less important that we did not feed their paranoia. The distinction between a good lover and a good hater, like Ulbricht, is that the lover is faithful; but the good hater knows no fidelity. He is promiscuous, and ready to consume with his freely floating aggression anyone who by his action is unwisely showing his wish to offer needless provocation. And there could not have been greater and more foolish provocation to the East German government leadership than to deny, by non-recognition, that they and the GDR existed.

In retrospect I realise that the East Berlin meeting was to act as a catalyst ensuring, whatever my preoccupations with domestic social policies, that during my 30 years in the Commons I could never forget that the future of Britain and Europe was dependent upon our political skill and understanding in relating to the emotional torments of the German people. Like a leper displaying his sores, Ulbricht, in the fury that was to emerge in our discussion, exhibited to me his gaping wounds; for the sufferings that belonged to him, and those he imposed upon others, were necessary scourges, warding off fears of disintegration, and giving to him corroboration of his own intactness. The flagellate syndrome that this fanatical and abstinent puritan displayed endures in many aspects of contemporary German public life, and often seems endemic to Germany. In May 1992 Kohl found the syndrome causing him political discomfort, and accurately identified it, complaining that 'Germans prefer to be morose Germans . . . they lack the capacity to rejoice.'

When, in 1959, the morose, unsmiling Ulbricht commenced his meeting with me, he did not begin by outlining his peace proposals but embarked upon a dogmatic cataloguing of the Nazi connections of the West German Republic. But as he developed his assault upon the Nazi past of what he described as the revanchist leadership of West Germany, I became increasingly disquieted as I saw his projection of guilt and collective responsibility upon the West Germans was a clumsy attempt to exculpate the people of his state from their terrible participation. The facts bore no resemblance to his thesis. Ulbricht was governing that part of Germany which had been the Nazis' electoral base: it was the Protestant north and east which had especially voted Hitler into power, and had subsequently loyally sustained him.

For some time I silently listened to him. I was initially inhibited, perhaps because of my awareness that the RAF had killed his father in an air raid; and knowing that, to his credit, he later placed a tombstone on his father's grave inscribed with Goethe's words: 'Let man be noble, helpful and good'. This was not the gesture of a hypocrite, for Ulbricht belonged, I believe, to that dangerous breed of politician, the sea-green incorruptibles, whose intentions are honourable and whose actions wreak havoc. In the year I met him, with messianic zeal he had proclaimed the ten commandments of socialist morality; one of them was: 'Thou shalt lead a clean decent life and respect the family'. He was expounding the creed of a man who was reacting fiercely against the promiscuity which had surrounded him in his infancy, for he had lived his hard childhood in the heart of the brothel area of his native city. Indeed, his abstemiousness and his strict spartan life as a young man were key factors in his wresting of power over the German Communist Party from Thaelmann and his hard-drinking companions. His successors were not as self-indulgent as they have been represented, but they were vacillators, lacking the hot certainties which possessed Ulbricht. He was a believer, and the Lenin beard he sported told of the endeavours he was making to emulate his hero.

My patience with him was not limitless, and there came a time when I had my fill of his diatribe against 'revanchists' and of his persuasions that 'neo-Fascism' and anti-Semitism were running wild on the fertile soil of Adenauer's 'military-clerical regime'. I interrupted the zealot to suggest that not all the millions of Jews thrown into the ovens were pitched there by those living in West Germany; that the Germans in his republic must share the guilt, even though I provocatively conceded that there was at least one difference between East and West Germany on this score: the West Germans were making financial reparations both to the surviving members of the slaughtered families and to Israel; the East Germans had not paid a single penny. My comment ensured that subsequently we had a dialogue, not Ulbricht's prepared monologue. The turbulence increased considerably when Ulbricht attacked the reparations as payments to an imperialist base, and I retorted that I had never seen British or American troops in Israel but I had observed many Russian troops in my days in East Germany. Not until these pleasantries were well over did we return to the purpose of my visit, to discuss at length his proposals for peaceful co-existence. But I left him knowing that his sensible proposals were pipe-dreams unless his fears of attack and subversions from the West were diminished by conciliatory gestures coming from the Allies.

Panzer troops on Welsh soil

I was therefore indignant when, not over-long after my visit to East Germany, the Conservative government announced its intention to bring in West German troops for training in Wales. Worse, by collusion with the Opposition front bench, this quaint contribution to international understanding was to be acquiesced to by the Parliamentary Labour Party. The decision was ill-received in pacific Wales. The placing of panzer troops on Welsh soil was widely considered a bizarre method for cementing British–German friendship, and, to many, a grim and offensive heralding of the formal burying of the war against Nazism. I was only too well aware from my encounter with Ulbricht how it could alarm and provoke the leadership in East Germany and, indeed, of all the other countries of Eastern Europe; and equally I was aware that the intended token force was a test of British public opinion.

I flung myself unreservedly into the protest movement that, led by the South Wales miners, speedily grew up. I spoke with studied intemperance at many protest meetings in the Principality; helped to cajole the Welsh Council of Labour, the regional governing body of the Labour Party, into acceptance of my point of view; flanked by hundreds of police, I led a demonstration of many thousands of trade unionists to the Pembrokeshire headquarters of the German Forces; and in the House, with a handful of other MPs, I defied the party whip. I was, with deliberation, vexatious and provocative.

Those who had given private assurances of an easy passage to the government naturally found my activities infuriating. The usually well-mannered shadow Foreign Secretary of those days, Patrick Gordon-Walker, was roused to such emotion that, failing to persuade me to abstain and not vote against the Tories, he excitedly pursued me, arguing, into the 'No' lobby, and I literally had to shake him off as physically he sought to restrain me from passing through the tellers and registering my vote.

My defiance of the whip on the German troops issue led me, together with the handful of the MPs also involved, being summoned individually to a disciplinary committee composed of Hugh Gaitskell, George Brown and the chief whip. My attendance upon them was short and pungent. Asked why I had defied the whip, I told Gaitskell and Brown – each of whom had married a Jewish woman – that they should not ask me for an explanation but should ask their wives; and in the momentary silence that followed my reply, I turned on my heel and walked out. The recommendation they subsequently made to the parliamentary party that I should be severely reprimanded, but that no further disciplinary action should be taken, was willingly accepted by the parliamentary Labour Party wishing to close the issue.

But I did not intend that the matter should be so ended. Not only was I to march with Michael Foot on the next annual visit of German troops in Pembrokeshire, at the head of an even larger demonstration but, meantime, I persuaded my good friends on the South Wales area committee of the Municipal and General Workers Union, where my professional links as a lawyer were strong, to raise the issue at the annual conference of their union. They did this with effect and, when the Trades Union Congress met, the usually accommodating Municipal and General Workers Union had been mandated to vote for the protest with the more militant unions. The TUC therefore lined up with those of us who had been reprimanded.

To underline the point, I surprised, by a stratagem, the Tory government and my own front bench on army estimates day in the House of Commons. By seizing upon a reference to the money spent on army recruiting publicity, I raised the whole question of the publicity presented to the nation by the army on the occasion of the panzer visits. I elevated the question to a constitutional issue, suggesting that the army was meddling in politics in seeking to persuade the public to accept visits which were abhorrent to the TUC. My co-rebels, delighted with my ruse, soon followed me in the Chamber to initiate a full-scale debate. The army, which had been reluctantly in any event dragged into the issue had, by the time the debate ended, more than enough.

From then on, the panzer unit slunk into the western part of Wales without any publicity, and no further German troops were deployed elsewhere in Britain. Soon the training in Britain totally ceased and I had successfully made my little contribution towards dampening down the Cold War. Almost 30 years later, however, there was to be a piquant postscript. When Margaret Thatcher, ever stirring up the Cold War, laid down as a condition of agreeing to unification, that British troops should be allowed to train in East Germany, Hans-Dietrich

Genscher, then German foreign minister, became enraged by the British stance. He clearly was not prepared to condone such obvious provocations to the Soviet Union; and in the end it was Thatcher who crumpled, and waived her attempted condition. Events had indeed turned full circle.

PART IV

Spreading Guilt Thinly

Erasing memories

During one of my many visits to Germany in 1991, I decided to visit the memorial centre at Dachau. The previous day I spent in nearby Munich. There is little to remind you of Toller's city, and overmuch to remind you of Hitler's. Munich, he had declared, was to be the capital of German art, and his commission of the Haus der Kunst, was an earnest of his intention. When the grandiose 'temple of art' was completed in 1937, the occasion was marked by a parade two miles long through the centre of Munich, led by the SS and SA contingents, flanked by 500 riders, and followed by floats representing the glories of the Roman Empire down to those of the present; the most significant contemporary contribution displayed was a huge model of the new Berlin designed by the Führer himself. In his opening speech of the first exhibition 'German Art for All', Hitler praised the trash it contained: the sculptures of nude Nordic warriors brandishing spears and swords, the sentimentalised renderings of idealised German landscapes, and of passive German motherhood, and excoriated the degenerate paintings of the rootless Jewish and Bolshevik modernists. Today the works of the painters he outlawed, Picasso, Beckmann, Kandinsky and Kirchner, line the walls of the pompous halls of the cavernous building; but theirs is a doubtful triumph. The paintings in such over-sized surroundings look like postage stamps floating on a vast expanse of wall. Their vitality is sapped, their restless anarchic work mortified, their colours drained; the great marble floors, the straight line of columns in the former 'hall of honour', the enormous corridors, bring death not enhancement. The Führer's favoured architect, Paul Troost, has had a posthumous victory. Hitler's slime, even after half a century, is not easily cleansed in Munich; and my morning's viewing left me melancholy.

My afternoon did not improve my spirits; perhaps the morrow's visit to Dachau cast its shadow before me. I walked across the vast Königsplatz, and, for me, it was difficult not to hear echoes of Hitler's voice haranguing the huge Munich gatherings of the Nazi faithful whom the party, whose national headquarters were nearby, was wont to assemble here. A poster displayed on one side of the square made me aware of an exhibition that was taking place not far away: for the first time in Munich a large collection of the works of the Jewish painter Chagall was being shown. The juxtaposition of Hitler's favourite forum with the paintings of the man who, above all, had evoked the world of the *shtetl*, the world of the dreamers, romantics, the fiddlers, the gentle zealots of the Pale, the world utterly destroyed by the Nazis, jarred upon me.

The exhibition had been discreetly assembled. No one could present a Chagall collection and completely blot out his mourning for the lost ghettos of Eastern Europe, but the selection was artful; the emphasis was upon the fantasies, the lovers, the folklore, not upon the more explicit excruciating and accusatory threnodies. The smooth, well-dressed Munich bourgeoisie moving around the gallery were in little danger of being reminded that they, or their parents, were exterminators of all the people and the Yiddish culture that Chagall depicted. The dissociation between the murderers and the victims was nicely corroborated by the gallery's catalogue: the paintings were put into an historical perspective that somehow omitted the Holocaust. They told us of 'both Russian folklore and the religious intensity of the gay and life-loving chassidim of eastern Judaism . . . they belong to the sources of an expressive art which was tangential to the big European style of art after 1900 but which did not abandon its characteristic features'. With such soothing and distractive prattle, the *gemütlichkeit* citizens of Munich looked at the paintings, blind to the indictment against their fathers which was spelt out in every stroke of Chagall's brush. On that afternoon they, unlike myself, had a pleasant hour with exotica.

My short train journey from Munich to Dachau was no less dispiriting. An elderly, bucolic, ingratiating passenger, noting I was watching for my stop, said he would alert me as we approached my destination; he proudly announced he was a citizen of Dachau, of old lineage, not like many who had come there after they had been forced out of Silesia. But why should I go to the camp, he prattled on; the old town of Dachau – 400 years older than Munich – was a charming place; not for nothing it had once been a famous artists' colony. The camp had unfairly given Dachau a bad name: people went there for cheap thrills. If I wished, he would act as my guide, steer me to a good restaurant, show me the fine St Jakob's Church and the multimillion-Deutschemark gallery showing the paintings of the Dachau artists. I found myself being drowned in what Nobel prizewinner Heinrich Böll has described as 'The sea of stupidity, the whole sea of infinite German talkativeness, unmatched anywhere in the world'. Losing patience with the chatter of my fellow-passenger, I firmly declined his invitation to the other Dachau, coloured brochures of which I was a little later to see prominently and tastelessly displayed in the concentration camp's museum.

But his monologue explained to me the conduct of the present burghers of Dachau who for eleven years refused permission for the building of a *Haus der Begegnung*, a house of encounter, where young Germans could explore together with other youngsters from other countries the tragedy of the Holocaust. Such a centre has been established in Poland in the town of Oswiecim, near the Auschwitz-Birkenau death camp, but Dachau rejected an invitation to twin with the Polish town, and adamantly refused to participate in this exercise in *Vergangenheitbewältigung*, recalling and coming to terms with the past; for they wish only to blot out memories. For them the centre would be accusatory not, as was intended, an international symbol of how to deal constructively with a gruesome legacy. The leader of the burghers said the mark of Cain was not to be pressed upon the brows of Dachau's residents, and defiant in refusal, and using the language of Goebbels when he attempted to bolster Germany's collapsing morale, the mayor declared: 'We will defend ourselves with all our might, to the very last drop of blood.' He and his colleagues were fighting a rearguard action, for they had similarly fought against the concentration camp itself being established as a memorial centre.

A shield from responsibility?

To the credit of the Bavarian government, who endowed the memorial, no sanitised version of the hell-hole is presented. From the moment the visitor passes through the original gate, still bearing the taunting greeting *Arbeit Macht Frei*, he is not spared. Defending criminals in Wales in my professional capacity has meant that entering a prison has been a commonplace in my life; and I have seen too refined cruelties in maximum-security prisons throughout the Western world. At one time, at the request of the Home Secretary, together with a distinguished criminologist, a bishop and a psychiatrist, I trawled prisons throughout the USA and Europe, charged with the almost impossible task of devising a regime for Britain's gaols under which prisoners sentenced to long or life imprisonment would live out their lives with no hope of escape, yet remain members of the human race. In some countries, as in Sweden, I encountered regimes as degrading to the gaoler as to the caged man, and others where, under the affectation that a prison must be escape-proof, technology became an instrument of state sadism. But Dachau belongs to no category of prison I have entered and, as when I first had sight of the surviving victims of a concentration camp, so again, in these reconstructed surroundings, I was stricken with horror. When I have visited a murderer in his cell, however much sympathy I felt for the wretch, distancing was possible; but with Dachau's victims, if empathy takes over it has no boundaries. There is nothing to do but weep; and alone, unobserved, I turned to a wall and, for the first time for many years, I cried.

Only by hardening the heart could I continue; becoming the observer meant deserting the victims, and as soon as some detachment was gained, misgivings commenced. They stemmed from a self-scrutiny, questioning my own motivation in embarking upon such a masochistic exercise, and a questioning too whether the memorial was there to comfort mourners, for repentance, to acknowledge guilt, to be a permanent and terrible reminder, or did it have a less creditable purpose; was I becoming paranoiac in sensing a sinister if unconscious attempt to use Dachau as a shield, to protect so many Germans from responsibility and focusing all guilt upon Hitler's henchmen? The history of Dachau makes possible such an abuse.

Dachau was no purpose-built abbatoir, as were Treblinka and Auschwitz. It was the first of the concentration camps. In 1933 Munich's police president, Heinrich Himmler, threw into it political opponents, mostly Communists and Socialists. Many of those, including Roman Catholics and Protestants of the Lutheran Confessing Sect, who entered its portals, never returned, while others after a short or long period of incarceration came out, often broken into acquiescence. As time went on and war commenced, other groups, not least many Polish priests, were to die there. With such a background it is not difficult to weave Dachau into a tapestry depicting German political and religious resistance against a regime imposing by violence its will upon a nation.

It would be a dishonour to belittle either the numbers or the courage of the thousands of anti-Nazis who suffered for their political and religious opinions; according to a Gestapo summary in April 1939, 160,000 were held in 'protective custody' and 25,000 were under indictment; by this time 225,000 had been sentenced to average gaol terms of three years. Half the members of the Communist Party, some 150,000, were subjected to imprisonment or worse during the Third

Reich. There certainly were not insignificant numbers of Germans held in concentration camps for political and religious reasons between 1933 and 1945. But it would be a treason to them to allow their courage to be used as a figleaf to cover the shame of the overwhelming majority of Germans who activated and condoned their sufferings. The Dachau memorial comes perilously close to clothing, even as it reveals, unspeakable barbarities.

To tell of the persecution of some of the Roman Catholic lower secular clergy by the Nazis is a recitation of facts: although most of the impositions of protective custody imposed upon them were fortunately of short duration, there was a handful of priests who suffered death sentences and more endured confinements in concentration camps; and the agonies at Dachau of many Polish priests cannot be minimised. But Dachau should not be used or be regarded as evidential proof of the so-called 'Church struggle'. There were rare defiant individuals like Bishop von Galen, Bishop of Münster, but as a whole, the Roman Catholic hierarchy in Germany, like the leaders of the German Protestant churches, was worse than pusillanimous. No German Roman Catholic bishop ever found himself incarcerated in Dachau or any other concentration camp. The obscene and unforgettable proclamation made by the Cardinal Archbishop of Vienna, and all the bishops of Austria, a week after the Anschluss, echoed and made explicit the similar proclamations being made from the pulpits in neighbouring Bavaria:

> From our innermost conviction and of our own free will we, the undersigned Bishops of the Austrian ecclesiastical province, proclaim on the occasion of the great historical events taking place in Deutsch-Osterreich: we acknowledge joyfully that the National Socialist movement has achieved and is achieving outstanding success in the domains of *Völkisch* and economic reconstruction and of social policy on behalf of the German Reich and nation, especially for the poorest sections of the nation ... The Bishops' best wishes and blessings go with this activity, and they will exhort the faithful accordingly. On the day of the national plebiscite we Bishops accept it as our indisputable duty to declare our allegiance as Germans to the German Reich, and we expect all believing Christians to know what they owe to their nation.

At the Dachau memorial in Catholic Bavaria, where tribute is paid to the Roman Catholic inmates who died, there are ominous reticences. Much is recalled, but not those bishops whose proclamation

spurred on the perpetration of the bestialities which killed their co-
religionists. In 1992 Ernst Klee, the distinguished documentary film-
maker, angered churchmen in Germany as he revealed from his
painstaking archival research how churchmen of both persuasions did
their best after the war to aid, abet and excuse appalling individuals,
many of whom had left their churches to join the SS, and none of
whom evinced the slightest remorse for crimes which tax the
imagination: a whole apparatus was created by clerics to assist Nazi
criminals by providing references, fake identity papers, and Red Cross
passports enabling them to be spirited away to Syria or South America.
Germany's clerics should not be permitted to shield themselves behind
the martyrdom suffered by rare pastors like Martin Niemöller who was
imprisoned in the Sachsenhausen and Dachau concentration camps
from 1937 to 1945, Paul Schneider who died in Buchenwald, and
Bernhard Lichtenburg who having offered public prayers for the Jews
died in transit to Dachau. Present-day clerics of Germany would be
better advised to agree to open their archives, or even to encourage
some of their fellows to write the history of their institutions during the
Nazi period. Such a history, placed in Dachau, would add considerably
to the significance of the memorial.

A triumphalist counter-revolution

While I was at Dachau, there were few visitors except for parties of
schoolchildren being conducted around by their teachers. Observing
the youngsters, I suspected that they, when looking at the depiction of
events so distant from them, were understandably responding even as
our schoolchildren do when visiting the chamber of horrors at Madame
Tussaud's or the Tower of London. But finding there were more
teachers present than those engaged with their charges, I entered into
conversation with them, curious to know how they instructed their
pupils in the history of the Nazi era. I was aware that, belatedly, after
a rash of vandalism throughout Germany by youngsters smearing
swastikas on public buildings and attacking synagogues, the ministers
of education of the ten federal states issued, in 1962, uniform directives
about how the history of the Third Reich was to be taught in schools,
and laid down a teaching plan that included stipulated curricula units
on Nazism as a political and administrative system, anti-Semitism and
the Holocaust, Hitler's foreign policy and his responsibility for the war.
Those enquiring conversations with the schoolmasters in 1991 arose

because I wondered how effectively those directives were being applied; my doubts were, a few years later, shown to be only too justified, for an authoritative survey showed that German schoolchildren knew no more about the Nazi era than they did of the Middle Ages. And, far from filling in the lacunae, official ambivalence meant that in 1993 a newly published comic book illustrating the barbarous truth of the Nazi era, praised by President von Weizsäcker as a 'worthy and impressive work', was peremptorily withdrawn from the schools. With such hesitant political education prevailing, it was unsurprising that my inquisitiveness at Dachau drew me into deep and unwelcome waters.

The schoolmasters were worthy young men, dedicated to their profession; but as our conversation expanded so did my apprehensions, for I found they were drenched in the teachings of the German professors of history who today are marginalising the German historians who, from the 1960s, often with great courage and always attracting extraordinary hostility, have broken away from the tradition of German historicism with its unswerving allegiance to a nationalist viewpoint. The conservative historicists had absolved Germany from any special responsibility for the outbreak of the First World War and placed the Third Reich as an unfortunate aberration from the sound traditions of German history. This was the history taught to the children of West Germany from the immediate post-war years until the 1960s. Then the Hamburg historian, Fritz Fischer, broke ranks and with intimidating documentation and scholarship, showed how far-reaching were Germany's plans for hegemony and world power between 1914 and 1918. Even more, to the dismay of the political and academic establishments, he insisted that the results of his research unequivocally demonstrated a continuity between Imperial Germany and the Third Reich.

Fischer was treated as a pariah for his presumption. He was accused of besmirching Germany's good name, and the government grant enabling him to lecture in the USA was withdrawn. But he held his ground in the ensuing debate which took place not only in academic conferences and learned journals but also throughout the mass media. In the end, by the early 1970s, it appeared that Fischer's work had inspired a wholesale revision of German historiography undertaken by a generation of younger historians; and the children of Germany were beginning to be taught that Germany must be assigned the lion's share of responsibility for the 1914 disaster, and that the Third Reich was not the negation of German nationalist historical tradition but was its culmination.

For a while – only too short – it appeared that German historical scholarship had established what was generally described as 'a change of paradigm'; we saw the intellectual dominance of a new orthodoxy highly critical of the German past, and an acceptance of the singularity of German history. It seemed that Germany's scholars were not only talking about *Vergangenheitbewältigung* – coming to terms with the past – but were genuinely engaged in the painful exploration. The mood did not last long. The ending of the Social Democratic-dominated government meant politics and scholarship speedily became entangled in the conservative intellectual atmosphere of Germany, and pressures began on historians in government-sponsored official history institutes. My dialogue with the young teachers at Dachau chasteningly spelt out to me that in triumphalist Germany, intoxicated with its reunification, a counter-revolution in the teaching of history has been achieved and, despite some resistance in some of the Social Democratic provinces, the children of Germany are being brought up with a perception of their country's past and a vision of its future replete with sinister overtones.

We forget, at our peril, that Hitler's whole cast of thought was historical, and his sense of vision derived from his sense of history. His talk was studded with historical references and interpretations of historical parallels: 'A man who has no sense of history,' he declared, 'is like a man who has no ears or eyes.' With such remembrances we should not dismiss the debate among German historians as mere academic squabbles. Kohl certainly did not when, deciding that 'more positive historical consciousness' was needed, he initiated the building of a German historical museum in Berlin and a house of the history of the federal republic in Bonn; in both museums it is intended that the Third Reich will substantially be omitted from consideration. The £46-million Bonn museum, planned to open this year, is an ostentatious attempt by Kohl to draw a 'final line' under the Nazi past, and bury its memories under a self-congratulatory symbol of the success of post-war Germany. Meanwhile the universities in former East Germany are being reformed and there seems little doubt that they will be free of any taint of followers of the Fischer school: the senate of Berlin University ordered the total closure of the history department of the East Berlin Humboldt's university and, by their selection of new professors and lecturers, will doubtless ensure that the history that Kohl finds acceptable will shape Humboldt's undergraduates.

When I left Dachau, and those teachers of the rewritten histories, it was no longer the sombre past that weighed me down: the innocent pedagogues were harbingers of a dangerous future. With the teaching

they are receiving, the young of united Germany are being cleansed of
guilt-ridden inhibitions, and without restraint could resume their
predatory designs on the east, which inspired and destroyed their
grandfathers; but this time the conquest would be an economic one,
and it would be upon countries of Eastern Europe and the prostrate
republics of the former Soviet Union. No British politician or diplomat
called upon to treat with contemporary Germany can be considered
qualified if he is unacquainted with the legerdemain being practised by
Germany's dominant historians; their extraordinary polemics against
any German scholar who demurs has led the media to label the
controversies stemming from the historians' battle over the nature of
the Nazi past as the *Historikerstreit*. Amidst the clamour of these
passionate and indiscreet quarrels we can learn of the snares which are
being set to ensure that not Britain, or Europe, but a resurgent
Germany will become the ultimate victor of the century.

Self-scrutiny, *Verboten*

Ulbricht, when he attempted to persuade me to exculpate the
population of East Germany from responsibility for the rise of Nazism,
was expounding the theses presented by all the East German
historians. In the GDR, up to the time of its collapse, an
impersonalistic Marxist-Leninist historiography prevailed: no biography of Hitler was ever published there, and, as there was no scrutiny
of the individual psychology of Hitler, it followed that the group
psychology of the Germans who had so enthusiastically responded to
him never came under review. The explanation for Hitler's rise to
power was dogmatically asserted: imperialist German finance capital
had reared him, and used him as their agent to destroy the might of
organised labour and to create a framework for the recovery of
capitalism from its unprecedented crisis; the poor German workers had
been intimidated or deceived. In the museums of the concentration
camps at Buchenwald and Ravensbruck, the children, now the adult
electorate of East Germany, were presented with exhibitions, still in
place in 1991, in which the common humanity of the victims was
subordinated to the twin aims of exalting Communism and suppressing
the word Nazism; the only alteration at the Buchenwald museum since
unification is that visitors now receive a pamphlet which announces,
with excruciating delicacy, that 'It has been decided to institute some

changes, as far as technically feasible, to overcome a certain one-sidedness in the presentation.' Meantime, the history lesson that continues to be taught there is that the murder camps were not run by German Nazis but by alien 'Fascists': the Brownshirts are referred to as if they were intruders from outer space. The population of the former GDR have been conditioned not to look at the German past shared with the West Germans but to look straight past the central issue in it: that Nazism was uniquely German and that its crimes were not done 'in the name of Germany' as Kohl so often says, but by Germans whose victims were overwhelmingly non-Germans.

The escape route from personal responsibility which the East German historians provided was indeed crude and roughly hewn. But in the West, down to the present, a tacitly or overtly apologetic historiography has provided smoother passages to enable the Germans to extricate themselves from the pit into which they had so avidly thrown themselves. There appears to have emerged two main schools of historical interpretation, the one described as intentionalist, the other as functional. The intentionalist, in depicting the history of Nazism, lays emphasis upon the programmed and consequent implementation of Hitler's ideological intentions; the functionalist tends to lay emphasis upon the exterior restraints, usually economic, sometimes geo-political, which bound Germany, creating special intractable problems which led to the disaster. Within these broad spectra of historical interpretation, one searches in vain for an explanation or hypothesis specifically directed to the unique and barbarous collective behaviour of twentieth century Germans. Elusively the issue of guilt is avoided; responsibility falls upon Hitler personally or upon unconquerable economic factors that had made the Weimar ungovernable and inexorably led to fatal consequences. The Germans, in short, were trapped, involuntarily; the fault was in the stars not themselves.

The ingenuity and scholarship displayed by today's leading German professors of modern history, as they retreat from self-scrutiny, is impressive. At Bremen, Immanuel Geiss, resentful of what he describes as the 'moral and ideological overtones that have crept into the debates' associated with Nazism, hampering discussion 'in a purely academic or detached way', has recently issued a clarion call to German historians calling for an end to 'self-critical introspection'. Dismissing what he describes as 'the absurd charge that there was or is a constantly wicked or aggressive German national character which has caused all the trouble', he tells his students that 'the time has come for Germans to move on to the next stage of historical synthesis with wider historical horizons'. Research and debate have placed 'too narrow a focus on Germany's part in World Wars One and Two, and too narrow a concept of continuity, particularly when this term is loaded with a conscious or subconscious tinge of moralising'. There must be 'a widening of historical perspectives to truly global horizons.'

His message, even if vulgarised, certainly had reached the youngsters I met when observing their aggressive 'peace' demonstrations against the Gulf war; their anti-American, anti-British and anti-Israeli sloganising may be seen by the generous and naïve as a healthy protest against militarism. In fact it also had, as in conversations with them I soon discovered, more disturbing implications. The wickedness of the Americans and British in their bombings of Iraqis, and the behaviour of the Israelis towards the Palestinians, were proofs for them that there was nothing special about Germany's Nazism: the Gulf war validated their belief that their fathers and grandfathers could be exempted from any singular crime. The 'global perspectives' of Geiss were certainly being curiously applied.

I found it sadly ironic but not surprising when, a few days later, I met in Hamburg some elderly German Jews, survivors who had returned to live on their pensions, who told me the peace demonstrations had convinced them that they must now re-emigrate. Bitterly they insisted that the mood of those demonstrations meant that the young Germans had learned nothing from the past and, for them, old fears had been revived.

These old Hamburg Jews were expressing a view which the German essayist Peter Schneider adopted when he set out, and condemned, the explanations given to him for the sloganising in the peace demonstrations which identified with the people of Iraq as victims of Allied bombing but not with Israelis who were also bombarded:

> Didn't all this come from bottled-up resentment and suffering that had practically never been expressed throughout the 45 years since World War Two? 'We too were bombarded by the Allies in a similarly senseless and barbaric fashion. And just as this war is unjust, so was the war that freed the world from Nazi fascism.'

It is perhaps unsurprising that the young demonstrators should take up such a stance: the teachings of their mentors are unlikely to correct them. Even a liberal anti-Nazi historian like Eberhard Jäckel, a history professor at the University of Stuttgart, enjoins his students not to believe that the last war can be adequately explained as being the consequence of Hitler's pursuit for *Lebensraum* and the elimination of the Jews. Jäckel, like Geiss, calls for a global approach: 'The Second World War was not a German war alone but a world war, a global conflict, and so the historian's approach has to be global as well.' Then, referring to Japan and Italy, he plays his trump: 'If *[sic]* we say that Hitler's war was a war of territorial conquest or of territorial expansion, we must not overlook the fact that two other countries fought similar wars for territorial expansion at the same time, and even started them before Hitler started his.' The subsequent development of Jäckel's theme seems more like justification than explanation: the Western powers, unlike the Johnnies-come-lately Germany, Japan and Italy, were satiated and wanted, by manipulating the League of Nations, to maintain the status quo. Becoming aware of the implicit apologia he is making for Hitler's war, he claims he is not seeking to minimise Germany's 'exceptional aggressiveness'; but that is precisely what he is doing. By unloading so much of Germany's guilt upon the Western powers, and sharing what is left with Italy and Japan, he lightens the load. German guilt, like butter, he evidently believes, can be spread thin.

The humanisation of atrocity

Certainly, extraordinary apologias are now proliferating among a substantial number of German historians bent on telling their younger generation that there is no need to feel ashamed for the recent past, that it should now be erased, and it is time now to learn to be proud of the German nation; these pedagogues include some of the leading professors in Germany who hitherto have been held in high esteem in international academic circles and who undoubtedly have a considerable influence over German public opinion. It is fortunate that their convoluted theses, belatedly translated into English in 1993, have happily been subjected to rigorous analysis by one of our leading scholars of German history, Richard Evans, who has written a devastating critique which one hopes will be read in Germany.

Richard Evans who, to the good fortune of his students, holds a chair at Birkbeck college, is an historian born after the Second World War. He is diffident about criticising those of my generation whose judgements on the Germans are determined by our experiences, but he nevertheless clearly thinks we are handicapped, for he believes our conclusions are vitiated by our dependence on German literature and art to which we turn for aid to unravel the complexities of Germany's collective behaviour; we lack, he believes, the advantage of his generation of being schooled in the social sciences, and consequently we are prone to generalisations which he cannot condone. This latter-day Platonist, with his hostility to the arts as a revealer of historical truths, his overvaluation of reason and his underestimate of the dynamic unconscious factors determining historical continuities and changes, would have us deploy the methodology of the social sciences when we make our assessment of Germany's history in this century. He is correct in implying many of my generation are suspicious of the claims of social scientists; the goal of natural science is the domination of nature by the use of scientific techniques, as the goal of the social scientists modelled on the natural science is prediction and control of human beings. But such an approach too easily discards divination and empathy; hermeneutic methods, as employed in psychoanalysis, give a depth of understanding often barred to those hemmed in by their social science training.

Fortunately, in applying his methodology, when scrutinising Germany's leading historians, Evans's weakness becomes a strength, for he is determined to examine only what these historians say and to avoid any survey of their motivations and to eschew personal biography. What he has succeeded in destroying is any claim to true scholarship which they may possess, for he has demonstrated how economical they have been with the facts in order to reach their distorted conclusions.

One of the historians whose work Richard Evans has so painstakingly examined is Ernst Nolte. His treatises contain the most blatant attempts to relativise Auschwitz and all it stands for; his is an attempt to 'humanise' Nazi atrocities by pointing indignantly at crimes committed by others, like the murders perpetrated by the Turks in 1915 when 1½ million Armenians were killed, or the behaviour of the Americans in Vietnam. But above all, he points an accusing finger at the Gulag archipelago created in Russia; and it was, he would claim, the fears that arose from that terrorism that brought about Hitler's response. Thus he seeks to rehabilitate the Germans, the Nazis, the bourgeoisie and Fascism in general by portraying Hitler's policy as a defensive reaction to the Soviet and Communist threat. Violence from the left within Germany, and the threats coming from outside from Russian exterminators, brought about the Nazi response. Nazism was basically a 'justified reaction' to Communism; it simply overshot the mark. As for the Jews, had not Chaim Weizmann, the Zionist leader, declared war, on behalf of the Jews of the world, against Germany when, at the outbreak of the war, he offered the support of the Jews in Palestine?

So Nolte sounds his rallying call to the Germans: they must not permit a mistaken belief in the uniqueness of Hitler's final solution to remain a major obstacle to the re-building of German national self-confidence. Predictably, given Nolte's stance, the events in the Soviet Union in August 1991 proved a godsend to him. As the hardline coup failed, the apologists for Nolte immediately used the occasion to claim this was corroboration of his thesis that the Nazi war against Russia was part of the 'European civil war' which had raged throughout the twentieth century against Communism. The German attack on Russia can thus be submerged in the prolonged struggle which has been taking place between civilised Europe and Communism, particularly in the Soviet Union. It is indeed a neat trick to use the burial of Soviet Communism to bury recollections of the true evils of Nazism. And throughout 1993 Nolte continued to play the same trickster's game, declaring in a lengthy press interview that the concentration camps were a Nazi realisation but compared to the Gulag they were a small thing: 'The moment has been reached to look at these things with a little more perspective and a little less emotion.'

A no less pernicious attempt to persuade the Germans and the world that it is time to stop blaming the Germans for the crimes of Nazism is that made by another of Germany's foremost historians, Andreas Hillgruber, who is also put under scrutiny by Richard Evans. Hillgruber has the same goal as Nolte – so to arrange the recounting of recent history that the way is open to Germans to reassert German national pride. His sophisticated effort is sometimes presented with breathtaking insouciance, for it leads him to call upon the young to have as their models those in the German army who, at so much sacrifice, fought heroically in the east against the Russian advance. Hillgruber, who was born in East Prussia and was a serving officer in the eastern campaign, urges the young in Germany to identify themselves with the heroes who were in that campaign and were in the German army of 1945; for they tried to protect the inhabitants of the 'centuries-old area of German settlement . . . the home of millions of Germans who lived in the core land of the German Empire – namely in Eastern Prussia, in the provinces of East Prussia, West Prussia, Silesia, East Brandenburg and Pomerania'. The German army, in short, was attempting to preserve the inhabitants from the terrible fate that awaited them at the hands of the barbaric Red Army.

To put forward such implicitly revanchist views, suggesting that

Germany's existing boundaries cannot be regarded as final in the light of the violent manner that they were imposed, Hillgruber requires us to accept the distinction between the German army and the Nazis. Only fabrication could sustain such an acceptance. Not only did the German army in the east behave, on the whole, with needless brutality to any who fell into their hands from the Red Army, they also laid waste whole areas of territories they occupied, and massacred or otherwise caused the death of millions of innocent civilians as a matter of policy; it is a travesty to suggest that they were just soldiers engaged in conventional military conflict and largely free from the taint of Nazism. From the commanding generals on the east front to the common soldier, they took full advantage of the battle orders, subsequently condemned as 'criminal orders' at the Nuremberg trials after the war. It was an army permeated with Nazi ideology. One-third of the junior officers were middle class and young enough to have been exposed for most of their adolescent and adult lives to the Nazi indoctrination which was a central part of Germany's education system from 1933. They, and specially appointed National Socialist officers, as the war progressed, increasingly instructed the troops in Nazi doctrine; they responded to their leadership by ever-increasing barbarity as the German eastern front deteriorated.

Nor was their conduct in other war theatres less obscene. Those of us who served in the Mediterranean area have different perceptions of the German officers from Hillgruber. Under Field-Marshal Kesselring's command, they committed appalling atrocities upon the Italians. The catalogue of their crimes against defenceless civilians and disarmed soldiers is awesome; it includes the wiping out of the whole population (including children) of the unoffending township Amarzaddoto and the massacre of 5,000 unarmed Italian soldiers who had surrendered at Cethalonia, an act of savagery which left the soil of the island a carpet of corpses. A call for such barbaric officers and troops to be models for today's young Germans is an insult to them and, indeed, a threat to neighbouring countries and, potentially, to all Europe.

When Germany's best-known contemporary philosopher, Jürgen Habermas, spelled out the dangers of history being so distorted for public use, the revisionist historians fell upon him like a pack of wolves. They were infuriated because Habermas spelled out what he believed to be the continuing liability of all those alive in Germany today. He insisted:

Our own life is connected with this context of life in which

Auschwitz is possible, not through contingent circumstances, but internally. Our way of life is connected with our parents' and grandparents' way of life through a web of family, local, political, and intellectual transmissions – through a historical milieu that has made us what we are today. Not one of us can sneak out of this milieu because our identity, both as individuals and as Germans, is permanently interwoven with it, from bodily gesture through the language to the rich interplay of intellectual customs. . . . But what follows from this existential linking with traditions and ways of life that have been poisoned by unspeakable crimes? A completely civilised populace, proud of its humanistic culture and its constitutional state, made itself liable for those crimes . . . Does something of this liability carry over to the next generation and the one after that?

Giving 'yes' as the answer to his own question was just the reply the revisionists did not want to hear.

And it is a reply which is unacceptable too to the German economic historians within whose theses, for my part, I find the most subtle evasions of Germany's guilt.

The apocalyptic road

Embedded here we find an amoral cynicism that exceeds that of the historians who follow Geiss. Geiss seeks to distance German responsibility by asserting that what occurred was the consequence of 'universal historical mechanisms'; the most influential German economic historian Knut Borchardt provides a different cop-out; one more particular and in some respects more sophisticated. He would persuade us that the economic difficulties of the Weimar Republic were insoluble within the context of Germany's parliamentary democracy. His profoundly pessimistic diagnosis of the German economy in the 1920s and 1930s gives him the opportunity to tempt us into believing that there was a tragic inevitability to the ending of the Weimar: economic imperatives permitted no alternative. Choices were not available to the government and the people of the republic: whatever direction they took, all roads led to but one destination – Armageddon.

These retrospective economic analyses would have us regard the people of Germany as helpless playthings in the hands of a destiny that has the form of irresistible economic forces and entrapped interest groups, all compulsively held back from creating a consensus; the characteristic features of the theses of these economic historians are the depersonalisation of German politics of the period, the reduction of evil to statistical tables of wage movements, productivity, taxation trends and levels of investment; and, above all, a secular apocalyptic philosophy that seems to be a dangerous part of Germany's cultural tradition. The density of their arguments, and of the dialogues between themselves as they lay different emphases upon Borchardt's economic models, does not always succeed in masking their unconscious motivations; their elaborate rationalisations can be sensed as defence mechanisms erected to protect them from the terror of genuine insight into the German *Geist*.

An example of this academic school is Harold James, who now lectures at Princeton and was formerly at Cambridge, and still provides readers of *The Times* with his views on German affairs. Sympathetic to the general thrust of Borchardt's thesis, he contends that Hitler came to power as a consequence of inevitably disintegrating 'corporate interest groups' and low economic growth; value judgements on the main protagonists involved in the political process are painstakingly eschewed, although the detached economic historian cannot forbear to opine that Hitler 'was certainly a more accurate economic forecaster than the majority of contemporary commentators'. James, however, appears to go even further down the apocalyptic road than Borchardt: not only was it not possible for the Weimar to solve what he describes as the 'distributional conflict', which many others would call class conflict, but the Nazis too were fated to be unable to resolve the problem:

> Only the complete destruction, in and after 1945, not of physical capital (much of which survived the war), but of the institutions and social habits that had produced the low-growth society made it possible for more rational combinations of labour and capital to produce faster development and, with this, a way out of distributional conflict.

Armageddon, in this view, was the prerequisite before Germany became the New Jerusalem.

Such views, although expressed in the vocabulary of the economist, are pale reflections of Jung's tenet that Nazism was but the necessary precursor of the wondrous qualities within the German collective unconscious which, after Wotan's storm had blown itself out, would 'ecstatically' emerge. Germanic peoples certainly seem singularly prone to apocalyptic thought. It is said that the original apocalypse idea sprang from Jewish communities during the second century before Christ, but their religious establishments, seeing the dangers of such eschatology, frowned upon them. Apart from Daniel and some suggestive apocalyptic themes that appear in the later Prophets, no apocalypses were accepted into the Jewish canon. But their exclusion was too late and nowhere, to the particular chagrin of the Jews, have they been more enthusiastically received than in Germany.

The history of the pogroms in Germany is a tale of persecutors possessed by apocalyptic zeal: the Flagellants, in fourteenth century Germany, slaughtering the Jews of the Rhineland, and the large groups from Western Germany recruited into the First and Second Crusades who massacred more Jews than Moslems, were gripped by the belief that apocalyptic deliverance was only possible after the infidels had been destroyed. Hitler and those who associated with him certainly had many precedents to support them. The infiltration of apocalyptic theories into the German economic historians' doom-laden analyses of Germany's recent past shows the tradition, in a milder but disquieting form, lingers on.

Not all these German economic historians belong to Hitler's generation. Most of them were children or were unborn at the time of the Nazi era, and one should be ever mindful that children do not choose their parents and cannot be held responsible for the deeds of their progenitors. Yet, unfairly, a parent's guilt can be encapsulated consciously or, more likely, unconsciously in the child: the child's sensitive antennae pick up the guilts the father endeavours to conceal. The father can leave huge gaps in the biography he presents to his child; but his attempts at concealment are in vain.

All of us who are parents well know that few of our secrets are not divined by our children: our embarrassments, failures and guilts are unspoken but the child has a profound understanding of the language of silence and that is a tongue lacking grammar and vocabulary. When communicated by a mother holding a child in loving arms it can convey bliss. In other circumstances, it can be terrifying and threatening. When it is deployed to emit the terrible guilts of a father, those guilts of the father are felt as even more terrible: crimes committed in daylight may be able to be faced, but what the child fears most is the dark. And the guilts of Nazi fathers are often buried in the blackest of dungeons.

So often, then, I feel there is a singular poignancy within the dense presentations, formidable charts and nicely assembled sums of the German economic historians: they are surely erecting barriers, brick by brick, statistic upon statistic, trying in vain to stem the tide of guilt which an unjust fate has decreed must engulf them. The statistics that are presented are often skewered; but even when they are seemingly scrupulously deployed, they can act as a bulwark against historical truths. The purpose of these afflicted German economic historians is not consciously to mislead their readers: rather it is to protect themselves from the terrors their fathers' guilts have implanted in them. Inevitably, in my view, the consequence is that their seemingly impersonal contributions are profoundly personal, becoming theses which can sometimes evade or minimise 'Germany's guilt'. From such German historians and German academics we cannot expect to be provided with guidance as to how to treat with the Germany of today.

Fanciful historians

Unfortunately, to the confusion of a British public, there are pontificating British historians, within Tory think-tanks or on television, who do not adequately take up the challenge set by the unfortunate theses of so many of Germany's political and economic historians. Norman Stone, a trustee of the Thatcher Foundation who holds the Oxford chair of modern history, castigates those on the left who have stressed the sinister implications of Ernst Nolte's work: and sometimes we find him expressing the most bizarre opinions as when, in July 1991, he obtrusely asserted: 'There is really no sign of any seriousness that German domination of central and eastern Europe would be anything other than beneficial.' Such extravagant views, sometimes accompanied with vulgar smears against those who do not share them, led Edward Heath to comment in the *Sunday Times* that 'many parents of Oxford students must be both horrified and disgusted that the higher education of our children should rest in the hands of such a man'.

As a young don at Cambridge, Stone was a frequent visitor to my London home and was a diverting guest when staying with me at my house in Tuscany. Then singularly good-looking, always playing the part of the little boy lost, I noted men at my dinner table found him unchallenging, exceedingly engaging, and women, as he teased out their protectiveness, found him appealing. His private life was ever in tumult, and his later moralistic stances, which led him, no doubt wrongly, to be accused of homophobic prejudices, were certainly not then in evidence. The personal disarray was mirrored in his speculations and opinions, few of which he held to for long; and they were indeed amusing as he laced them, as fantasists do, with little embellishments of truth, capturing his fellow-guests whose responses reflected and enhanced his false self-image, no doubt making him, at least intermittently, feel real.

Of course such a personality, not known for abstemiousness, inevitably had moments of suicidal despair as some rebuff threatened fragmentation or total dissolution of his fragile self. More usually, however, he was maniacally buoyed up; his grandiosity kept him afloat. The shifts of opinion, like the multiplication of roles he played in short periods of time, all bore the impress of his early deprivation as a fatherless child; he lacked the confidence and certainty which can sometimes come through an identification in childhood with a fixed and well-defined male parental figure; and no doubt from the same initial handicap sprang both the attractive fictional element in his skill as a raconteur and an elasticity in historical judgements not overburdened by respect for facts. Since at that time the repertoire of this working-class lad did not yet include the role of the heavyweight besieged Establishment defender of the Tory right fighting against carping left-wing academe, his effervescences sometimes made him a sparkling court jester at my dinner table, and doubtless at others.

He was then, as now, politically jejune. He accompanied me for a few days on what I believe was his first visit to the Commons while I did my parliamentary work and engaged in the usual rounds of meetings, delegations and lobbying groups. I remain with misgivings that this introduction to Westminster may have acted as the precipitate to his miscasting himself as a serious political commentator able to bring his claimed historical knowledge to bear upon international issues. His pretensions reached their apogee in the meeting at Chequers in March 1990 when Thatcher asked him, along with three other historians, for advice on how Britain should deal with the newly united Germany. The leaked minutes of the gathering revealed the unsurprising – given Stone's presence – lack of intellectual rigour governing the symposium; falling into the trap, so attractive to German historians seeking to claim Nazism as a disjunction in Germany's history, the group favoured the view that our perception of Germany was distorted by an excessive focus upon the period running from Bismarck to 1945 and the predominant view emerged that 'there was an innocence of and about the past by the new generation of Germans ... We need not worry about them.'

Illiterate in the field of dynamic psychology they, quite unabashed, expressed misgivings about certain aspects of German 'character' such as 'a capacity for excess, to overdo things, to kick over the traces and a tendency to overestimate their own strengths and capabilities'. After similar excursions into pop psychiatry, they concluded, however, that if these characteristics did emerge troublesomely then we should remember 'the more certain Germany became, the easier it ought to become to construct alliances against it'. However, this necessity could be avoided; there was an answer. 'The overall message was unmistakable;' the minute told us, 'we should be nice to the Germans.' Stone's hand in the conclusion is unmistakable, echoing not only the fatal appeasement policies of the 1930s but also his own 1990 articles mocking the fears of the older generation that 'the Germans were going to be almighty again'. We should understand, he opined, 'the Germans are now an exceedingly democratic and pacific-minded people'.

By the end of 1992, however, belatedly catching up on events, he shamelessly sang a different tune: 'There is a great crisis looming in Germany . . . Xenophobia seems to have taken a grip . . . the fact is that Germany is divided and rudderless. This is the end of what used to be a stable, prosperous state . . . a German problem once again. Friends of Germany, among whom I firmly place myself, see troubles ahead.' By Armistice Day 1993, reflecting his mood swings, he was again back in step with the old Establishment figures lulling us into a false security. On the same day that in *The Times* William Rees-Mogg, after 'an excellent lunch in Hamburg' informed his readers that 'those who see Germany as a threat . . . seem to me completely mistaken', Stone, in the *Guardian*, declared: 'It is certainly quite striking that, today, we have a Europe that amounts to a *Mitteleuropa* with a human face: a dominant Germany, but one run in almost impeccably democratic style, and with an almost paranoid fear of using her weight in political matters. With that Germany, the partnership is obvious and sensible . . .' So he switches, characteristically, from one extravagance to another. One of his lesser extravagances, revealing insight, was his acknowledgement in *The Times* in December 1993, that he was 'a bit of a near-lunatic Germanophile'.

The fact is that, whatever academic reputation Stone gained from his early work, before he became a journalist, it was not as a German historian. His one excursus into German history of which I am aware was a book he wrote on Hitler in 1980. He sent it to me inscribed 'with love', a display of affection that most certainly did not seduce me into valuing its content. Its shallowness becomes painfully obvious when compared with the *Hitler* published by another professor of history, Ian Kershaw, at Sheffield, whose study of a charismatic leader offering not limited options but a tempting though illusory and empty chialistic vision of political redemption, shows rare understanding; it is to be hoped that some of the students whose fate Heath mourns will turn from Oxford to Sheffield for an authentic instruction in the recent German past. Historians in interdisciplinary studies of Germany's conduct, as Kershaw's book illustrates, could contribute much guidance to British politicians but the work of too many of Germany's contemporary historians, and not a few of ours, reveals the need for discrimination.

The heart of darkness

It is a need passionately felt by a small group of young historians, sociologists and physicians based in Berlin and Hamburg; this is a team which receives no research funds from state institutions and has no formal link with any university. These self-conscious outsiders on the west German historical scene regard Germany's organised academic life as corrupt and corrupting. Their well-documented charges against the establishment's historians, although often intemperate, cannot be brushed aside. They accuse them of ignoring in their studies and hypotheses the 'inner structure of the Nazi state' and of overlaying the tracts of deskbound Nazi criminals with arid academic debates which blur the continuities between the Third Reich and today's republic.

Predictably, the academics have sought to discredit these Young Turks who are alleging that they are contributing to Nazi methods of rule in the federal state. The heat and the personalisation of the debates match the violence of their own internal academic politics; observers from outside Germany never cease to be astounded by the poisonous onslaughts with which German historians, even with apparently only marginal differences between themselves, conduct their arguments. The cacophony enveloping these controversies tells us not only how politicised is historical instruction in today's Germany: it tells us too of the emotional turbulence afflicting the protagonists. In their studies of Nazi Germany, as they approach the heart of darkness, their anxieties mount and consequently so does their aggression to one another. In their well-publicised common room battles, they avoid the self-scrutiny which alone could correct the distortions in their scrutinies of the country's recent history. There are bold exceptions like Wolfgang Wippermann who holds the chair at the Freie University; but far too many of them only churlishly acknowledge the significance of the psychic forces at work.

And the presumptuousness and, sometimes, arrogance of some of our own historians, posturing as detached Olympian observers above the battle, does not encourage the German historians to make that acknowledgement. There are young professors of history, like Richard Overy of London's King's College, who, affecting a tolerant stance, advertise their liberal credentials by telling us there is merit in the arguments on both sides of those involved in these German debates; the only trouble, Overy tells us in 1993, is that the protagonists 'overstate' their case; all would be well if only they adopted 'a middle way' for 'Germany is unrecognisable from the age of Hitler' and now behaves with 'moderation and understanding in world affairs'. And, more, ignoring how such illusions held by my pre-war generation were shattered, he beseeches us to remember 'there is another German history of democrats, liberals, socialists, of men of conscience and discrimination'. I find it hard to forgive myself that as a teenager in the 1930s I held such superficial and fatally flawed views. An historian today should surely not have to live through painful disillusionment in order to understand the real source of the ill-tempered debates of the German historians. The fact is that many of them carry within themselves too many detonators to dare handle such explosive material as recent German history. For bomb disposal we need another expertise; perchance we may find German psychoanalysts who offer us more than the German historians.

At first sight this hope seems improbable, for the history of German psychoanalysis in the Nazi period is an ignoble one; after the Jewish psychoanalysts fled, or were killed off, the psychoanalyst rump organisation accommodated itself to the Nazi creed. Only now, in the last few years, have the young German analysts very consciously begun to free themselves from the shabby compromises made by most of their mentors. Fortunately, however, a few German physicians remained untainted, and their insights into the condition of their people, and the illumination provided by many in the international psychoanalytical community, help us, far more than do most historians, to explain Germany's descent in the twentieth century into barbarism.

PART V

The Borrowed Sense of Guilt

When love is blind

Are the Germans capable of mature love? Or is their capacity limited to abject love, to infatuation? In mature love, the lover identifies himself only partially with his beloved one; his ego, enriched with some of his woman's qualities, undergoes a partial change using his chosen one as a model. But the critical ego maintains its function. It is otherwise when love is total abandonment: then love is blind, and just as the consequences can be awesome for the sightless infatuated individual, so when a similar process takes place, simultaneously, in millions of people, disaster can follow.

Freud, anticipating Hitler's Germany in his work on group psychology in 1922, spelled out the results of total abandonment to a beloved leader: 'Conscience has no application to anything that is done for the sake of the love object; in the blindness of love, remorselessness is carried to the pitch of crime. The whole situation can be completely summarised in the formula: the love object has been put in the place of the ego ideal.'

Such a surrender by the German of his ego to Hitler was placed under scrutiny by two German psychoanalysts, Alexander and Margarete Mitscherlich, a generation later, when they published a seminal work, *The Inability to Mourn*. Publication of the book initially had an astounding impact. Though a dense and discursive work, unsparing in its condemnation of German conduct both under the Nazis and in the post-war world, more than 100,000 copies were sold in the first edition; and, as passages became incorporated into Germany's school textbooks, for a short time it seemed that it could act to bring about the shattering cathartic re-experience Germany needed in order to overcome its past.

Mitscherlich was not a detached physician putting forward arresting hypotheses on the basis of hundreds of case histories of his patients: he also brought to his assessments his own painful experiences. As a student in the 1930s he had been actively engaged in left-wing anti-Nazi activities and when the Nazis assumed power, his house was searched and his library confiscated; he went into exile in Switzerland. In 1937 he returned to try to arrange for the legal defence of his political group leader; he was arrested for his pains, and gaoled. When ultimately released, he was permitted to continue his medical studies only on condition that he reported twice a day to the Gestapo, and it was under such fraught surveillance that he qualified as a neurologist. The end of the war brought him even closer to his captors. Having been made a minister in the first German government formed by the Allied Occupation, he became the head of the German medical commission to the American military tribunal dealing with the medical war crimes of 23 German physician defendants. No one, therefore, is likely to have more experience of the corruption and evil that can exist under the guise of national loyalty and neutral professionalism. It was his exposure to such sicknesses that led him, as he sought to find their poisoned source, to psychoanalysis.

The 'biological' reaction

His search evidently led him to conclude that his fellow-countrymen required blunt and brutal warnings. He told them: 'We Germans do not understand either ourselves or our actions during the most terrible chapter of our history ... Our behaviour is determined by denials which have now become unconscious.' Far from applauding the German's economic success, he deplored the manic quality of their drive and warned that their unswerving dedication to the present sprang from sick and dangerous denials of their past; these repudiations, Mitscherlich asserted, were the consequences of the German way of loving, for the overwhelming majority of them knew only self-love; their choices of a love object were narcissistic and lacked genuine empathic quality. Such was the love between them and Hitler when the Germans and the Führer chose each other.

And when Hitler committed suicide, so encapsulated were the egos of the Germans within Hitler's, so total had their surrender been to him, that to protect themselves from following his example and falling into melancholia and worse, survival demanded that the leader should be treated as a foreign body and be totally expelled from their psychic household. No memory of the man must remain, and the crimes committed in his name must be blotted out, de-realised, behind a veil of denial. Only thus, in an emergency 'biological' reaction, could the Germans continue uncrushed by guilt and shame; by not accepting that their defeat was an occasion for mourning, in terms of psychical energy, they were making a global retreat from their past. They had resolved that it was useless to brood over what had been; all their energy should be focused on their present tasks and that should be their only preoccupation.

Such a stratagem to avoid mass melancholia which otherwise would have engulfed them was, Mitscherlich seems to believe, justifiable and understandable as a temporary emergency measure. What he cannot countenance, and what he fears, is that so many of his fellow-countrymen have continued to be frozen into the position they took up immediately they found themselves belonging to a defeated nation; his fears are surely well-founded for, if the German people will not retrieve the terrible memories of the Nazi era, they, and all of us, are in danger, because then they will never accept or learn what truly happened, and could act out again the components embedded in their psyche which they cannot bear to accept into their conscious minds, not least what Mitscherlich has identified as 'a capacity to hate as deadly as it is foolish'. If the defence procedure which they adopted in 1945 to ward off melancholia persists, and is never to be sufficiently corrected by insight and understanding, then we shall have the most powerful nation in Europe psychically disabled.

We could usefully recall Freud's observation that neurosis does not deny reality but merely wishes to know nothing about it, and apply that comment to the collective conduct of so many in newly united Germany. In 1992, as I wandered through West Germany and the territory of the former GDR, I found the disturbing tactic was now being used to stifle recall of Germany's Nazi past. Under the affectation that *Vergangenheitsbewältigung*, the overcoming of the past, required that the files of the Stasi be opened up, the informers of the GDR's secret police were now to be exposed; they were to be pursued with a zeal which was in striking contrast to the German reluctance to root out Nazi criminals in the post-war world. Germans who had responded to Mitscherlich's admonitions, and understood the dismaying results that could stem from Germany's proneness to selective amnesia, repeatedly expressed to me their dismay that the revelations of the oppressiveness of the GDR were being used to vitiate the memory of the horrors of the Nazis. Shame was being heaped upon the Communist stool pigeons; the complicities of all those who had supported the Nazi state were now projected away from themselves upon the wretched sneaks.

Predictably, Chancellor Kohl led the pack: urged on by his guru, the egregious historian Michael Stürmer, an expert in relativising Nazi crimes by equating them with the crimes of Stalinism, Kohl, in

February 1992, laid a wreath at Bautzen, the notorious Stasi gaol: 'In memory of the victims of Communist injustice'. He brushed aside the condemnations and denunciations of left-wing intellectuals Günter Grass, Stefan Heym and Christa Wolf, and those of Professor Jens Reich, the civil rights campaigner and co-founder of New Forum, which triggered the East German revolution. Reich pinpointed the issue: West Germany was using the debate as 'an easy excuse to avoid tackling its own past'. As the controversy increased, even the tabloids, fearing it would provoke too many uncomfortable recollections of Nazis left in high places during Adenauer's regime, had cold feet. 'Germans, stop persecuting yourselves!' screamed *Der Bild*, belatedly frightened of the consequences of chasing Stasi informers, so many of whom are in the limelight living their lives in united Germany as senior medical consultants, trendy poets and prominent politicians, even as so many Nazis, unscathed by any punishment, lived their lives in post-war Germany. The motivation of those now wishing to still the denunciations was far different from those of Reich. They preferred to smother the stink of an immediate German putrid past lest the odours should be a reminder of another stench of 50 years ago.

Omnipotence: the infantile fantasy

Those of us placing such interpretations upon Germany's contemporary moods often meet the accusation that the emphases we place upon the Germans' infatuation with the Nazis and with Hitler are exaggerations, and that it was only special social and economic conditions that allowed Hitler to emerge, and now that those factors are entirely changed, we are misleading ourselves in viewing current German stances as the continuing bitter aftermath of a failed love affair. Our thinking, in short, is anachronistic: we are old men locked into our experiences of the thirties and forties; our vision is failing us and we cannot see the enormous differences between those living in today's democratic Germany and those who lived under the Third Reich; and that we are being vexatious when we acknowledge the existence of considerable differences but insist that, if the depths of the German psyche are plumbed, we find many of the differences are deceptive, and are only on the surface.

It would indeed be fortunate if we were in error but the research and sensibility of younger British historians belonging to the post-war generation tells us otherwise. Professor Ian Kershaw in his 1991 publication *Hitler* explored how Hitler came to take control of the machinery of a complex modern state, unchecked by institutional restraints and without curtailment by traditional ruling classes. Only too chasteningly, he shows how Hitler became the fatal attraction of the German people; that Hitler was the embodiment of a wide range of social expectations and resentments; that all forms of legality and of rationally ordered government were undermined by the passionate desire to divine the wishes of the beloved leader and then to 'work towards the Führer' to ensure the execution of his presumed intentions. There is little comfort in Kershaw's publication for those who would exclude personal biography from history and present us with impersonal determinants as explanations for extraordinary events; but there is too no yielding by Kershaw to simplistic versions which would persuade us that Hitler was, as the odious Albert Speer, Hitler's architect, described him, 'a demonic figure, one of those inexplicable historical phenomena which emerge at rare intervals among mankind', a view which would have us erase the complicities of the German people.

Kershaw demonstrates that large swathes of the German population endowed Hitler with charismatic qualities, and that the consequent charismatic domination was for many a willing submission; it was certainly not the case of a nation being hijacked by the diabolical influence of a single man. The description of the intense interrelationships between Germany and Hitler, as unravelled by Kershaw, shows a considerable congruence with Mitscherlich's illustration; although one uses the vocabulary of the historian, and the other that of the psychoanalyst, both speak the same language.

The quiddity of their findings is the nature of the coalescence between Hitler and the Germans. The love the Germans gave so lavishly to Hitler was, as Mitscherlich describes, 'an early infantile self-love': they gave to him the cherished ideas of omnipotence we all possess in our infancy. All responsibility was transferred to him as together, in unison, their infantile fantasies of omnipotence were barbarously acted out; they gave him everything, including their conscience.

A nation afraid of itself

There are those who acknowledge, albeit often churlishly, that, given the societal conditions of the time, the Germans were temporarily

enveloped in a love affair so compulsive and obsessional that reason
and discretion were abandoned; but that was childish folly, and now,
in maturity, in an ordered society, their relationships with their
political leaders and other countries are those of adults who have long
since renounced their dangerous onanistic and omnipotent fantasies of
infancy. And, to support that view, we are sometimes presented with a
much-quoted opinion poll for the *Suddeutsche Zeitung* taken early in
1991. That revealed that more than 42 per cent of Germans, from East
and West, then looked to Switzerland as the role model for their
country; of the rest, few indeed wished to assume the role now held by
any of the great powers. Those who present this as evidence of how
changed is today's Germany are guilty of a generous but dangerous
naïveté: there is something worse than absurdity in a country, large
and powerful, affecting the wish to be small and politically powerless.
The flight from responsibility, the desire to be 'a little one' and a
shirking from international commitments that may involve participation in a United Nations force, are not signs of a nation that has gone
through a needed rite of passage and is now ready to assume the
burdens of adulthood.

The poll response gives every sign of being over-determined, of a
nation afraid of itself, of its power and aggressivity; a nation that had
overcome its past would hardly be claiming it wished to be as a child
among adult nations. Fear of themselves is justified, for large sections
of today's German citizens, in my opinion, continue to nurse uneasily
the murderous prejudices of the Third Reich, and are capable of
dealing with them not by adequate insight but by utilising disavowal,
projection or repudiation, all frail defence mechanisms against
unconscious psychic forces threatening to overwhelm them. Another
authoritative poll, taken by *Der Spiegel* in 1992, on the fiftieth
anniversary of the Nazis' Wannsee conference which decided how all
Jews were to be murdered, showed that one-third of Germans now
believe that Jews carry all or part of the blame for their persecution;
almost half insist that the Third Reich had its good side as well as its
bad; and 42 per cent play Pontius Pilate, preferring to believe that only
a minority of Germans knew about the Holocaust. Such poll
protestations explain to me the comment of a German rabbi: 'The
Germans,' he said, 'will never forgive us for their having gassed us at
Auschwitz.'

The portrait that emerges, of a nation so refusing to slough off its
past, is ugly. John Ardagh, a writer who has striven valiantly to
interpret the Germans to Britain, would have us believe today that

Germans are 'a people possessing solid post-war virtues, concerned above all with ecology, peace and stability'. One suspects that the reconciliations he has successfully made in his personal life as a son of a Viennese Jewess married to a German prompts his generous but over-romantic judgement. In fact, the Germans of the 1990s clearly have a genuine fear of the potential of their own aggression and that may prompt daydreams that they can be conflict-free Peter Pans playing in Swiss treetops; but such fragile escapist idylls, without difficulty, can be, and are being, swept away by Germany's political leadership which is reawakening atavistic emotions that those yearnings so inadequately camouflage.

Timothy Garton Ash, in his recent, minutely researched publication, tells us: 'One of Germany's most distinguished former diplomats said in 1992 that the aim of German foreign policy must be to prevent German hegemony.' That is advice demonstrably unacceptable to Chancellor Kohl.

Dodging the confrontation

Even as the results of the Wannsee anniversary polls were being published, Chancellor Kohl, ever a seismograph registering majority opinion in Germany, was expressing his determination that Germany henceforward must take an assertive role. He counselled Germans to revel in themselves, not to seek to love and hence to be loved: 'To deny Germany's new strength is about as useful as denying the weather is overcast . . . If you only ever want to be loved, you can never be a shaker or a mover,' he swaggered. Love, he evidently believed, was best bought: 'The best way to counter the image of the "Ugly German" is through practical aid for other countries, notably Eastern Europe.' Like all who buy 'love', he expected, and was getting, value for his money: having used the consolidation of German economic power to whip his European partners into line on the issue of recognition of Croatia and Slovenia, he made the doubtful claim in his speech that European acceptance of German policy in Yugoslavia was a great triumph for peace. The word he used, however, to describe this great victory is *Sieg*, a word for many of us reminiscent of Hitler's promised *Endsieg*, or final victory, in the Second World War. No wonder voices were raised from thrice-occupied France that Bonn's support for Croatia was a bid to revive some Reich in Mitteleuropa. The Serbians placed no other interpretation upon Germany's precipitate action, and were choked with anger when the Croatians, thus encouraged, provocatively adopted as their national flag the symbol of the vile *Ustasha*, the Nazis' enthusiastic wartime allies.

Germany's austere and principled president, Richard von Weizächer, warned his fellow-countrymen that there are 'some concerns abroad about the new German might', but his lonely voice went unheard and Kohl pressed on, declaring that the European Community decision was 'a great victory for German foreign policy' as indeed it was – as great a victory as it was disaster for millions living within Yugoslavia. The German-led intervention has there incited every ethnic group to wide-scale racial murder. And our hands are not clean, for we yielded to Kohl's importunings, who was ready to give us a disreputable pay-off: 'The Germans,' said Gerald Kaufman, the former shadow Foreign Secretary, in a Commons speech which brought forth no denial, 'played a far from guilt-free role in cobbling together the British opt-out on the social chapter of the Maastricht Treaty as a swap for British connivance in the policy of blanket recognition of the Yugoslav republics.'

The terrible events that flowed from those precipitate recognitions gave Kohl an opportunity to mobilise his Bavarian Catholic pro-Croat electorate and to exploit the divisions within the German Social Democratic party, torn between the desire to preserve a pacifist stance and a desire to participate in the international military 'peace' mission to the Balkans. In August 1992 Kohl deliberately started to talk even tougher, wishing to embarrass his opposition: 'It is just not possible,' he opined, 'that we in the middle of Europe are looking on, saying that others must do something.' Kohl's eye was clearly on the next election; he was on the warpath domestically as well as in the foreign field.

Subsequent events in Somalia enabled him to press home his advantage, and by July 1993 he was able to persuade his parliament to approve the Bundeswehr's deployment there. Hans-Ulrich Klose, the SDP leader, accused the government of colluding with the United Nations Secretariat to ensure that the Bundeswehr's function in Somalia went beyond humanitarian aid to become a combat mission, and he insisted that the real purpose of the mission was to erase the experience of the Gulf war, when German troops stayed at home, and so demonstrate Germany's 'fitness' to take a permanent seat on the UN Security Council.

Klose's speeches, like the Chancellor's, were now significantly containing explicit intimations of the battle-lines that were to be drawn between the Christian Democrats and the Social Democrats in the next election; such party polemics lend weight to the Freudian view that party politics are often mere epiphenomena, pale reflections of the struggles being enacted within man's psyche. The 'central issue' in the election, Kohl indicated, was to be the challenge to the existing constitution which inhibits Germany from taking any military action outside Nato, a course which his opponents, holding to a near-Swiss neutralism fearful of military adventures, opposed. Yet again we are witnessing Germany's wild oscillations of mood, switching between its yearning to possess an assertive foreign policy, and its reaction-formation represented in near or absolute pacifism: and the choice to be put to the electorate is to be between grandiosity and infantilism. These polarised programmes of the political parties tell us of a morbidity within Germany's body politic: it presents itself in this incapacity of the Germans to handle their own persistent domineering.

Mitscherlich identified the ætiology of their agonising. As long as they failed to acknowledge and work through their guilt, and the attendant anxieties, he prognosticated that they would be at the mercy of their explosive unresolved conflicts, condemned to thrash around in their rationalisations and political conduct as they dodged the needed confrontation with themselves: the condition would remain untreated and festering until they overcame their inability to mourn, the title he gave to his seminal work. When a loved one dies, even an evil loved one, there can be no moving beyond the psychic numbing of the loss without the experience of mourning. As one psychoanalyst put it: 'To be unable to mourn is to be unable to enter into the great human cycle of death and rebirth – to be unable, that is, to "live again".' And the collective life of Germany will not have its needed new start until it mourns; the Germans need to mourn the loss of Hitler who was part of themselves, they need to mourn too for all their own selves, for the millions of slain German soldiers and for millions of Russian, Polish and Jewish victims. Twenty-five years after Mitscherlich made his diagnosis of Germany's sickness and classified it as an inability to mourn, it remains a malady infecting much of Germany's intellectual life and political behaviour.

Addiction to guilt

But will they ever accept treatment? In Erfurt in the spring of 1992 a sardonic German criminal lawyer mocked at my expressed hope that more Germans could belatedly be persuaded to enter into the rituals of mourning: that, he said, was impossible. It was not because the mourning required, as a prerequisite, acknowledgement of guilt; rather, it was because such a course could lead to the diminution of the now unacknowledged guilt feelings which so oppressed them. Their addiction to guilt, he scoffed, was too pleasurable for them to be prepared to suffer withdrawal symptoms.

Our conversation had taken this turn while we were sharing our experiences of the masochism that afflicted so many of the hardened criminals that he in Germany, and I in Wales, had defended. Both of us had found that when we had succeeded, through some defects in the prosecution case or by some legal technicality, in obtaining an acquittal for our clients, that we received no thanks from them; they left us with only a surly goodbye. But when, despite our spirited defences, they were found guilty and received heavy sentences, they wrote to us from gaol expressing the warmest appreciation for our work. These were men who have been described by psychoanalysts as criminals through a sense of guilt: some early maladjustments in their childhood had left them with a neurotic sense of guilt so severe that only by committing, in their adulthood, a crime that could attract punishment could their guilt feelings be temporarily assuaged. When we obtained their acquittal, we cheated them of their unconscious desire.

My cynical lawyer acquaintance transposed such bizarre individual conduct to the collective behaviour of Germans. He was implying that their pleasure through pain, their masochism, was too intense for them ever to relinquish voluptuous punishing guilt feelings. I could not dismiss his disquieting and defeatist hypothesis, for few can doubt the existence within German culture of what Mitscherlich has described as the 'traditional command and obey principles'; in such a culture, submission can bring with it morbid delights and that was how millions of Germans enjoyed their relationship with Hitler.

The lawyer's pessimism particularly disturbed me since it brought about a recall of the illuminating explanations I had obtained from a reading of the American psychoanalyst Franz Alexander when, as a young solicitor, I found myself bewildered by the irrational responses of my criminal clients. Alexander had taken as a starting-point Diderot's statement that the very small child would be the most destructive of criminals if only he had the physical power to carry out his aggression; and Alexander spelled out the consequence if the child renounced these non-social tendencies only on account of fear of intimidating parents or educators. Then the child, incorporating the images of his punishing parents into his own personality, could be governed, as an adult, by a pseudo-conscience, by a pathological superego, which needed to be appeased and warded off by the same tricks and compromises as he had been forced to adopt against his original severe preceptors. The child had learned that a certain amount of punishment was considered as an atonement for a forbidden act. Then, as an adult:

> ... he will assume the same technique in dealing with his own conscience – he will inflict on himself punishment which allays his sense of guilt, makes him quits, with his own conscience. He treats his own conscience like some foreign agency. He has learnt that with a certain amount of punishment he can pay for his misdeeds and therefore he will voluntarily endure sufferings or even provoke punishments in order to get rid of his guilty conscience. The danger which lies in such an attitude is obvious. Suffering becomes not only atonement but provides an emotional justification for discarding the restrictions required by the conscience.

The sick games of this nature I had seen in criminals who felt frustrated if my attempts to obtain them acquittals cheated them of their punishment. And now I wonder what proportionate punishment – if such is conceivable – could those feeling guilty of complicity in Nazi criminality unconsciously desire to inflict upon themselves? Could these men, so often the children of severe authoritarian fathers, ever forgo their punishment? Would they masochistically and for evermore cling to their guilt rather than daring, by adopting Mitscherlich's mourning prescription, to release themselves from their morbid, unconscious but deliciously-felt flagellation?

I would not dismiss the German lawyer's dismal prognosis, for I have too often seen the pervasive influence of masochism in politics. It is certainly not peculiar to Germany, and I have sought elsewhere to show its operation in Britain, where, for a decade, bondage to Thatcher cost us dear; but the swings between sadism and masochism have in this century's politics been more overt and intense in Germany than in any other Western country. Freud always insisted that the ebb-tide dragging man back from maturity to dismal perversity was regulated by a dark moon which he names as the death instinct. If Freud is right and if indeed masochism is, as he believed, older than sadism, then it must be taken into account when we examine man's history of wars and persecution, for they may well be part of his frantic attempt to ward off his yearning for the ultimate delight of self-destruction. By resisting the temptation of a still and lifeless Nirvana, and directing his erotically loaded sadism outwards, away from the interior life, man may postpone, for a little while, the joy of his submission to death. But the challenge Freud gave this century in illuminating the importance of sexuality in our lives has been only superficially met. Gripped with panic, we dodge the awful implications of an hypothesis which states that a biologically determined instinct, bathed in exciting sensuality, draws us to our nemesis, and that we can only advance the date of our masturbatory death by directing some of the force of this terrible instinct into sensually inspired sadistic fantasies, and in actual cruelty against our fellow-man; and nowhere at any time in history has such cruelty been exceeded than in the Holocaust.

Within the unpleasant raillery of that German lawyer there was more than an element of self-mockery. He was signalling me that there were many older Germans beyond redemption; and that their sadism, now that it was blocked and unable to be expressed in war and genocide, had turned in upon themselves. They would never acknowledge and work through their guilt, for that would mean they would forfeit the pleasures of self-inflicted punishment.

A flawed heritage

Sombre prognostications of this order, if made in Britain, meet fierce condemnation by the political establishment. The response to Nicholas Ridley's notorious comments on contemporary Germany, which led to his enforced resignation from the Cabinet in 1990, shows how unacceptable are views affirming that very many older Germans are well-nigh intractable and irredeemable. Such views are certainly undiplomatic and highly inconvenient but that does not necessarily invalidate them. Ridley had a knack of expressing, often clumsily, awkward views, as I well recall when he was, to the discredit of the Commons, savaged because, after a visit to the Falklands, he was guilty of the offence of suggesting to the House a sensible negotiated settlement with Argentina which would have prevented that avoidable war.

For my part, unlike almost all my Labour colleagues, I always enjoyed Ridley when, as ally or opponent, we sat together on many meetings of standing Commons' committees. When he came, as a young man, into the House, he was a refreshing *enfant terrible*, as became the younger son of a viscount. I began to find his continuation of this role into middle age a little tiresome, but soon I appreciated his functional value in a Commons that increasingly became swollen with the oleaginous professional members, circumspect and odiously labile in their politics. He had a patrician's disdain for the compromises of the smoothies and always remained his own man; far removed as I was from his radical right-wing economic views, I respected his authenticity. His unequivocal Whiggish credo meant that his form of libertarianism was not confined to a detestation of Statist intervention in economic affairs. He no less passionately hated those laws which he regarded as impertinent interferences in the private conduct of citizens; and consequently I often found him a vigorous supporter of my social legislation which he rightly interpreted as designed to free people from legal prohibitions which only added to the burdens of their personal predilections and dilemmas. My only difficulty with Ridley was persuading him to curb his delicious wit and to subdue his provocations which could inflame opponents and estranged waverers whose support I needed. He certainly did not fall into the Neanderthal man stereotype in which many have cast him, and the carapace he affected of misanthropy and curmudgeonliness was too thin and luminous to conceal the sensitive and tense inner man; indeed, his water-colours tell us more of him than the provocative swashbuckling which so often infuriated my Labour colleagues. Ridley had, of course, in the opinion of the young interviewer, Dominic Lawson, to whom he addressed the comments on Germany, one great fault: he was too old, and his age disqualified him from forgetting the last war, and his visit, shortly before the interview, to Auschwitz had reactivated all his mistrust of the Germans.

Lawson had resentfully asked him: 'Aren't your views coloured by the fact that you can remember the Second World War?' Lawson then disparagingly tells us: 'I would have sworn I saw a spasm of emotion cross Mr Ridley's face,' and then Ridley replied: 'Jolly good thing too. Only two months ago I was in Auschwitz, Poland, next week I am in Czechoslovakia. You ask them what they think about the Second World War. It's useful to remember.' Lawson in his repugnant commentary, unworthy of repetition, on Ridley's response, shows how violently he disliked the minister's references to the past, to Auschwitz. It is unfortunate that this young man has so little recollection of his own Jewish ancestry. Perhaps then he would not have so evidently relished his entrapment of Ridley.

However, the more serious charge that has to be met by those of us whose recollections of the Nazi era are etched permanently in our memories, is that we are talking of Germans who are already dead, or soon will be, and that even younger men like Kohl whose childhood may have been seared by the impact of the war, will soon leave the political stage, and the new generation, to whom Hitler and the last war are the distant past, will govern Germany. It is argued that to persist in visiting the sins of the fathers upon the children is bigotry; and that our pessimism is clouding our judgement upon future British–German relationships. It is urged upon us that it is time to draw the line: as John Ardagh persuasively suggests: 'Forty-five years after the war's end, that now ought to be possible.' We should 'look at Germany not just as some peculiar problem child, but as a normal modern society.'

Sometimes the well-intended exhortation, with its comfortable but spurious assumptions, is obeyed at our peril; large numbers of adult Germans today are the children of Nazis. Shortly before they were born, or when they were infants, their fathers had acquiesced or had been actively engaged in the murdering of $1^1/_2$ million children throughout German-occupied Europe. As a criminal lawyer, I have seen, as do our probation officers daily, how devastating is the burden that can fall upon the children of criminals; it is naïve to believe that, although Nazi fathers would have attempted to mask from their children, as so many did, their complicities in child-killing, that these children, today's adults, have been left unaffected.

More, my own experience, as a serviceman, of the conditions existing in devastated Germany as the war ended, is always with me when I meet Germans in their mid–fifties and sixties, men born in the immediate pre-war years. As little children and young teenagers, they had so often experienced separation from parents and abandonment by their caretakers. They were exposed to air-raids and fire, hunger and typhoid epidemics. They witnessed their companions turn into corpses. And then, later, as a few Germans felt able to reveal to me, another sort of abandonment was inflicted upon them. Their frightful experiences were not allowed to become a topic of conversation in their homes, nor in their schools. They were required to bury their own past even as did their fathers. They were doubly afflicted: they were required to collude with their fathers in an attempt to erase the past.

But 80 years ago Freud spelled out in his *Totem and Taboo* how vain is the notion that parents can cover up grim pasts, leaving the next generation the freedom to make a completely fresh start; he wrote:

> We may safely assume that no generation is able to conceal any of its more important mental processes from its successor. For

psychoanalysis has shown that everyone possesses in his unconscious mental activity an apparatus which enables him to interpret other people's reactions, that is, to undo the distortions which other people have imposed on the expression of their feelings. An unconscious understanding such as this of all the . . . dogmas left behind by the original relation to the father . . . make it possible for later generations to take over their heritage of emotion.

And now psychoanalysts, not least German practitioners, reviewing their clinical work, sadly but truthfully tell us how maiming is the emotional heritage bequeathed to today's Germans by their guilty fathers.

The German analyst Eickhoff does not blink at the facts when he presents illuminating clinical material demonstrating how the pathology of dead Nazis can permeate and influence both the real circumstances and the emotional side of the lives of his patients across the generations; he has been startled to find how trans-generational pathology can be so transmitted that even two-year-olds can be seen as displaying depersonalising symptoms that have their source in the destructiveness of their dead Nazi grandfathers. For a considerable time there has been investigated in the United States a grim plenitude of clinical material showing how far-reaching are the deleterious effects of the traumatic experiences of scarred survivors of the Holocaust upon their children. More attention has been paid to the children of victims than has been paid to the children of the persecutors; but they are no less haunted by fearsome ghosts, and we will not exorcise them if, out of political delicacy, we pretend that they do not stalk modern Germany.

Even, or perhaps particularly, those younger Germans who are dedicated to absolute pacifism or 'green' movements, and appear to be rebelling against everything their fathers and grandfathers stood for, are by no means fully emancipated from the immediate past. Eric Simenauer, the only Jewish analyst who left Germany under Hitler to have returned after the war, has told of his younger patients:

> However paradoxical it may seem, we find that the same young people who rebel against their fathers and everything they represent are caught up in the very ideologies they oppose. I conclude that these young men have relinquished only the ego identifications with the father, the initial constitution never having been changed in the superego and in the ideals.

Most German adults who are the children of Nazis do not reveal themselves so exotically; yet, although appearing to be reserving all their enthusiasms for their work and the pleasures of the consumer society, their apparent disengagement from the world of their committed fathers is often even more superficial. Those who begat us cannot be so easily blotted out.

The unadmitted responsibility

What the children of the Nazi generation can suffer from, some German analysts tell us, is a 'borrowed sense of guilt'. The fathers have brought down the curtain on their shameful past: for those fathers did not tell, as my father did to me and as I did to my children, tales of wartime hazards and valour of which we were proud. Only exceptionally would the defeated Nazi father boast of his past involvement; and by his very silence, his unadmitted responsibility, he bequeathed his unmetabolised guilt to his children who, I have observed, sometimes stagger under its burden.

A child, if blessed with a father, will usually idolise him when a little one and rage against him in adolescence; but to find his own identity and work through his ambivalences, to be his own man, he needs the presence of a father who in the end he may see as he is, with virtues and warts. Since I took the initiative in altering the divorce laws of Britain in 1969, I have, with limited success, urged the need to bring in conciliation services that will mean the death of a marriage will not also mean the death of the family; so that, unlike now, all children of broken marriages will be likely to see and remain in touch with their fathers. Without the presence of a father, the child can be at risk; too often the child becomes lost and, in adulthood, his emotional life a shambles. In a sense, many men of the Nazi era became absent fathers, physically present but remote from their children from whom they withheld a whole segment of their lives.

Nor does it seem likely that the mothers of so many of today's German adults would have filled the dangerous vacuum the fathers had created. Mitscherlich has reminded us of how the German mother of my generation liked to see herself in relation to the child in the role of the father's deputy, as a dispenser of punishment; and a typical reaction, as Mitscherlich points out, was that of the many mothers who were proud to be allowed to sacrifice their sons on the altar of the Fatherland or for the great Führer. It is an error to treat the women of the Third Reich as passive and innocent victims of a male-dominated Nazi movement. The voting pattern reveals that increasingly, as the 1930s advanced, German women, particularly the younger women, voted, especially in Protestant areas, for the Nazis. A significant number of women were ready to acquiesce in the surrender of their recently won political rights in return for the honour and prestige bestowed on them as mothers in the Fatherland. Such mothers have been no less tight-lipped with their children than their husbands.

The schools too would often have failed to provide teachers who could have acted as father surrogates, telling the pupils of the evils of the Nazi regime, bringing them into touch with a black period in the country's history, and helping them to face and overcome the dilemmas which guilty and withholding parents were creating for them. Even although younger adults of today's Germany may have escaped from the more autocratic teachers inevitably moulded in the rigid disciplines of the authoritarian pre-war educational system, they nevertheless came under the influence of the traditional German view of school education that its function is to train the mind rather than to indulge in character-building or to promote civic responsibility. These are matters seen to be the responsibility of parents; the austere utilitarian schools then, as now, finish at 1 p.m. and then the children are sent off home. What was absent was the warm sense of community, the buzz of valuable non-academic activity, all the elements which could have healed the scars that the cold, frightened and defeated fathers were inflicting upon their children. Today's German adults rarely found role models in their school which would have freed them from the oppression of their fathers' unspoken guilt.

Nor is it probable that those of today's German adults who passed their *Abitur* exam and entered the overcrowded universities would have found there admired and outspoken anti-Nazi professors, from whom they might have found the courage to face and overcome the past. The craven subservience of the universities to Hitler left a pall over the college life which was lived by Germany's graduates: 4,000 of those teaching in the universities were ejected from their posts in the de-Nazification era, but right up to the student uprisings of 1967, the old hierarchies remained rigid, with old-fashioned senior professors stifling any move by junior lecturers for change, and ensuring that little or no illumination was granted to students wrestling with their fathers' past.

And today, unhappily, the ramshackle universities with their overcrowded lecture halls, accommodation shortages, and poor study facilities, all worsening as spending cuts take place to help pay for unification, are certainly not turning out students who know and understand the shames of their grandparents; little of the left-wing idealism displayed by their parents' rebellious 1960s generation seems to have rubbed off on them. The majority appear to be concerned only to adapt successfully to Germany's materialist society, and look away from the disturbing past, and any ugly symptoms of that past currently displayed; a significant minority, however, are finding an identity within the right-wing *Burschenschaften*, reactionary student clubs, steeped in masonic-like rituals with 'Honour, Freedom and Fatherland' as their slogan, and with ritualised beer-drinking, fencing without face-guards, and gatherings where extremist politicians and historians are invited to address them, as their main activities. The chaos and disorganisation within so many of the universities give opportunities to those fostering such clubs, and I have encountered genuine fears amongst liberal German professors that the 'fraternities' could haul the wave of neo-Nazi extremism off the street on to the campuses. The young men joining these clubs, dressed in their brightly coloured, cavalry-style uniforms and pinbox hats, hitherto bereft of any framework, are now acquiring a menacing identity.

The writings of British apologists of contemporary Germany acknowledge the central problem confronting the Germans, which is reflected in a ceaseless stream of books, articles and media debates about their national identity. And in 1986 the historians' debate, *Historikerstreit*, burst like a storm over German academe. Although the argument centred on Nolte's provocative reflections on the Holocaust, the underlying theme, as Professor Kershaw in an arresting 1992 memorial lecture has emphasised, was that of national identity. John Ardagh has succintly made the same point: 'It often occurs to me that nothing identifies a German so much as this search for his identity.' But he, as many others sympathetic to modern Germany, whilst honest enough, when noting this restless quest, to acknowledge in general and vague terms that 'the principal cause is obviously the Nazi legacy', nevertheless seems anxious to evade what is even more obvious: that we attain a confident and certain self only when we have had the opportunity, particularly in childhood and adolescence, of identifying with parents or surrogates whom we can trust, whom we can love and whom, without excessive fear we can, as we develop, if needs be, temporarily hate and against whom we can rebel. Without such opportunities the disadvantaged son or daughter is left bereft, undefined; and that is the lot of so many Germans today.

The predicaments of the generation born during or immediately after the Hitler period are painfully clear. Growing up without their fathers during the war years, many of this generation remained without a father for a long time afterwards if he was a prisoner-of-war. From an early age everything prompted them to identify with a Führer who was held up to them as ideal and unconquerable. Their absent father himself partook of the glory of the victorious hero. When their Führer fell, and if and when their fathers returned, the children were left rudderless with no real and tangible opportunity for identification anywhere. And those born later, those now in their thirties and forties, have fared little better for they have had fathers who, vainly attempting to conceal complicities and guilt feelings, left them as children too often bewildered and confused as they attempted to decode their parents' pregnant silences. It is not, therefore, surprising that Ardagh finds the Germans riddled with identity problems.

These problems are often acutely personal; when their parents, shattered by Hitler's defeat, sought to avoid intolerable emotions by breaking all affective bridges linking them to the immediate past, they rendered themselves so numb that their strangulation of affect extended also to their own enquiring children. The perceptive can often sense the suffering of many of those children, now adults who, however successful their working careers may be, regard serious personal relationships as threatening: fears of encroaching upon the parents' menacing and ominous silences has left them, as adults, emotionally immobilised, frozen. I have no difficulty in accepting the belief of some German physicians that they are presented with more problems of impotence than doctors in other European countries.

Collective confusion

Now, however, the German identity confusions are increasingly finding collective expression within the foreign and economic policies being pursued by Kohl on the international stage. At one moment, in 1991, the Germans were insisting that Europe move to establish a collective foreign policy, and the next moment they infuriated their fellow EC members by embarking upon a unilateral intervention in the Balkans. Insisting in 1991 upon the necessity of continuous international co-operation in the monetary sphere, they then, in 1992, to the detriment of all the economies of their allies, raised German interest rates and affirmed that this was what the German economy required. In 1993 whilst manoeuvring to obtain a place on the UN Security Council, the

Germans shrank from any military commitment to a UN peace mission outside Europe. This schizophrenic conduct as Germany swings from an assertive nationalist role to a benign international role is being interpreted as cynicism. After the meeting in December 1991 of the leading industrial countries, the G7, Germany's sabotage of the bid for international co-operation to surmount the world depression caused *The Times* to comment: 'Not since the war has Europe been so in thrall to Germany. Not since the signing of the Treaty of Rome has Germany's commitment to true European "union" been so cynical.'

There are historical precedents which *The Times* could call in aid to justify the charge. The young German historian, Detlev Peukart, who died tragically, shortly before his major book was published in Britain in 1991, fearlessly set out the cynicism of the Brüning government in 1931 who, at the time of the world crisis, deliberately behaved passively, adding to international difficulties, 'because it wished to use the crisis to secure its objectives in domestic and foreign policy'. That government, and the German employers, by making Germany insolvent believed it would make it easier finally to shake off the burden of reparations and, within the crisis, obtain the exclusion from the coalition of the Social Democrats, and consequently be able to bypass parliament and set up an authoritarian government. It cannot be gainsaid that the Machiavellian tactics generally used by the Germans to cheat upon their reparation obligations, ultimately led to the situation summed up by Peukert: 'Reparations did not in fact bleed the German economy. Indeed their net effect was to leave the economy in rather better shape.' With such recollections of nationalist economic policies, careless of the international consequences, it may be difficult to challenge *The Times*. Yet I find myself reluctant to be so condemnatory; rather I think the dichotomies within the current German economic and foreign policies are primarily reflections of their identity confusions which many politicians like Edmund Stoiber, Prime Minister of Bavaria, are currently exploiting.

In November 1993 Stoiber poured scorn on Kohl's European enthusiasm, treating him as if he were a dodo, and declaring that Kohl had grown up in a post-war Germany gripped by guilt about Hitler and the war. Ominously, Stoiber declared: 'We hoped that the then divided German nation would be subsumed in a European nation and that thereby we would be free of our historical responsibilities . . . all this has been changed by reunification. The German people were no longer in step with the European ideal.' What the Germans now had to do was to work out 'what the German identity actually is'. The identity which Stoiber is inviting the Germans to assume is unequivocal and can be singularly attractive to those who, hot for certainty, long for the unambiguous. He wished the Germans to turn their eyes to the East and, free from entanglements in a European Union, unilaterally, to dominate economically Eastern Europe and, if possible, the republics of the former Soviet Union; he wants a strong nationalist Germany engaged in colonial exploitation. Even Stoiber is now being outflanked; the former chairman of the Bavarian Free Democrats and champion of the anti-Maastricht cause, Manfred Brunner, set up in January 1994 a new national anti-European party. He too looks East and his stance is receiving enthusiastic support from his close friend Jörg Haider, the leader of the Austrian far Right and a man known for his praise of Hitler's employment policy.

Increasingly I found in Germany in 1993 among the business community a new mood, showing that Stoiber and Brunner are no mere eccentrics, engaged in political tactics to gain extreme right-wing support in the coming elections; there are many in commercial circles who are now attracted to the option of a Germany, with its European ardour cooled, and with East Germany, over the decade, metabolised, finding its economic destiny in the East.

The ardour of some, far from being quenched by the threat of a Fascist Russia, has been fuelled; for immediately after his electoral success in December 1993, Vladimir Zhirinovsky the Russian Fascist leader, flaunting his views in the neo-Nazi Munich-based *Nationale Zeitung*, pledged himself to build up links with extreme right-wing bodies in Germany and back their challenge to the post-war German-Polish borders; and he made clear his readiness to negotiate back to Germany the return of Köningsberg, now Russia's Kaliningrad. Those of us who lived through the shock of the Nazi–Soviet Pact believe that those British Germanophiles who deny that any serious body of opinion in Germany supports Stoiber's opinions are whistling in the dark.

We can be misled by such Germanophiles. One of the most devoted, Alan Watson, who shares many of Ardagh's views and who, like him, has the advantage of a German wife, has in a recent over-eager and affirmative book and television series about the 'new' Germany, wistfully sought to use the German penchant for metamorphosis – a favourite word of Goethe's – to suggest that a transformation has taken place; and that now we have a Germany which hates the nationalist state and is possessed by idealistic beliefs in a united Europe. Such an appraisement does more credit to Watson's romanticism than his sense of reality. He is indisputably correct when he contends that perhaps the most characteristic concept in German philosophy and literature is the idea of metamorphosis with which, at a more developed level, struggles between opposites are exquisitely resolved. Germany's philosophy and literature is certainly focused to an unusual degree on the processes of such changes, changes within people and things that bring about dramatic alterations from what they have been in the past to something new. But I doubt if this particular cultural heritage, as Watson contends, is now operating so benignly in modern Germany that a confident sense of identity will be gained.

In the past, from Kant to Marx, all the emphases placed upon various theses and antitheses which the German thinkers postulated, found their political resolution within most dangerous metamorphoses: thus the notion of Hegel who saw that man's awareness of his spiritual self would meet the material world of the scientist within a collective will, finding its highest expression in the state. 'The State,' wrote Hegel, 'is the Divine Idea as it exists on Earth.' Not surprisingly, Hegel's yearned-for metamorphosis was appropriated by the Nazis. Now, however, Watson would seek to persuade us that a new metamorphosis is being enacted: that the German restlessness, the ceaseless strivings for yet further metamorphoses, is finding expression in a German advocacy of European integration. It is from this 'treasure' of Germany's intellectual heritage, Watson tells us, that Kohl is drawing when he advocates the progressive transfer of sovereignty from the nation-state to democratic institutions of the community Europe: 'He is in this sense speaking from deep within the German cultural tradition. His idealism has this Hegelian dimension to it.'

Not all will yield to Watson's effusions. I belong to the generation that was seared by the political philosophy which is certainly possessed by 'the Hegelian dimension'; by Marxism. When I was sixteen, like so many of the bright youngsters of the time, I was introduced by our left-wing intellectual gurus, so often products of public school and Oxbridge, to Marx's dialectical materialism, and I was seduced into the belief that an irresistible dynamic was at work which would lead to an explosion, releasing vital social forces which would transform the whole basis of society. The metamorphosis was to be wondrous. As the Communist *Manifesto* puts it:

Centralisation of the means of production and socialisation of labour reach a point where they become incompatible with their capitalist integument. This integument is burst asunder. The knell

of capitalist private property sounds. The expropriators are
expropriated.

And we believed the millenium would follow. Now, 60 years later, I
cannot cease to be astonished how during the 1930s so many British
intellectuals became obsessed with the German 'treasure', and deserted
their own political traditions, lured by an alien culture. Away from
theory, in practice the metamorphosis was fated to be witnessed in
Stalin's Soviet Union, in the archipelago, and in states like the GDR.

Watson encourages the German assertion by claiming: 'The
characteristic insights of the German philosphers . . . a better society
can be born and Germany and the Germans can play a part in that
creative process, a process within history.' For my part, I doubt if a
reintegration of such philosophical 'insights' into contemporary
German thought is the route to a confident and benevolent German
identity. No incantations drawn from the thaumaturgical texts of
German philosophers will still the identity confusions of today's
Germany. No magic metamorphosis will liberate the Germans from
their enslavement to the insistent demands from their borrowed and
unconscious sense of guilt which can, despite themselves, so distort
their decision-making that other countries conclude that the Germans
are being cynical, deliberately provocative and uncaring.

Digging up repressed roots

Their freedom to make needed objective and balanced political choices
will only come when, arduously, they dredge from their unconscious
their monstrous sense of guilt, one which is proportionate to the
terrible crimes committed by their parents and for which they are not
personally responsible. We can be encouraged by Freud to believe the
task is not impossible. Telling of the battle facing psychoanalysts
dealing with a patient's sense of guilt, he distinguishes between those
whose guilt is their own and those who have borrowed it from someone
like a father or mother who, in his vocabulary, he describes as 'an
object of an erotic cathexis':

> The battle with the obstacle of an unconscious sense of guilt is not
> made easy for the analyst. Nothing can be done against it directly,
> and nothing indirectly but the slow procedure of unmasking its
> unconscious repressed roots, and of thus gradually changing it
> into a conscious sense of guilt. One has a special opportunity for

charge of mental energy

influencing it when this unconscious sense of guilt is a 'borrowed' one – when it is the product of an identification with some other person who was once the object of an erotic cathexis. A sense of guilt that has been adopted in this way is often the sole remaining trace of the abandoned love relation and not at all easy to recognise as such. If one can unmask this former object cathexis behind the unconscious sense of guilt, the therapeutic success is often brilliant.

The overwhelming majority of Germans alive today are innocent of any crimes; yet they are afflicted with a neurotic sense of guilt which comes from poisoned 'repressed roots' of the kind Freud is describing. To bring those roots into the light of day, into consciousness, a task which Freud insists is the prerequisite to successful therapy, will not be done even by the Germans making the painful acknowledgement that their fathers, directly or vicariously, were murderers. They will have to dig deeper, for the killings were fulfilments of terrible lusts and desires, and it is those cravings which have to be levered out of German soil.

Hitler craved for racial domination which he believed would guarantee German supremacy, and his other irresistible desire was for *Lebensraum*, living space; and the German people joined him in boundless indulgences in these perverted passions. It was the ungovernable appetite for racial superiority and *Lebensraum* which brought disaster to Germany, caused the Holocaust and led to the death of millions of Germans, Russians and Poles. The transmitted guilt which continues to cripple emotionally so many Germans today comes from their fathers' abandonment to those terrible twin passions; the pulsating primal Wotan-like energies within those lusts burst the crust of civilisation.

However, it is not our task to taunt the Germans with the debauchery of their fathers; nor, indeed, would it help them or ourselves to invite them to disavow their parents, for psychoanalysis has long since taught us that the disavowed will come back in other guises. What we are asking them collectively to go through is the similar agony that an individual patient has to endure when he suffers 'the slow procedure of unmasking unconscious repressed roots'. When the sons, therefore, ask: 'What are we to do with our Nazi fathers?' the answer is not that their fathers must be utterly rejected. Rather, the solution lies along the clear path outlined by one of France's leading psychoanalysts, Janine Chasseguet-Smirgel; outrageous as it may seem, the son has to identify with his father, and only when he has first done that is he likely, as a result, to achieve his own humanity. Chasseguet-Smirgel has written:

> If you speak of the need to integrate your identifications with that father, you are immediately treated as a Nazi yourself. But in the absence of identification, where there is only counter-identification, there can be no genuine choice between acceptance and rejection, and sublimation becomes totally impossible. In order to become a human being in the full sense of the term, we have to be able to discover, confront and own the Hitler in us, otherwise the repressed will return and the disavowed will come back in various guises.

Only one German politician, the elderly Christian Democrat Speaker of the Bundestag, Philipp Jenninger, has dared to act as Chasseguet-Smirgel counselled; it cost him his political life. On the occasion of the fiftieth anniversary of *Reichskristallnacht* – the night of the broken glass, the brutal pogrom heralding the extermination of the Jews – before a parliament filled with deputies and representatives of Israel and the pathetic remnant of German Jewry, in the most remarkable speech delivered in post-war Germany, Jenninger called upon the nation to follow his example. He tried to force today's Germans to identify with their fathers, and in an extraordinary surgical probe, to make them unblinkingly see how and why their forebears had acted as they did. His listeners became choked with anger and, as he developed his oration, the cowardly deputies walked out in droves; they had come to say they were sorry, and then to depart speedily from an uncomfortable occasion.

But Jenninger had come to delve into the psyche of the nation in 1938 and to do this he first recited:

> . . . the triumphal procession of Hitler's early years: reincorporation into the Reich of the Saar, introduction of general national service, an enormous armaments drive, the signature of an accord with Great Britain on the size of fleets, the occupation of the Rhineland, the Olympic Games in Berlin, the *Anschluss* of Austria to the Reich, and finally, only a few weeks before the November pogrom, the Munich Accord allowing the dismemberment of Czechoslovakia. At last the Versailles Treaty was indeed no more than a scrap of paper and the German Reich was the dominant power on the European continent . . . For Germans, who had seen the Weimar Republic as little more than a series of foreign policy

defeats, all this must have seemed a miracle. And that was not all: mass unemployment had been transformed into full employment, mass poverty had been turned into something approaching decent living standards for broad levels of society. In the place of doubt and hopelessness, there was an atmosphere of optimism and self-confidence. Had Hitler not done what Kaiser Wilhelm had only promised, brought the Germans wonderful times? Was he not really chosen by Providence, the leader a nation receives only once in a thousand years?

And only when Jenninger had thus made his listeners identify with the previous generation, did he proceed by giving his eyewitness accounts of the barbarity of their fathers as they dog-whipped, suffocated and shot Jewish children. The form of his speech, using the classical rhetorical device of building up in order to knock down, gave an added power to this most intellectually compelling and rhetorically structured damnation of Nazism ever delivered by a German. The response he provoked fulfilled Chasseguet-Smirgel's prophecy that an insistence that the present generation of Germans must first identify with the Nazi parents would bring the charge that this was an advocacy of Nazism. Jenninger was stigmatised as a Nazi apologist. One of the few fully understanding the significance of the occasion was the former Reuter correspondent in Berlin, Peter Millar. He has written of that strange commemoration ceremony:

> The horror of the Nazi atrocities became the more chilling when one understood how the ordinary, decent German man or woman was seduced into believing Hitler was a messiah. It cost Jenninger his political career. No one wanted even to try to understand the phenomenon of Nazism; it was easier to apologise. West Germany was like a psychiatric patient prepared to rehearse and repent the horrors of his past endlessly, but not to examine and exorcise them.

Such public repentance without exorcism, the syndrome which Millar identifies, so often takes exotic forms in Germany, even by Germans who suffered under the Nazis. There is an illustrative story, not apocryphal, of a Protestant clergyman who having survived a short period in a concentration camp, delivered a fulminating sermon of repentance to an international congregation. He wallowed in accusations against himself, his country and his church. A Swiss theologian who grew tired of listening remarked: 'Those are the Germans. First they are the greatest criminals and then the greatest penitents. What matters is that they are the greatest.'

Jenninger, unlike that clergyman and so many Germans, did not shrink from the step that can bring about a confident self, free from neurotic guilt; to reach that state, the Germans first must have the courage to plunge into Wotan's cesspit. They must swim in the pool in which their fathers were wont to revel, amongst the detritus of racialist and *Lebensraum* doctrines; and only after they have suffered this unholy baptism will they be able to gain their full humanity and will Germany cease in its present restless and dangerous confused search for an identity.

The purification of blood

In his bunker, beneath the ashes and collapsing masonry of Berlin, Hitler dictated the last few sentences of his political testament: 'Above all, I charge the leadership of the nation to a rigorous adherence to our racial laws and to a merciless resistance against the poisoner of all peoples – international Jewry.' As he began, so he ended. The dream of a racialist state was the Nazis' dynamic; and its creation was the ultimate fulfilment. Today's Germans will not find themselves until, without equivocation or mitigation, they accept that their fathers totally surrendered to a barbaric racialism and gave it the highest priority, over-riding all other policy considerations. This is an acceptance the Germans have resisted. Even a liberal German historian like Eberhard Jäckel, whom we sometimes see on our television screens seeking to explain modern Germany to us, cannot tolerate the burden of sole German responsibility for the awful fact; he complains that it was our lack of determination that enabled Hitler to embark upon his war of conquest and elimination, a complaint which has no more or less justification than the blame attached to careless householders for the burglaries inflicted upon them. Such projections of blame, or marginalisation of the significance of Hitler's racialist policies, have been commonplace for decades in Germany. It took until 1991 for a German professor, Wolfgang Wippermann, with an English academic, Michael Burleigh, at last squarely to face the Germans with the reality that their fathers created in the Third Reich a government that was fundamentally different from any other totalitarian regime that has ever existed; and that it was different precisely because of the all-encompassing nature of its racial policies.

Wippermann clarifies how dangerously naïve it is to present Nazi racialist doctrine as a jumble of crazy outpourings, or as a cynical and opportunist political tactic. It was never a concealing mask used to gain and perpetuate Nazi power, never a smokescreen for a classic appetite for conquest; it was no diversion, no mere fistula, no secondary feature of the body politic. Wippermann demonstrates how social policy, military and foreign policy, were all subordinate to the creation of hierarchical racial new order. Long before Hitler came to power, the vision of the barbaric utopia founded upon the alleged verities of race had been presented to the fathers of today's Germans, and received their endorsement.

The Third Reich distinguished itself from all other authoritarian states, past or present, not only because of its racialism, but because of the singular form of racialism it ruthlessly practised. Hitler's racialism was no mere rationalisation for anti-Semitism; 'traditional' anti-Semitism with all its multi-causal impetuses, not least the religious divide, has and does exist in other countries, and racial prejudices have entered into its expression in other lands, but always peripherally. Because the race issue was so central to the Hitlerian creed, Germans today have to question whether the form of racialism expressed by the Nazis is peculiar to Germany, is endemic; and, to find the answers, an interpretation of the underlying fantasies behind Nazi racialism must be attempted, for although those fantasies may not be particular to Germans, their overt expression most certainly has been, for nowhere else have they been acted out in state policy.

At their 'purest' they can be clearly seen in the Nazi treatment of homosexuals: there, disengaged from conventional historical expressions of anti-Semitism, we see them, starkly, in most florid form. In all the years of my struggle to end the criminality of homosexuality in Britain, despite the diversity of the moralist and bizarre arguments which fell upon me, never did I once encounter any one analagous to the German contention that was to send tens of thousands of pink-triangled homosexuals to their deaths in concentration camps. It was Himmler who, in 1937, put the case for their slaying, calling upon a policy to be adopted in accordance with the 'Nordic-German people's purer consciousness of the "idea of race"' which had led to the 'primæval Germanic view' that homosexuality was 'a degenerate and racially destructive view' and that those offending should be 'drowned in the bogs, clothes and all'.

Accompanying this display of arcane wisdom, were illustrations of his thesis. As a consequence of the First World War, Germany had lost two million men. There were also, Himmler calculated, two million homosexuals in the population. This meant that Germany's 'sexual balance sheet' had gone into deficit, because 'four million men capable of sex' had either died or had 'renounced their duty to procreate' on account of their sexual proclivities. A 'people of good race' could not afford this imbalance. Instead of fulfilling its 'candidature for world power and world domination', Germany would sink into 'insignificance' within 50 years because some of its 'racially pure' and 'sexually capable' male population did not want to produce children or have sexual contact with women. Sexual behaviour was no longer a matter for the individual for it involved 'the life and death of a people, world power or "Swissification" ... I hope finally to have done with persons of this type ... so that ... the increasingly healthy blood which we are cultivating for Germany, will be kept pure.' Like the Jews, the homosexuals went to their death because of their blood.

This blood theme haunts the German culture; it did not begin with the Nazis. The yearning for the fusion of pure unadulterated blood with the replenishing soil, the cult of *Blut und Boden*, has been an operant in a tradition of which German romanticism and the nineteenth century revival of paganism are only more recent expressions. In another culture, the writings of the Nazi racial exponents and the speeches of Hitler would have been treated as the ravings of madmen; but in Germany the pseudo-biological dimensions of the Nazi creed are not innovative but corroboration of irrational myths that may well be as old as their founding fathers, the Germanic tribes possessed of the Nordic strain to which so often the Germans have described their 'heroic', Faustian and endlessly roving nature.

Walther Darre, the Nazi racial theorist and Hitler's minister of agriculture, was therefore addressing a receptive audience when he wrote:

> Our goal using all the means in our possession is to produce a condition in which the supply of blood, the agent of creativity in the body of our nation, is maintained and increased. Upon this depends the consolidation and development of the quality of being German ... We acknowledge that for the German nation the earth is as much a healthy basis for the maintenance and renewal of its blood as a means of producing its food.

And this farrago of nonsense, the theme of the need for the admixture of pure blood and soil, was ceaselessly expounded by Hitler. As early as 1924 he was declaring: 'What has been profitably Germanised in history is the soil which our ancestors acquired by the sword and settled with German peasants. Insofar as they directed foreign blood into our national body in this process, they contributed to the catastrophic splintering of our inner being.'

To end that 'splintering' was, as Darre put it, 'to purify the inherited German protoplasm of elements of non-Nordic blood by a process of selection . . . this systematic concentration of pure blood, together with expulsion of all that is foreign or undesirable, is the only way to succeed in eliminating impurities in the body of the nation.'

Returning to the womb

Despite their tragic consequences, there is an extraordinary refusal outside Germany to take these Nazi racial doctrines seriously; they are simply dismissed as crazy. If this attitude is maintained, there is little possibility of the Germans themselves extirpating the unconscious fantasies which have so repetitively enveloped their culture and which attained their apogee in the racial state of 1933-45; such fantasies left uninterpreted, left buried, could emerge again in one form or another, a menace to the Germans and the rest of Europe. One of the few who have warned against leaving the Nazi racial policies so uninterpreted is Chasseguet-Smirgel; and using her clinical material, and not least the dreams of her pre-psychotic and borderline patients, she has illuminated an area which half a century after the Holocaust has remained strangely neglected. Her work has led her to postulate that the infant has a primary wish – immediate and inborn – to strip the mother's body of its contents in order to regain possession of the place once occupied before birth, and that all obstacles which, after birth, made access to the mother's body impossible, have to be removed: the wish is that 'of returning to a world without organisation, to primæval chaos, to a universe marked by homogeneity and the continuum present before birth'. It is this schema, much elaborated, that she applies in her scrutiny of the Nazi racial doctrine and, under her tutelage, it cannot be doubted the gobbledegook of Nazi racialism assumes a coherence that, otherwise, leaves one despondently bewildered.

The racialists offered the German people a utopian bliss when the desired unity, the *Blut und Boden*, was achieved; with terrifying alacrity, upon the well-watered culture, the subliminal message flourished. The Germans were being proffered the regressive choice of a return to the

womb, and eager to live out, untrammelled, their fantasy, all exponents
of harsh reality had to be exterminated. Again and again in *Mein Kampf*
the self-described 'idealist' Hitler assaults the 'materialism' of the Jews;
the reality principle had to be denied by him and, indeed, as the former
Nazi Rauschning recorded, Hitler accused the Jews of having invented
reason. Rosenberg, the Nazis' philosopher, made all explicit: for him
'the flaw in the Jews is their intellectualism, that fatal separation which
comes between our natural instinctive roots composed of blood and
race, and our soul, our thoughts and our action'. Thought was the
enemy, for it shattered the delusion that the intra-uterine bliss could be
regained. It denied the possibility of fusion of mother and child; it
challenged the essential tenet of Hitler's racial theory, that of
consubstantiality, for he applied the same concept of consubstantiality
to the Reich which Christians apply to the Church when they refer to
the mystical body of Christ.

Impatient, Hitler could not wait for the great merger which would
come about when the racial purity had been attained. On the way to
that goal, at Kehlstein, Berchtesgaden, he had caused to be created a
personal shrine which monumentally exteriorised his fantasy. It was
Martin Bormann, the faithful servant ever anticipating the most
profound needs of his master, who understood Hitler's wish for a
rebirth: Berchtesgaden was built by Bormann with the intention of it
being a gift to Hitler on his fiftieth birthday. The perplexed non-
German observers at the time of its construction commented that only
madmen could conceive of such a place, let alone build it; they were
too dismissive, for Hitler at Berchtesgaden was revealing all. This was
the materialisation of the child's conception of the return to the womb.
First there is the approach by a winding upwards road some nine miles
long cut out of the mountain, then after reaching a heavily-guarded
entrance there is a long tunnel leading to a wide copper-panelled lift
rising hundreds of feet right through the rock, taking one to a strong
and massive circular hall with windows all round: the impression there
is of being suspended in space. Here Hitler believed he could be alone,
safe, undisturbed in his eyrie, able to revel in the joys that mother
nature bestows.

His fantasy had a fateful consonance with that of the German
people; the personal fantasy was the static sparking off of the group
fantasy that in *Blutgemeinschaft*, a community of blood, all pure
Germans would, in a single body, come together inside the national
soil. The horde of German brothers, homogenised, would take
possession of the mother; and in such a dream the father, the separator,

thwarting the consummation, must at all costs be excluded. It is that corollary to the fantasy enveloping the Germans that was to lead to the extermination of six million Jews for, to Hitler, the Jew, correctly, symbolised the separator; and when Hitler so designated him, Hitler was echoing a dominant theme in traditional German philosophy with its passion for mystical unities. Hegel, Feuerbach, Nietzsche and Marx all attacked the father God of the Jews and even as they, often intemperately, praised Greek polytheism, it is clear that if they accepted Christianity in any form it was because in the incarnation of the Word, man is less separated from God than he is in Judaism which regards doctrines of incarnation as blasphemies, and those of transubstantiation as heathen. For Hitler, of course, even Christian doctrine contained no such mitigations: it was hopelessly Judaised. 'It is deplorable,' he said, 'that the Bible should have been translated into German and that the whole of the German people have thus become exposed to the whole of this Jewish mumbo-jumbo.' In his *Table Talk* he always equated St Paul with Trotsky, both destructive forces causing decay whose only 'providential' roles were that they provoked a 'defensive reaction' of the 'attacked organism . . . the healthy German body'; both must be overcome so that, uninfected, the ultimate consummation could be achieved. Hitler told his table companions that 'the heaviest blow that ever struck humanity was the coming of Christianity'.

Hitler's impatience with Christianity is more than understandable, once the distinction between his racial anti-Semitism and Christian anti-Semitism is acknowledged. The teachings of the Christ myth require the continued existence of that oft-used paradigm of the Jewish people, Judas, which has been deployed by Christian anti-Semites throughout the ages; nowhere has Judas, often in the guise of a character in the folktale of the accursed wandering Jew, unpenitent and malevolent, been depicted more cruelly than in the legends, sculptures, passion plays and paintings of Germany. Between Christ and Judas, however, there is a symbiotic relationship, a fundamental interdependence: for the Judas story is prophesied to have a happy ending because, at the end of time, the Jew would expiate his sin, become a convert and thus provide the indispensable preliminary to the Second Coming of Christ. So long as Christianity retained its vitality, so long did the Judas-Jew, often labelled the 'black Christ', the agent without whose betrayal mankind would never have salvation, remain an imperative need.

But Hitler had no time for the Passion; he was essentially a misshapen creature of the Enlightenment, affirming that science had overthrown such beliefs. His creed, a spurious science of eugenics, vibrated with paganism, but it was presented in modern garb. The Christian anti-Semite saw the Judas-Jew as an evil, but as a necessary evil; but Hitler was a modern man, a fundamentalist convinced by his 'science' of pseudo-biology, and for him, and the Germans who followed him, the Jew no longer represented a necessary evil but an unmitigated evil, totally dispensable, who, hence, without inhibition, could be annihilated.

If the German hold on Christianity had been firmer than their pagan yearnings, they would have resisted Hitler's 'final solution'. In my childhood I was forever involved in playground fights, usually with the children of Roman Catholic families, as I responded to the taunt that I was the killer of Christ; that was a form of anti-Semitism to be unknown to my children, for Hitler and the Germans had all but buried it in Europe beneath the debris of their 'biocracy'. Keeping the Jew alive, even in torment, in order to ensure the Redeemer's arrival, was no part of the Nazi ideology: for the majority of Germans, Hitler *was* the Redeemer, and neither he nor they would defer to the Jew Jesus Christ, and await His coming. They eagerly exploited all the prejudices that Christian anti-Semitism had deeply embossed upon German culture, but they would never yield to the doctrines of a Levantine interloper.

Hitler therefore opted for an alternative and more regressive doctrine. The German cultural tradition, with its passion for unity and its yearnings for fusion with mother nature, reflected an attempt to expel the hated father from the psyche; and the harsh and brutal home environment endured by Hitler as a child meant his ideology had a congruence with such a tradition, for when the upbringing is harsh, the small child can envy the passivity and security the unborn child enjoys with the mother, and he fantasises about finding a way to the longed-for claustrum and ousting and supplanting his hated rival.

The racialist virus re-emerges

But, more, Hitler's particular personal predicament became enmeshed with socially resonating conditions: the First World War left many Germans in a state of profound dereliction, like that of an infant abandoned by his mother. To return to pre-natal bliss was a fantasy that was singularly attractive to a people despairing of the here and now. That was the mood which led to Nazism among so many in the Weimar Republic suffering inflation and unemployment on a massive scale. Today, with an unemployment rate of 15 per cent and six million under-employed, the conditions in East Germany bear uncomfortable resemblances to that period. In the former GDR a joyless disillusionment afflicts millions; the collapse of the Nazi and Communist states, the failure of the cynical West German politicians to fulfil their reckless promises, and the collapse of the social welfare support of the least unsuccessful of the Soviet-Communist models, have left so many East Germans feeling worthless and abandoned. To move around eastern Germany is to encounter not only terrible environmental dereliction, it is also to meet emotional desolation.

No one can tolerate such feelings of helplessness for long: the incidence of suicide increases, but another option beckons. Self-esteem can be regained, feelings of intactness can be reclaimed, by proclamations of superiority and by physical action demonstrating that others are subordinate: the neo-Nazi groups attack the dark-skinned people originally imported for menial labour and turn upon other non-Germans seeking asylum; and their racialism finds resonances in ever-widening circles in the eastern provinces. And meantime, the efforts by Gregor Gysi, the ex-Communist leader of the Party of Democratic Socialism, and former GDR Christian Democrats, to create a new East German grouping able unitedly to counter this extreme right-wing resurgence, are met with hostility. Bonn wishes to erase totally any distinctive political alliances within the former GDR and assumes the affectation, despite all the evidence to the contrary, that there is one seamless State now, and that no political action must be taken which revives memories of the GDR.

With swirling large-scale movements of population now enveloping Europe, social tensions shot through with racism are certainly not confined to Germany; but nowhere are they more potentially threatening, for there the body politic appears to lack the strength to resist the virus of racialism. The State insists that reliance must be placed upon existing democratic institutions and the opinions they generate to eliminate the infection; Bonn also relies upon money, the capital investment and the free market, to create in East Germany a society where, before the state is in danger of being overwhelmed, dissent informed by racial prejudice will be stifled under an avalanche of consumer goods.

But, unless one believes in political homeopathy, these responses, as a therapy, are suspect for, within the interstices of West Germany's own political and economic doctrines, the poison of racial prejudice remains. The ambivalence displayed within the present treatment of the four million *Gastarbeiter*, the so-called guest workers, reveals the consequences of the German failure to summon enough courage to explore in depth the ætiology of the racial state which was the unique contribution made by their fathers to the twentieth century. Despite the reparative and supportive action taken by churches, many young liberals and a few large companies, to assist the immigrant communities, the dominant attitude remains the assertion and protection of German exclusivity.

Labour immigrations, history tells us, have, unless forcibly prevented, always led to permanent settlement. In Europe those who came from Indonesia to Holland are accepted as Dutch citizens, as are Polish miners in France, and as the Asians and West Indians are in Britain; but the Germans are still locked into their past and, so encumbered, they cannot cope with alien cultures. They claim their policy is one of integration; in practice their laws and regulations ensure that millions who have now lived in Germany for decades are voteless, lacking security of residence, and barred from acquiring German nationality by insuperable obstacles such as the need to pass stiff language tests which may even include local dialects like Bavarian.

This response is not simply xenophobic: with considerable justification it is claimed that large sections of the young German population are the least chauvinist in Europe. The response is worse; it is the old sickness: racialism. Germans positively fawn over Scandinavians and receive Britons warmly; but the darker-skinned cannot belong to the *Volk*. Nor are they accorded the protection of a Racial Discrimination Act such as we have in Britain; advertisements for job vacancies and flat lets abound with *Nur für Deutsche* or *Nur Europäer* caveats, and many discos and pubs refuse entry to any Turk or black man. And meantime, the mass-selling tabloid *Bild Zeitung* is openly racialist in its headlines and selected stories, printing material that would be unlawful in Britain. Most Germans who know legislation is needed lack the political courage to advocate its introduction, fearing what the ensuing debates would trawl up from the depths; they know and fear the dangerous undercurrents that run beneath the surface.

No pusillanimity, however, has been shown by federal Germany's politicians in encouraging the ingathering of the *Aussiedler*, the resettlers, descendants of Germans who settled in other lands – usually centuries ago: in recent years, from Romania and Poland to Transylvania and Kazakhstan, one of the largest migrations in

Europe's history of such descendants has been taking place. There
have been some mutterings by the German taxpayer at their
resettlement which is costing ten billion Deutschmarks a year, and
very recently unemployment and housing fears have led to an attempt
being made to put some brake on this extraordinary influx by, among
other restraints, sending up satellites for German channels to be made
available to 'kith and kin' abroad; but all who arrive with a visa
proving their ethnic origin remain welcome. They are distributed
amongst the *Länder* where they are tolerably well-housed, given full
unemployment benefit, retraining and German language courses, and
helped to find jobs. Their blood is their passport and qualification.

About nine out of every ten ethnic Germans from Poland now being
so distributed and given full German citizen rights were provided with
a sinister mechanism to overcome their difficulty in proving the blood
of their ancestors. Lacking proof that they possessed a German parent
or grandparent, they have been admitted because they can show a
parent or grandparent collaborated with the Nazis by applying, on the
grounds of their Germanness, to be inscribed in the Nazi 1939 register
which, despite their Polish citizenship, made them eligible to serve in
the German army. In practice, therefore, today's Germany recognises
as eligible for asylum on blood grounds those whose parent or
grandparent acquired the Nazi worker's certificate, while a compatriot
whose father or grandfather died in the Warsaw uprising against the
Nazi barbarians is barred from entry. This appears to be one of the few
exceptions when blood alone does not determine the issue: collaboration with the Nazis is the necessary additive to a successful application.
Indeed, collaboration with the Nazis can bring other rewards. In
Latvia, now that those who served with the Germans in the SS Waffen
can declare themselves, they have been awarded German pensions –
while the pathetic handful of old Jews who survived these murderers
are denied any help; their blood and victimisation disqualifies them.

Asylum-seekers and accusatory ghosts

All the differentiation in the treatment accorded to the *Gastarbeiter* and
to the *Aussiedler* is an obvious legacy of Nazi racialist doctrine; but it no
less pervades and obscures the arguments presented in the fierce debate
being conducted over those flooding in from Romania, mostly gypsies,
from the former Yugoslavia, the Lebanon and Poland. This is an issue
that touches a raw nerve, for it recalls the treatment of the gypsies

under the Nazis. The gypsies or, as they less pejoratively describe themselves, the *Sinti* and *Roma*, were an acute embarrassment to Nazi racial theory, for they came originally from North India and belonged to the Indo-German-speaking or, as Nazi racial anthropologists would have it, Aryan people. The tangle in which the Nazis found themselves led to many convolutions in policy and disputes between Himmler and Martin Bormann; but with the aid of the 'research' done by the egregious Professor Robert Ritter, the specialist in 'criminal biology', it was 'proved' that nearly all of them had, in their migration west, interbred with lesser breeds and, as such, were a threat to the racial-hygienic measures taken to protect the purity of Aryan blood; consequently they were to be eliminated – as they were, by the hundreds of thousands. Post-war Germany has displayed even more reluctance to acknowledge its responsibilities for their extermination than for the Holocaust. Not until 1982 was the fact of Nazi genocide against the gypsies officially acknowledged by Chancellor Helmut Schmidt. Now the gypsies entering Germany, despite their colourful costumes and bright scarves, are seen by many as accusatory ghosts, and are met with particular hostility. The shameful onslaught upon the gypsies in Rostock in August 1992 is not to be seen as the work of a small group of alienated adolescent skinheads: many of Rostock's inhabitants, members of all classes, stood by cheering or acquiescing as, with police complicity, the gypsies were forced out of the town. History does sometimes repeat itself in a deadly fashion.

The cause of the guilty unease stirred by the entry of the gypsies into Germany is obvious; but from the self-same source come the perturbations felt by the coming of other asylum-seekers; the German anguish arises because the Germans are trapped in the coils of their fathers' guilt. The basic right to asylum enshrined in their constitution was an anxious attempt to make amends for the treatment meted out to the Jews to whom little asylum was offered by the world when they attempted to escape from the Nazis. Now that that basic right to asylum is inappropriate to the present situation, the Germans are divided about how to proceed, fearful that any serious modification of their liberal immigration legislation would renew, however unjustly, charges of suspected racialism. The problem, as John Ardagh has put it, is that: 'On the one hand, the politicians are under popular pressure to be tougher with the flood of entrants. On the other, they are saddled with this liberal legislation that Germany, because of its black past, could not make more stringent without causing an outcry at home and abroad.'

Once again, the lack of insight into the nature and dynamics of the racialism which possessed their fathers means that German political decision-making becomes dangerously indecisive, frozen with fear of any steps which could compel them to look into the abyss. Inevitably, as a consequence, the confused discourse of the debate has been an imperfect palimpsest: the original accursed text written by their grandfathers has not been erased and the inscriptions of the present protagonists are not legible. As a result, throughout 1992 and 1993, a discordant medley emerged. Federal and *Länder* governments and the political parties were locked in disputes over the issue; the SDP tore itself apart and the government was severely buffeted as the different wings of the Alliance collided with each other. When, in June 1993, after agonising negotiations between the leaders of the main parties, institutional amendments were passed, the appropriate German authorities and provincial governments were almost totally unprepared and confused, and practical plans to implement the new regulations were almost totally lacking; all was muddle.

Kohl, knowing the wishes and prejudices of so many of his supporters, and ever mindful of the coming 1994 elections, exacerbated the difficulties. After Rostock, despite persistent calls for him to show solidarity with the harassed refugees by visiting another asylum home, he stayed resolutely away. It was again the president, Richard von Weizsäcker, who braved the wrath of those overtly or secretly sympathising with the bullying rioters by visiting a refugee home in Mecklenburg. And it was von Weizsäcker who addressed the German nation unequivocally after race riots spread further throughout Germany, and after the Jewish memorial at the former concentration camp at Sachsenhausen was partially burnt to the ground in an arson attack. He spelled out the dangers in language from which the leaders of the mainstream political parties shrank: 'Each and every one of us is called upon to protect our legally constituted, humanitarian democracy . . . or will it befall Germany once more that we look away or even stand by and watch as people are hunted down?'

This was not the language Kohl wished to hear from his president. He sought to replace von Weizsäcker, on his retirement, by someone pliant and accommodating, acceptable to the right. His chosen candidate was the distasteful Steffen Heitmann, a former East German priest who had no serious difficulty in reaching a *modus vivendi* with the Communist rulers of East Germany, and whose view on the Holocaust so differs from that of von Weizsäcker. Heitmann had declared: 'The time has come – the post-war era has finally come to an end with German unity – to put this event in its proper place.' Such comments happily provoked sufficient storm in Germany to make Heitmann unelectable and, bowing to the storm, Kohl prompted Heitmann's withdrawal.

In the meantime, however, with von Weizsäcker still in place, his initiative forced the political establishment to make a bid to obtain a consensus decision on the asylum question, and with a view to making constitutional changes. By May 1993 a compromise between the government and part of the Social Democratic Party was cobbled together, and amidst tumultuous scenes, with thousands surrounding the Bundestag protesting that the legislation was only designed to placate neo-Nazism feeding on xenophobia, the vote to make changes was passed. Many in Germany, while not sharing the protesters' views, felt the legislators' proposals were defective and would result in little diminution in the numbers of asylum-seekers but would increase the numbers who will enter illegally; a social problem would be turned into a police problem.

Now that that ill-thought-through asylum legislation has been passed, will the measures regarded by a minority of Germans as lamentable responses to Molotov cocktails thrown by rabbles at minorities, quench racialism? Or, as often happens with instant legislation made in response to a particular clamorous problem, are we witnessing a containment exercise, an abortive attempt by political élites to smother symptoms, leaving deeper causes untouched? All my legislative experience has taught me that instant legislation, like shabby instant politics which often prompt it, usually lacks efficacy; not only does it lead to unanticipated administrative snarl-ups but, more seriously, it may, acting as a catharsis, give relief to the indignant or frightened leading protagonists involved in the issue but leave the wider public untouched, with attitudes and convictions remaining undented.

Similarly, although it may be regarded as churlish, it is difficult for me not to place within this dangerous instant politics genre the huge anti-race demonstration staged in Berlin in November 1992 by both the mainstream parties. I share the disquiet expressed by Janet Daley in *The Times* when she pertinently commented on the rally: 'It was, arguably, an attempt to gloss over a deeply divisive and difficult moral question with which Germany . . . must come to grips.' Warning that German politicians arranging mass rallies should remember the brutal rise of the Nazis, she stigmatised the demonstration as one of the 'public manifestations (which is what the French call them) that are necessarily imprecise, incoherent and unstable . . . When they are

staged, by a ruling government, they become absurdly contrived.'
There was indeed an uncomfortable logic in the description of this rally
as a 'piece of hypocrisy' by the leaders of the right-wing Bavarian
Christian Social Union, ally of Kohl's Christian Democrats, even as
there was in the chanting of 'Hypocrite! Hypocrite!' by the left-wing
extremists who threw eggs at the leaders of the demonstrations; for the
extreme right and left well knew that the rally was, to a considerable
extent, an attempt to avoid the real crux of the problem. Perhaps that
crux was, ironically, more visible in the reputable opinion poll
published on the eve of the demonstration: it told us that one in three
Germans believe that Jews are wholly or partly to blame for having
been persecuted throughout history.

It is not only British observers who have expressed unease as the
large anti-racist demonstrations, following Berlin's lead, have taken
place in many German cities. Micha Brunlik, professor of education in
Frankfurt and Heidelberg, expresses the view of many liberal-minded
Germans when he stresses that these candlelit processions recall Nazi
rallies, and that turning politics into theatre will not help the
immigrant they pretend to defend: 'This kind of anti-racialism turns
politics into æsthetics.' He tells of his distaste of 'staged pieces of
collective emotion, the use of people as props in their *Gestantkunstwerk* of
politicised æsthetic.' For him, '. . . this candle-illuminated world view
is a myth. It obscures history and contemporary reality alike and yet
remains vague and indefinable. The light of the Enlightenment,
however, is always the light of the day in the clarity of which the
testimony of the present and of the past can be read.'

My particular concern with these demonstrations is that they appear
to be laced with the ambivalences that have for some time been the
hallmark of much German anti-racialist propaganda. I first became
aware of them when, shortly before the Rostock riots, I observed
posters on the Berlin underground, part of a well-intentioned campaign
against racist violence, which depicted prominent German icons like
rock star Peter Maffray and football manager Ulie Hoeness announcing: 'I am a foreigner'. Later, in 1993, after the outbreak of racial riots,
I noticed in Stuttgart that protesting anti-racialist taxi-drivers laudably
formed a convoy of some 300 vehicles adorned with the slogan 'My
friend is a foreigner'. These odd 'I am a foreigner' campaigns are
deliberately intended to encourage identification with the victims. But
the question has to be posed whether such campaigns are governed by
an avoidance technique, as the psychologist Birgit Ronnelspacher, a
professor of women's studies in Berlin, has explicated:

The 'I am a foreigner' campaign encourages identification with the victims. The acts of violence perpetrated by Germans are thus not addressed and people avoid confronting themselves. This is a defence mechanism frequently found in attempts in Germany to come to terms with our history. In this way the issues of German arrogance, violence, or the German superpower mentality and of racism are not raised . . . The very concept of racism is taboo in Germany. This has a lot to do with our Nazi past . . . If we talk of specifically German factors, then one has to talk about National Socialism. This feeds into contemporary racism to the extent that the possibility of total annihilation and dehumanisation is always present. Germans are more afraid of Germans, and thus of themselves, than people are afraid of each other in other countries.

And, underlining Ronnelspacher's point, the poet Hans Magnus Enzensberger has angrily lambasted the 'I am a foreigner' campaign. He insists it is part of a 'condition of self-loathing, which is evident not only in the hostility to foreigners, but also in the opposition to it. . . . Self-hatred is projected on to others − most notably in the insidious assertion "I am a foreigner" which numerous German "celebrities" have adopted.'

This type of anti-racist propaganda does not appear to be succeeding; nor, as Brunlik has commented, have the anti-racist demonstrations. 'One might say that despite all the candlelit processions, just as many attacks are happening.' The Federal Intelligence Agency recorded 1,480 racial attacks in the first nine months of 1993. No less significantly, there has been no turning around of the electoral gains made by the neo-Nazi parties. In the 1992 *Länder* elections, more than 500,000 voters in Baden Württemberg and a further 100,000 in Schleswig-Holstein voted for the neo-Nazi parties. At Dachau, ominously and significantly, they received 17 per cent of the vote. Unhappily, the far right Republican party, fighting in Hesse, one of the wealthiest regions in Germany, on an overt anti-foreigner ticket, made substantial advances at the expense of the main parties. Attempts to isolate the party have failed. Now, as a result of these elections, it is represented in three state governments, and in Frankfurt, Germany's financial capital, it has gained ten seats on the city council. Even in areas regarded as left-leaning, the far right have made significant advances: in the 1993 Hamburg state elections, the electorate, inert and gripped by *Verdrossenheit* ('fed-upness' or disillusionment), allowed the racialists to obtain 8 per cent of the vote. And by 1994 a new word had been coined and hardly a day passed without the term appearing in print or on television, *Partieverdrossenheit*, or PV: it is a word describing the phenomenon of the growing weariness of the electorate with the established political parties. It is a dangerous condition which can only be of benefit to the far right.

But apart from those who, disenchanted, voluntarily abstain from voting, there have been in recent elections, as there will be in the elections of 1994, notable absentees. Turks, Croats and other foreigners who settled in Germany twenty or more years ago remain non-citizens. In all these elections, seen as a barometer of support for the racialist far right, the *Ausländer* had no access to the ballot box, for the laws governing citizenship are saturated with racialism. The obstacles for Turks to obtain full citizenship are many and various: an applicant must have lived in Germany for at least fifteen years, must be able to pay fees of up to DM 5,000 for naturalisation, and must be able to prove he has a 'morally irreproachable life'; he is denied, unlike in most EC countries, the right to hold dual nationality – a denial which compels him to abandon his inheritance rights in his native country. As Cornelia Schmalz-Jacobson, the government-appointed Commissioner for Foreigners, who is spearheading a campaign for easier citizenship, has unequivocally stated: 'Nowhere has blood dripped so thickly into law.'

But Kohl rejected her proposals for easier citizenship as too radical. Only when the murder by neo-Nazis of Turkish women and girls in Solingen took place in May 1993, and the Turkish community took to the streets protesting against the inertia of the police, did Kohl tentatively move and, under pressure from Turkey and world opinion, permit his ministers to canvass possible legal changes such as a 'temporary' citizenship for the Turks. Kohl, however, moves slowly, fearing the growing strength of the far right and the unrelenting opposition to status changes by his coalition partner, the Bavarian-based Christian Social Union. He lacks the will, or wish, to invite his electorate genuinely to confront its racialism. Rather, he yields to the right and seeks to allay their concerns by gestures such as attending the reconsecration of the Berlin Protestant cathedral, symbol of German imperialism, even as in the same week, despite criticism, he refused to attend the memorial service for the victims of the Solingen arson attack. Meantime, Germany continues to define its nationals as people with at least one German parent; the *jus sanguinis*, the blood law, remains supreme. 'The fact remains,' a *Times* editorial in June 1993 commented, 'that the laws on citizenship – in Germany, of all countries – are based on blood. Until this is changed, the ghosts of Germany's past will not be exorcised, nor its current crisis properly addressed.' But Kohl, faced with such international comment, remained defiant and responded by assailing the foreign press for such interventions; he told his Parliament that he was not prepared to countenance double citizenship for the Turks, and the most he would consider was to ease the citizenship laws so that foreigners who had lived in Germany for two or three generations may be permitted to apply for naturalisation.

Kohl may resent what he regards as foreign intervention, but German racialism cannot be regarded as a domestic issue; for unless the Germans find the courage to confront racism they will never be at ease with themselves, and their unease and disease can disturb all Europe. For, in Germany, racialism has a terrible twin, the *Lebensraum* syndrome. The 'master race' wants exclusive living-space. On the Mediterranean beaches and around the pools the German holiday-makers' anxiety to stake out their space in the sun notoriously causes vexation and friction; on the battlefield of Europe, it has caused the death of millions. It is not enough, therefore, to seek, by insight, to extirpate racialism; we need, and the enlightened German needs, to ask why, in the past, the lure of *Lebensraum* proved so irresistible to Germany.

Expansionist dreams

Hitler's ministration of two magic potions gave him the power to enchant the Germans. The uniqueness of Nazism as a phenomenon in human history lies in the Germans' frenzied response to his two drugs: racialism and *Lebensraum*. Already predisposed to such poisonous prescriptions, they became the most dangerous addicts the world has ever known. Have today's Germans freed themselves from their fathers' twin addictions, the one that led to the death of millions of the mentally disabled, the aged, the sick, of the gypsies and of the Jews, and the other which led directly to the Second World War?

In Hitler's speeches and *Table Talk*, as in almost all the work of the most perceptive of British and German historians, the two maladies are forever conjoined; yet, although their linkage is observed, and their fateful consequences catalogued, and although tardily, as in this essay, more and more efforts are made to explore the sources of the madness of Aryan racialism, no adequate scrutiny of the ætiology of the German obsessive and seemingly compulsive search for living-space appears to have been made. An array of explanations, and oftimes justifications, have been proffered to suggest there was a rationale behind Germany's persistent drive to expand territorially: demographic factors, economic necessity, military security, protection of German minorities outside the Reich's borders, have all been cited as prompters of the ceaseless desire to erase the boundaries. But other than those whose expositions are tainted by their evident wish to defend Germany's actions, increasingly the historians acknowledge the inadequacy of theses claiming Germany was at social, economic or military risk if it had rested content within the borders it had created for itself in 1938; for, by that time, Hitler had, through aggressive expansion, united all the main contiguous German-speaking areas into one unitary nation-state.

He had created a Germany that was no longer a Prussian empire; the imbalance between north and south had been redressed, the eastern frontier rounded off on its southern flank. The British appeasers, believing then, as indeed now, that the nation-state was the only stable form of government, foolishly believed that in helping Hitler to attain such an integration, peace would be assured and Germany would be stabilised. Their calculation was hopelessly flawed psychologically; as Professor Kershaw emphasises: 'Continuing limitless expansion was the very essence of Nazism . . . The "system" could simply not "come to rest".' The Nazi regime was 'incapable of drawing a line under victories and settling down to consolidate existing gains'. Indeed Hitler recoiled from any such consolidation. He told his military senior command in 1944:

> The psychological aspects must be added . . . It is impossible to keep enthusiasm and readiness for sacrifice placed in a jar and preserved. Enthusiasm and readiness for sacrifice appear once in the context of revolution, and then they wither. Grey day-to-day routine, comfort, cause the magic to fade and turn the people back into satiated bourgeoisie.

What then, we may ask, if no rational economic or social imperative existed, was the unconscious need that Hitler was attempting to assuage when he unleashed his forces upon Eastern Europe? What dream, far removed from reality, was he inviting the Germans to people as he embarked upon the adventure which led to the slaughter of tens of millions? And why did the Germans so enthusiastically and often so heroically respond to his call to create a German world without end, without any restricting boundaries? And, no less pertinently today, when German expansion is taking place in other forms and when disquiet is so evident in Serbia, Denmark, Poland and the Czech Republic, we should ask if we are justified in fearing that a new German hegemony over Europe is emerging that is not innocent of the evil motivations that prompted Nazi German yearnings for *Lebensraum*.

To understand that yearning, that frantic denial of boundaries, we must, I believe, indeed begin at the beginning, for it is in our infancy that we first endure the anguish of the discovery that boundaries do exist. The bliss within the illusion that we have a perfect fusion with our mother and the surrounding environment, that we enjoy absolute self-sufficiency, is shattered by our discovery that we are dependent on external sources of care and nourishment. Then, tragically, we must quit our Garden of Eden, knowing henceforth that a boundary exists between the self and the not-self; it is a boundary that hardens as increasingly we understand our helplessness and consequent dependency.

But still we feel exiles, away from our lost paradise when we were omnipotent and there was no other. 'Man,' Freud told us, 'is an ailing animal seeking after a time when he was his own ideal.' He is involved, throughout his life, psychoanalysts have taught us, in a constant quest for that part of his narcissism that was wrested from him at the time of his primary loss of fusion; and he rages against the frontiers which have been created telling him that he is no longer the ruler and possessor of the whole world which once moved entirely and only at his command: no longer are his thoughts, and his alone, omnipotent.

It was such omnipotent delusions that possessed primitive societies. Freud, in his *Totem and Taboo*, traces the fate of the omnipotence of thought in the three phases of the evolution of man's view of the universe:

> At the animistic stage men ascribe omnipotence to themselves. At the religious phase they transfer it to the gods but do not seriously abandon it themselves, for they reserve the power of influencing the gods in a variety of ways according to their wishes. The scientific view of the universe no longer affords any room for human omnipotence; men have acknowledged their smallness and submitted resignedly to death.

In practice rarely does the individual or the group reach the stage of maturity in which there is such complete acceptance of the exigencies of reality. The tug pulling the individual or group backwards never slackens. Individuals and groups can yield to their nostalgia, and willingly are dragged backwards; then the individual or group myths which temporarily enveloped them in their ascent to greater maturity again reassert their dominion.

In Nazi Germany the early Germanic gods, to whom the Germans had affected to transfer their omnipotence, once again held sway; and the dominant myth, that of blood and soil, tells us of the drive to return to the goddess 'Mother Earth'. *Lebensraum*, causing the battle for living-space as practised by the Nazi Germans, was but a metaphor, a terrible metaphor resulting in the brutalisation and death of millions of young Germans; the true *Lebensraum* they were striving to gain was unattainable, no matter how much territory was conquered. It was a place of total and limitless security, ever impervious to any invasive force, where every wish was anticipated and granted, where boundless intra-uterine bliss would be recaptured, and where the narcissism of our earliest days in this world would again reign unchallenged; and where there would be no restricting boundaries.

This Nazi concept of *Lebensraum* was certainly no dressed-up version of nineteenth century colonial exploitation: Hitler's war was of a different order, and with a different goal: 'War has returned,' said Hitler in 1941, 'to its primitive form. The war of people against people is giving place to another war – a war for the possession of the great spaces . . . today, war is nothing but a struggle for the riches of nature.' And, determined to justify it, and to emphasise its 'biological' character and distance it from mere wars of economic exploitation, he added: 'By virtue of an inherent law, these riches belong to him who conquers them . . . the law of selection justifies this incessant struggle by allowing the survival of the fittest.' The fittest, of course, for Hitler, were the Germans and those whose blood qualified them to join the Germans as they filled the empty spaces created by the elimination or expulsion of the Slavs in the eastern territories. Danes, Norwegians, Dutch and, 'after screening', Swedes, would be permitted to join in the fertilisation of the conquered territories.

Hitler's personal biography found a consonance with Germany's dominant myth, for *Lebensraum* had, for him, a deadly significance associated as it was with his own maternal traumas. His mother, Klara, had three children, all of whom died in quick succession before Adolf was born. As an infant he was consequently over-indulged and suffused with his mother's worries lest she should lose him. The ensuing symbiotic relationship was doubtless severely tested by the birth of two more children, by his mother's widowhood, and by her final illness from breast cancer during his teens. Adolf nursed her in vain, day and night; but he could never accept the finality of her death.

He was bent on restoring the 'motherland' within whose embrace he would be nurtured limitlessly for ever. His attempt to obtain the Ukraine, in particular, was no mere geo-political adventure: there was the breadbasket that would feed the Germans for evermore, and the German would there have a land for himself to be shared with no unclean rivals. Hitler's personal needs, like the nation's needs, were replete with these incestuous overtones.

Racialism and *Lebensraum*, therefore, were the basic components of Nazi doctrine, and should not be seen as fortuitously conjoined. Both offered the same fetish; both proffered the perversion of incest; purity of race was the certificate required to gain entry into the living-space within the uterus. The blood and soil myths clinging to the doctrines required the denial of the reality of a prohibiting father: he was eliminated. What was being offered by the Nazis, and accepted by the Germans, was a regressive choice, a pre-Oedipal choice, where the return to the mother could take place without facing the obstruction which in real life the father symbolises. There could inevitably be no accommodation between the German myth and the Jewish legend. Abraham had acknowledged the power of the father and in a symbolic castration, by circumcision, had made the great renunciation of the mother, and, in return for his obedience, the father had made him and his descendants the chosen ones. By that contract with God the Father, man's perception of the universe changed; there were to be no other gods, and man advanced to monotheism. But the Nazis fled from the confrontation which in the childhood of peoples as of infants has to be faced; they would not endure the terror of the Oedipal situation and the difficult compromises needed to advance to adulthood. They retreated, fantasised a consummation which would lead to a magic rebirth, and deceived themselves that they had found a short cut; it was a route that led only to barbarism.

Lebensraum, yet again

Unhappily, the unification of Germany, far from stilling these old longings for *Lebensraum*, appears to have reawakened them. From the time the GDR was established, Bonn refused to accept or acknowledge the permanence of a divided Germany. The Mitscherlichs, erroneously as it was to be proved, were persistently critical of West German attitudes, which reflected their denial of the then status quo: the psychoanalysts saw dangers in the sinister refusal to accept the reality,

and were understandably fearful of political thought that avoided
reality-testing and depended upon a magical fulfilment of the fusion of
the two Germanies. Yet it was indeed by 'magic', in the form of
intervention by the wizard Gorbachev, that the desired fusion took
place and Germany euphorically celebrated the consummation. But an
explanation is required as to why in a remarkably short period of time
disenchantment has taken place, and why the unification of Germany
has brought not joy to the Germans, but discontent; and why, when
faced with the formidable problems of East Germany which, it would
be thought, would engage all West Germany's energies, Bonn does not
husband its resources and concentrate attention upon its domestic
scene, but, on the contrary, following unification, has become
disturbingly activated and has commenced pursuing economic and
diplomatic policies perceived as expansionist which are stirring old
fears.

   In the last few years I have encountered many Germans who dispute
the German Establishment's denial that a unified Germany is reverting
to an assertive unilateralism aimed at expansion and ultimately the
triumphant economic domination of a trembling Europe from Berlin.
These are Germans profoundly dissatisfied with the ripostes given to
them by the German government when they have protested that
economic resources should be concentrated in the eastern part of the
country: Kohl has insisted that an 'economic iron curtain' at the Oder
and the Neisse would not serve Germany's security interests and,
consequently, under the guise of such 'security' needs, economic
expansion continues apace. Kohl's apologia prompts a recall of a
statement once made by Theodore Heuss, the first president of Western
Germany: 'The Germans find it very hard to remain sober when they
get close again to the sweet delights of hubris.'

   The economic stranglehold on Germany's eastern neighbours is
tightening. Ninety-five per cent of the registered value of foreign
investment in former Czechoslovakia is German and some 30 per cent
of such investment in Poland; already more than half of Russia's £55-
billion foreign debt is owed to German banks. Everything points to a
further acceleration of German investment as current Polish, Czech,
Slovak and Hungarian labour costs are a fraction of eastern
Germany's, a situation unlikely to change significantly in the next

decade. Indeed, it is more likely that Germany's eastern neighbours
will be further exploited as they become investment locations where
German capital and expanded production will be used to satisfy the
needs of heavily subsidised East German consumers. And, meantime,

under a cloak of goodwill, Central and Eastern Europeans are reduced to dependence as Germany provides 25 per cent of all aid going to the region, in addition to some 50 per cent for Russia and other successor states of the former Soviet Union; debt forgiveness for Poland has now reached 70 per cent of the total the Poles owe to German lenders. Parallel with the aid comes the trade. Trade in volume overall with Hungary and the former Czechoslovakia has doubled since 1989 to some 40 billion Deutschmarks. And the German banks are acting as pace-setters. Already the Dresdner Bank has opened a network of representative offices from Kiev to Alma Ata; Germany, through its banks, is slowly but with certainty, moving towards the Urals. It is the lands of Eastern Europe, as in Hitler's time, that lure present-day Germany. Although, rationally, Germany would be expected to be concerned with the Asian markets from which today's economic growth impulse comes, Germany, in fact, is doing less trade with the whole of South-East Asia than it is with Austria.

If Britain is not speedily within the heart of the Community, able to examine, exercise constraints, and be involved in co-operation with its partners, including Germany, in joint investments in Eastern Europe and Russia, then we are inviting Germany to achieve unilaterally, by economic means, a domination which it failed to achieve by arms in the last war. Its economic power is not to be underestimated; it is a country with a gross national product roughly one-and-a-half times that of Britain and a good one-third larger than that of France or Italy. For the present, however reluctantly, some absorption by the Germans in intra-German economic issues, cannot be avoided; but once Germany has settled those issues, its economic dynamism and its expansionist desires will determine that it will establish an unchallengeable hegemony. Time is short for Britain to ensure that the whole Community, not Germany alone, becomes intermeshed in Eastern Europe.

It is evident that economic expansion outside Germany is felt to be more fulfilling than metabolising Eastern Germany. The political tumult in 1993 which accompanied all moves to finance the huge cash transfers, some £65 billion a year, from west to east, needed to revive the collapsed East Germany and to integrate the eastern states into an overall system which shares out tax revenues between central and local government, is ominous; the German taxpayer acquiesces in economic expansion outside Germany but protests vigorously against making the sacrifices which German unification requires. It is an odd set of priorities and one which has contributed to Germany's failure to make the capital investment to effect a much-needed re-structuring of its automobile and chemical industries upon which it has been so economically dependent.

The explanation for this curious choice of precedence became more manifest to me as in 1992 and in 1993 I wandered throughout West and East Germany. After the promises held out, I found it was not only the desolate East Germans who, as unemployment has spread and the old welfare state agencies have collapsed, feel cheated; the West too is infuriated by the failure of the expectation which they dreamed united Germany would fulfil. For their impossible dream was again of *Lebensraum*, and the desires of that dream, like the desires of all perversions, are insatiable. A rough takeover of East Germany – more a rape than a wooing – totally lacking in solicitude, has left West Germany like the unsatisfied client of a bought whore whose seductive promises have not been fulfilled and therefore should be given only a niggardly pay-off. I believe the totally disproportionate anger that has arisen in West Germany over the payment of increased taxes for aid to East Germany, like the industrial unrest springing from workers refusing to rein in wage increases to assist the rehabilitation of East Germany, comes from a profound disappointment that is not necessarily related to avarice; the regaining of East Germany has given the Germans more land, but the territories gained are not enough; the possession of 'mother earth' has eluded them. The merger has fallen short of the impossible incest-ridden Ideal. The unattainable Ideal was a consummation which would yield a conception: it was to have resulted in the rebirth of the nation. The West Germans, full of anger, blame the East Germans for the consummation producing only a miscarriage. The dedicated West German social administrator, seconded to East Germany and trying to put in place a counselling structure unknown to the GDR, was not far offbeam when, in despair, she told me the West Germans know only how to hate, not to assist the East Germans.

Unsatisfied, too many appear to be casting around for other objects of desire, some of them lost following the war. One notes how, even when formal acknowledgements have been made of existing boundaries, the federal government does not hesitate to fund organisations intent on subverting them. The Deportee League which still, in violent language, continues to lay claim to regions lost in the east, received from the Kohl government five times as much money in 1990 as in 1983, more than 20 million Deutschmarks, said to be for 'preserving the cultural heritage of Germany'; in fact, the sum is earmarked for the

German minority in Poland, and the League demands that the federal government in no way interferes with any of its 'collaborative relations' with this minority. Meantime, too, the well-funded Bavarian-based Sudeten German Association with its 100,000 membership and its declared purpose of *Rückgewinnung der Heimat*, winning back the homeland, is disturbing the residents of today's Bohemia as it makes new demands that the recently concluded 'forgive and forget' agreement between Czechoslovakia and Germany be renegotiated now that Czechoslovakia has split into two. The unification of Germany appears to have done little to dampen the expansionist ambitions of millions of Germans. In November 1992 President Walesa of Poland was expressing the fears of many in Eastern Europe when he warned: 'There are demons at work in post-unification Germany.'

Some German responses to disenchantment with reunification remind me of the moods of disappointed wealthy clients I have encountered in my law practice. Faced with the collapse of a business venture, upon which these clients had embarked with high hopes, they found difficulty in coping with the anxiety the subsequent débâcle engendered. They had always measured their manhood by the success of their commercial abilities, and could only recover their poise by a display of phallic power which is often suffused with omnipotent fantasy; and I have sometimes therefore failed to rein them back as they were compelled, immediately after the initial failure, to plunge recklessly into another even more grandiose commercial venture probably equally doomed to fail. I consider the Germans' expansionist response to their profound disappointment that unification has not resulted in regeneration analogous to the conduct of those businessmen.

Nowhere, so far, has their expansionist response been more blatantly shown than in their determination, irrespective of the wishes of their allies, to move opportunistically into the Yugoslavia maelstrom. There they have from the beginning been defiant and aggressive, presenting as a reason for their unilateralist stances the need to protect Germany's security. They broke ranks with the European Community and gave recognition to Slovenia and Croatia without initially even asking for guarantees for the protection of the Serb minority. They cared not that their backing of an independent Croatia would recall the alliance between Nazi Germany and the infamous Croatia Ustasta regime of the Second World War. In the face of the avowed opposition of the United Nations' Secretary-General and the United States, they used their economic muscle to dragoon their EC partners into accepting their position; and always, as their actions were stirring the pot, they claimed that their interference in the internal affairs of the former Yugoslavia was proper, affirming, on the basis of reports by pliant leading German international lawyers, that all their actions were lawful.

When challenging their role in the Balkan tumult, I have frequently been met with heated denials that expansionism is the motivation. For my part I find the explanations proffered for German assertiveness as unconvincing as they are varied. Some Germans have apologetically suggested that it came from a specific domestic political pressure, that I should understand the difficulties of a coalition government under pressure both from 500,000 Croats living in Germany and from the Bavarian CSU who use their leverage within the government to insist upon actions which express their deep sympathies for the Catholic trans-Alpine republic – sympathies that were centuries old and had nothing to do with any reassertion of the horrendous Second World War 'episode'. Others have said, to justify claims that German security was involved, that speedy intervention was needed to prevent waves of refugees falling upon Germany, an explanation which certainly seems droll when one witnesses the terrible plight of the Moslems and others that has resulted from Germany's enthusiasm to give legitimacy to the break-up of Yugoslavia. Even more far-fetched is the argument I have met that Bonn feared that a military victory for the Serbs would serve as a signal to ambitious leaders and groups in the former Soviet Union, and so threaten Germany. The lack of force in all these justifications lead me to look for a deeper cause, and that I find in the desire of Germany to continue its restless search for a regeneration when it found that reunification of Germany had left it bitterly disappointed.

Those who believe such an interpretation of Germany's current disillusionment and assertive mood as extravagant should ponder on the indisputable fact that it was Hitler's regeneration offer to Germany which was the key to his electoral success. The German electorate of 1933 found the lure of rebirth irresistible. As the historian Ian Kershaw has accurately recalled:

> . . . the Nazi movement, acting as a type of 'super interest group',
> linked quite different, sometimes even incompatible, social
> demands to a unifying vision of national regeneration. The spread
> of its organisational framework from 1929–1930 onwards made
> the Nazi party far more capable than any other contemporary

political party of appealing to a wide range of the population, above all but not merely in the fragmented middle-classes, by incorporating their material anxieties and expectations into the psychological, idealistic belief that the problems could be resolved by the national rebirth which Nazism alone, under Hitler, was able to bring about.

With the defeat of Nazi Germany the dream of rebirth was temporarily shattered, but never totally relinquished: the belief was tenaciously held that, out of the ultimate fusion of the two Germanies, the nation would be reborn.

Rebirth and disillusionment

Now, yet again, as reality does not match the fantasy, the disillusionment is found to be intolerable. The German political scene becomes enveloped in bitterness and recrimination; the voters, finding that unification has not showered them with a cornucopia of blessings, have turned upon their leaders. In May 1992 both Wolfgang Schäuble, the leader of the Christian Democratic parliamentary group, and Björn Engholm, then the Social Democratic leader, said people had lost faith in politicians, and Engholm expressed his fears that the whole democratic system would be challenged. This lack of confidence in their own democracy was, a year later, strikingly illustrated when a suspected urban guerrilla was shot at point-blank range by the police; a storm arose which forced the resignation of the German Minister for the Interior; a widespread fear gripped Germany that a culture of violence, destabilising democracy, was emerging. That disillusioned post-unification Germany is so fraught is more understandable when one notes the critical assassinations which since reunification have taken place. In Parliament, Wolfgang Schäuble, the Christian Democratic leader in the Bundestag, speaks from a wheelchair after being shot at a rally and, in the Upper House, the Bundesrat, Oskar Lafontaine, the prime minister of the Saarland, has a long scar visible on his throat, the result of an attack when he was nearly killed in a 1990 meeting.

Meanwhile, the disenchanted electorate, feeling cheated of their dreams of regeneration that were to accompany reunification, continues to show its anger and to register contempt for the government and other major parties. Right-wing groups have made gains in the local elections, and in East Berlin the former Communist Party obtained almost the highest vote of all political parties; in March 1993, large sections of the electorate refused to vote in Hesse, and those who did shifted to the right, away from the established parties. The main parties, apprehensive of the mood of their electorates, at last, after six months of bitter wrangling, formed a 'solidarity pact' agreeing on some increased taxation to service the former East Germany's debt and the borrowing run up by the Treuhand, the government agency responsible for turning around and privatising the outmoded industries in the East. Otto Lambsdoff, formerly chairman of Kohl's junior coalition partners, the Free Democrats, made clear that the agreement did not spring from the partners' real readiness to agree but came from 'fear of public failure'. The partners are frightened of being overwhelmed by a disillusioned electorate. Only the naïve can believe that such turbulence sprang from a debate over the method of financing unification; a dispute over the amount of taxation to be levied and how it should be shared between central government and the *Länder* would not in itself bring about a condition where the leaders of the main political parties are fearful that the political system is at stake. The taxation arguments are mere inferior librettos; the underlying emotions, the music, profound and threatening, is replete with intimations of the unattainable, of being born again.

Born again

The nature of the rebirth interplay between the fantasy and the individual life of their patients was already spelled out by German psychiatrists in the early part of this century; Jung too assigned to the fantasy a dominating position in the imaginative life of neurotics. But it is in the work of early unconventional psychoanalysts, like Viktor Tausk and Otto Rank, that we find an abundance of clues to the restlessness of today's Germany; those psychoanalysts never ceased to emphasise the importance of the universal experience of the birth trauma, and explored the manoeuvres made by man, in his adult life, when, as an individual or in his group, he still sought to overcome the buried terrors of emerging from intra-uterine bliss to face the world.

They were impatient of Jung's persistent attempts to endow the widespread rebirth myths, so common to peoples in the east and west, with anagogic-ethical sentiments; for them it was a primitive mode of thought. They saw the yearning to cancel out the real birth, and to have a new, imagined birth where the umbilical cord is never cut and where, joined with the mother, an extra-uterine life would be lived even as it was in an intra-uterine shelter, as a wholly regressive phenomenon. And it was as such that it expressed itself in Nazi doctrine and practice. Today it seems to be simmering dangerously beneath the surface of Germany's political life. Fusion of the two Germanies has resulted in a miscarriage, not a birth; yet still, stubbornly, as if under some sinister repetition-compulsion, immediately a new search for a rebirth appears to be going on as *Lebensraum* assumes forms of economic domination and penetration. And, unhappily, the East Germans who have joined the enlarged state bring with them conditioning that is more likely to stimulate rather than quench the sick yearning; for they have been brought up on hymns of praise to the party which was saturated with Germany's ancient paganism. Anne McElvoy recently pertinently noted, in her review of the East German Communist Party domestic propaganda: 'Its imagery of the party as earth mother, a subconscious return to the notion of the pagan goddess of the Wagnerian variety, nourishing and dominating the nation with her eternal power, was far from new.'

Since the rebirth fantasy is common to all mankind and is embedded in the myths in the childhood of so many peoples, one is bound to ask why it seems uniquely difficult for the Germans to relinquish the infantile dream. One hypothesis is suggested by Germany's geography: probably no other nation in the world has borders with as many as nine other states. Freud has stated that all anxiety goes back originally to the anxiety experienced at birth, and Rank developed the view that all constricting situations later in life evoked that primal anxiety. Our unconscious wish to return to the bliss of the womb is blocked by the terror of re-experiencing the constricting paroxysms of birth; and Rank would persuade us that even the character of individuals is determined by the incidental individual peculiarities of parturition, as to whether they had easy or difficult births. Whatever the validity of many of Rank's theories may be, it is perhaps possible that the constricting evocative geography of Germany provokes a particular terror of returning to the mother's womb by the same road as was taken on birth. Indeed, Alan Watson believes the origin of what he describes as the 'German *Angst* of containment' is to be found in the peace settlement which ended the Thirty Years War in 1648: then, Germany was deprived of her access to the sea as her great rivers ran into the absolute blockade of the foreign powers and became, as the 'land in the middle', totally trapped. Given this historical background, it may be that the geography of shrunken contemporary Germany is particularly provocative: it is now confined to an area far smaller than that encompassed within the dream of its national anthem 'Deutschland, Deutschland über Alles' whose original first verse is now rarely sung:

> Germany, Germany above everything,
> Above all else in the world,
> Whenever we stand together
> As brothers in defence and defiance
> From the Maas to the Memel,
> From the Etsch to the Belt –
> Germany, Germany above everything,
> Above all else in the world.

did not exist

When the song was composed, Germany occupied an enormous portion of Europe: from the Maas in the west to the Memel in the east, from the Etsch in the south to the Belt in the north, people spoke and felt German. Now the Maas is in Holland, the Memel in Lithuania, while the Etsch runs through the Italian Tyrol. And the boundary revisions at the end of the last war have left Germany deprived of the old Prussia and Silesia. To my discomfort, I have often been plaintively told by Germans that I must understand that, even with reunification, the federal republic is now smaller than all previous German Reichs, covering 140,000 square miles, less land than France or Sweden. Restrictive anxieties, in such circumstances, could well be operating subliminally, and so make the search for a rebirth an ever more terrifying quest. In the past the attempt to resolve the dilemma was to find the escape route within *Blut und Bloden* dreams, when consummation and the resultant rebirth could take place without going backwards and re-experiencing the birth trauma. If there is substance in such speculations, then the ideology of *Lebensraum*, and its persistence, could be regarded as such escape routes.

There are also other speculations that may help us and the Germans to diagnose the dangerous malady. The wild oscillations in political moods in contemporary Germany, between passivity and aggression, between a passive desire for non-responsibility in a near or absolute pacifist foreign policy and, on the other hand, its wish simultaneously to have an assertive expansive stance, recall, of course, the Churchillian adage of the Germans being either at your feet or at your throat; but the mood change too is a relevant pointer to the operant behind the *Lebensraum* compulsion, for Freud, more than 75 years ago, when scrutinising the return to the womb and the rebirth fantasies of his patients, noted that 'in them homosexuality has found its furthest and most intimate expression', and traced both the passive and active homosexual elements within the fantasies.

In what psychoanalysts now regard as Freud's most important and elaborate of case histories, Freud wrote of one of his patients:

> . . . he wished he could be back in the womb, not simply that he might then be reborn, but in order that he might be copulated with there by his father, might obtain sexual satisfaction from him and might bear him a child . . . this instance, I think, throws light on the meaning and origin of the womb fantasy as well as that of rebirth. The former, the womb-fantasy, is frequently derived (as it was in the present case) from an attachment to the father. There is a wish to be inside the mother's womb in order to replace her during intercourse – in order to take her place in regard to the father. The fantasy of rebirth, on the other hand, is in all probability regularly a softened substitute (a euphemism, one might say) for the fantasy of incestuous intercourse with the mother.

Given the way these fantasies have woven their way into Germany's politics, Freud's stress on the linkage between homosexuality and womb and rebirth fantasies prompts the uncomfortable question of whether there is an unresolved homo-erotic element endemic to German culture. Alexander and Margarete Mitscherlich pointed out that there is 'a type of aggressive subordination that is no stranger to our German national culture', and how 'German culture relies so emphatically on the exploitation of obedience in innumerable social relationships'. Passive homosexuality clings to the so-readily assumed subordinate roles, even as more aggressive homosexuality lurks behind the martinet relationships between superior and subordinate: in so many of Germany's institutions we see subtle inter-meshings of homosexual sado-masochistic inclinations and gratifications. Ernst Röhm, the notorious homosexual creator of the *Sturmabteilung*, the SA, and an enthusiast for Nordic folklore, exotically presented all the morbid symptoms of the syndrome until Hitler, in the 1934 purge following Röhm's arrest while disporting himself with his young men, had him killed; but Röhm, in many respects, is but a caricature of a mood that in more mortified and covert form can still be found pervading some areas of contemporary Germany's institutional and political life.

The authoritarian family

The source of such a mood, and the explanation of its persistence, surely lies in the German authoritarian family system which, although much modified in recent decades, still has inadequately yielded to democratisation. Such an authoritarian family system where a feared and hated dominating father reigns, inevitably means that obedience and 'aggressive subordination' continues to operate in German public as well as private life; and out of such a snarled-up family system, strewn with unresolved Oedipal problems, the son, funking the challenge to the father, necessary if he is to attain mature adulthood, takes refuge in dream; and no dream is more dangerous than the impossible dream of the vengeful son, eliminating his father, being reborn of his own conception with his mother; for that private perversion moved into the public arena can, and has been, expressed, as we have chasteningly witnessed, in a fantasised regeneration of a nation and in the ideology of *Lebensraum*.

The character of this German family system is brought home to me each time I drive through Germany, back to London, from my Tuscany house. In Italy the child, in a hotel, restaurant, train or supermarket, is warmly received, everyone ready to indulge, play with, or to admire the little one; but in Germany I see confirmation of the long-standing reputation Germany possesses for *Kinderfeindlichkeit*, hostility to children. If a small child cries in a restaurant or even in a supermarket, people make an angry fuss; no tolerance appears to be extended to children who are brought into public places where every child, behaving as a child, noisy or restless, provokes disproportionate anger. I am not surprised to learn that because children are equated with noise, many young families find it difficult to rent flats and resort to buying houses at a cost they can barely afford; nor am I surprised that statistics show that child abuse in Germany is well above the European average. A 1988 survey conducted by the Institut für Kindheit revealed a horrendous molestation rate of 80 per cent among contemporary Berlin schoolchildren. Discipline and authority seem to have a greater priority in many a German household than love.

Some Germans of the young generation have urged upon me that rapid changes are, however, taking place, that the father-dominated household is fading out and that, within the family, rights, hitherto denied, are being extended to wives and children: that a democratic family system is being inaugurated where children are not regarded as chattels, and where women are freed from the constraints of the old

Kinder, Kirche, Küche ideal once accepted as the female role. It is to be hoped that such optimism is well-founded, for the traditional German family has been a cradle of discontents resulting in so many private travails being acted out disastrously on a wide political stage. For my part, I remain sceptical of the extent of the claimed changes. Women psychiatrists in West Germany have told me that their hospital outpatient departments are full of wives with young children who are cracking under the strain of working full-time and having to accept the non-sharing role of husbands who follow the bad example of their authoritarian fathers. And, incredible as it first seemed to me, such is the prevailing misogynist culture that some West German employers, treating the unemployed women of East Germany as cattle, insist, as a condition of their employment, in order that no maternity benefits are paid and continuity of work is assured, that medical certificates of their sterilisation are produced.

Such attitudes on the part of the West German male suggest that women's status still lags behind that reluctantly, and only partly, conceded to women in Britain. Those surviving of my generation have a vivid recall of the point at which in Britain a huge emancipatory step was taken: it was during the war. I can still remember how disconcerted were those of us who had served some years abroad and returned to find a new woman had emerged in Britain. She possessed a freedom, including financial independence, that came from her involvement in the war effort, principally from her engagement in the factories, farms and services. No similar liberation took place in Germany. Albert Speer, Hitler's minister of armaments and munitions, repeatedly urged the total mobilisation of women for war production; but Hitler would have none of it, insisting that factory work would inflict physical and moral harm upon women, damage their psychic and emotional life and their potential as mothers. Speer calculated that the mobilisation of the 5,000,000 women capable of war work would release 3,000,000 men for war service. But Hitler remained adamant in his refusal, which was strenuously backed by the *Gauleiters*. The German male feared a liberated woman far more than the enemy. I believe the failure of the German woman to make the breakthrough which was achieved by British women in wartime still shows in today's West Germany.

Meantime, the mass unemployment of the women of East Germany assuredly means too we cannot expect any stimulus to come from the east which would activate any benign modifications of the family system in West Germany. Full employment of women, giving economic

independence, was their only raft to save them from the notorious
machismo of the men of the GDR, where the authoritarian Communist
state matured the authoritarian family. Indeed, so acculturated are
many of the women of the east to their subordinate role in the family
that it has been remarked to me by young West German men,
evidently disconcerted by their failure in making advances to them,
that East German women are strongly masochistic and treat with
suspicion and distaste any courtesy or respect accorded to them.
Germany's discerning and witty essayist Peter Schneider recently
commented on the phenomenon when he recorded that East German
women have a different taste in men from those in the West:

> The East German woman will admit that when it comes to
> housework and child-rearing she is still living in the nineteenth
> century, but she doesn't see the answer to her problem in western-
> style domestic equality. The new sensitive man who has become
> so common in Western Europe and the northern United States is
> anathema to her – she will take the first East German roughneck
> over him any day. In fact, under the wings of the strong yet
> domestically traditional East German woman, a prehistoric male
> species has survived: the East German macho.

In any event, whatever changes may come about in the family
system as the two cultures collide, we have no present alternative but
to take things as they are, and to remember that the authoritarian
family, where women and children have been relegated to second
place, is the family in which today's West German adults were reared;
indeed, up to 1977 the civil code contained a clause that placed sole
responsibility for the household on the wife and permitted her to take a
job only if the husband agreed and if it were compatible with her
domestic duties. In 1983, revealing the male chauvinism that still
persists, Kohl had no hesitation in his election campaign in declaring:
'Our pretty women are one of Germany's natural resources.'

A Europe of tribes?

Spelling out the concatenation of determinants that from within the
non-democratic family link up ultimately with *Lebensraum* foreign
policies is no doubt an unwelcome complication to the politicians and
journalists who prefer simpler analyses of international relationships;
but such superficial soundings mean that, with no awareness of the

hazards lurking in the depths, many well-intentioned plans can be shipwrecked. Nowhere has this been more dramatically evidenced than in the first referendum in Denmark when the Danes refused to endorse the Maastricht Treaty. There were many reasons why the Danes took this stand, but there is no doubt that the determinant factor was fear of the expansionist mood that has emerged in post-unification Germany. As *The Times* reported on the morrow of the referendum: 'There is evidence that fear in Denmark of the power of the united Germany was a contributory, even decisive, factor in the close result of the referendum.' Along the Danish side of the German border the resentful folk memories of the two wars fought over Schleswig-Holstein, and the conduct of the Germans during their occupation of Denmark in the last war, are speedily reawakened when Germany's policies are seen to be dangerously assertive. Such occupation memories also determined the close result of the French referendum; to the embarrassment of the German political establishment the debate became overwhelmed by arguments as to whether it was best to lock Germany into the Community lest worse befell, or whether further integration would mean German domination of France.

When Margaret Thatcher, activating similar British memories on the eve of the Commons debate on Maastricht, made her notorious swashbuckling speech upon what she saw as Germany's efforts to dominate Europe, Edward Heath reacted fiercely. Affirming that today's Germany was now a democratic peaceful nation, he said: 'I have been absolutely disgusted at the bigotry and xenophobic, rabid statements which have been made about Germany . . . As one of those who had fought against, and helped in the rebuilding of Germany, and as a member of this House, I feel quite ashamed of the things which have been said.'

Although sharing Heath's European goals, I believe their achievement is made less, not more, likely by attempting, as he does, to repudiate so totally the incipient dangers that contemporary Germany presents; those dangers will not be overcome by denying their existence.

Of course Thatcher's rage against Germany is the familiar anger of a Caliban viewing the face to be seen in the mirror; for all those doctrines of blood, and sacrifice and grandeur, which have in the past laced German politics, and which make us fearful, are certainly not alien to her. Her fidelity to her father is total, and she never strays from his injunctions. His revealing inaugural mayoral address in 1945 could have been made by any petty German *Gauleiter*; there he epitomised the philosophy which he has bequeathed to his daughter. He saw war as an inescapable therapy in this vale of tears. 'Again and again in our human life we learn that without the shedding of blood there is no remission,' he declaimed. Thus indoctrinated, it is not surprising that Margaret Thatcher is quick to find fellow-travellers in Germany and then, by projection, to compound her prejudices with theirs, and to denounce them. Possessed as she is by her belief, expressed so vividly during the debates on nuclear disarmament and the Falklands war, that 'this is no ordinary country' and that this is because 'the people of the UK are an island race', her capacity to sabotage the building of a European community almost matches those who in Germany have not emancipated themselves from racialism and expansionism.

Attempting therefore to illuminate the sick dynamic that lies behind such attitudes is no mere academic exercise. If the dark, often subliminal, forces that still operate in Germany, and less vigorously in Britain, are not exposed, then the danger for all of us, Germans and Britons, is chasteningly clear. Europe will fall apart and what we shall bequeath to our children will be a Europe of tribes.

PART VI

An Abiding Flaw

Legalism and obedience

Thomas Mann, in his novel *The Magic Mountain*, has an exotic Russian woman give a famed bilingual reply to her German admirer who has asked her if she considers the Germans pedantic: 'Mais c'est vrai,' is the damning reply; 'you are a little bourgeois. Vous aimez l'ordre mieux que la liberté, tout l'Europe le sait.' It is this overruling passion for order which so often in the past Europe has known and suffered; and, subsidiary to concerns for freedom, it continues to pervade the German culture.

The rule of law to which Britain subscribes has as its goal the protection of liberties and the guarantee of justice; Germany has very different emphases, a deficiency of moral quality but replete in legalism. Obedience, enforced by law and regulation, is seen as the cement binding society together and preventing disorder. The philosopher Immanuel Kant's injunction has continued throughout the centuries and was followed by the parents of most of today's German adults:

> The characteristics of a child must include, above all, obedience. This obedience may be obtained by force – then it is absolute; or by confidence – then it is voluntary. The latter is important, but the former is an absolute necessity because it prepares the child for adherence to the laws he will have to obey as a future citizen, whether he likes them or not.

This is the doctrine – far removed from the advice given by the paediatrician Spock and accepted by the parents of many of today's British adults – which is a significant determinant in the personal conduct of a large number of Germans, and which plays an important part in Germany's political life. The old tag that in Germany everything is forbidden except what is specifically allowed while in Britain everything is allowed except what is specifically forbidden, is more than a half truth.

John Ardagh has engagingly presented us with a host of examples, some sad, some tragic, some uproarious, of the consequences of the torrent of ever more complex legislation pouring out from the

ministries in Bonn and in the *Länder*, but he optimistically believes that
the traditional rigidity in relationships between Germans and even
between the average *Beamte* (petty official) and the citizen is gradually
being modified. German lawyers I have encountered seem, however, to
continue to garner a large harvest as the Germans eschew compromise
and negotiation, and stick to their interpretation of the law; litigation
flourishes. In the political field too, Germans obediently and
punctiliously go to the polls, even in local elections, in numbers which
are the envy of those of us who have so often fought political apathy
among our own electorates; but what is remarkable is the manner in
which their citizenship abruptly ceases after the vote has been
registered. From then on it would seem to be regarded as unseemly,
disorderly, to seek to intervene in any way with the representatives
appointed: they must be left to carry on their work without interference
or pressure.

And this insulation from commitment beyond the strict limitation
required by duty invades the personal domain. 'One of the most
striking differences I have noticed between the British and the
Germans,' Ardagh has commented, 'is that if you ask a person you do
not know for a small favour, she is likely to reply indignantly "That's
not my business – the officials are paid for that."' Each must stick to
his last, otherwise disarray is bound to follow. Even within the
domestic sphere it is not unknown for couples, married or unwed, to
draft their own formal treaty, clearly setting down the day-to-day
rights and duties of each partner – who is to do the washing-up and
when, and what days and hours each partner can go out alone, and, in
some cases, the amount of sexual freedom each will permit to the other;
thus domestic life seeks to avoid the intrusion of unruly passion, and
everything is neatly under control.

In the closing days of the GDR, this singular German social
characteristic meant that the very revolution itself could only be
permitted provided it was legitimated by those whom the reformers
wished to depose. A Lenin prophecy thus came true; he once said that
a German revolutionary, if required to storm a railway station, would
first queue for a platform ticket. And so it came about that even as the
country was paralysed, the main opposition group, the New Forum,
applied for permission from the ruling Communists to be registered.
'Only, one suspects, in East Germany could an opposition on the verge
of a major breakthrough worry about not being officially approved by
its opponents,' McElvoy has tartly commented. A not dissimilar
display of punctiliousness was displayed in West Germany in the

summer of 1992 when the German president firmly and with reason admonished the main political parties for opportunism and reckless handling of East German's problems; his comments prompted resentment from unexpected quarters. A group of apolitical, liberal-minded young executives in Berlin had no hesitation in conveying to me their condemnation of their president's intervention; they solemnly told me they agreed entirely with the president's views, but he was violating the constitution, stepping out of his ceremonial role. This was indeed most disorderly conduct.

The generational rebellion

This oppressive ethos has in post-war Germany thrice provoked a generational rebellion by those unable to tolerate the insistence that order must be the dominant societal value. We have seen the student rebellions of 1968, the assassinations of the *Rote Armee Fraktion*, and the emergence of a strong 'green' movement in the 1980s. All three protests have had some effect, at least for a little while, upon the self-confidence of the compact majority, and led to some modifications of the prevailing legalism, although this can often take droll forms – as in the introduction of a Bill to reduce bureaucracy with the ominous title, almost enough in itself to crush hope of change, the *Entbürokratisierun-gesetz*, a law against laws.

All these three major protests, all essentially middle-class in origin, had embossed upon them the impress of adolescent strivings; a rebellion against the parents, a feature of adolescence everywhere, simply took more extreme forms in Germany, where the state organisations and so many guilty parents lacked the confidence, tact and elasticity, and tolerance, to contain the protestations. But such effervescences, even in their most violent forms, tend to end when the vociferous young leave their own adolescence; and so it seems they have in Germany. And the present generation of the very young, the under 22s, have not followed the example of their immediate predecessors: more recent polls show that, among them, there are clear signs today of a return to more conservative values.

The Green Party in Germany, with its essential philosophy of libertarianism, anti-materialism, anti-authority values, and suspicion of discipline, initially had greater political success than green movements elsewhere in Europe, and its functional value as a corrective to German conformism was considerable. Unhappily it is now a shambles, a victim of its own prolonged unworked-through adolescence: the insistence that no one in the organisation should become a parental surrogate by remaining in any official post except for a short while has left the Green Party rudderless and, lacking leadership, it has lost all the West German seats it had obtained in the Bundestag.

That a green movement in Germany, with its former despairing leaders committing suicide, should appear to be ending in turmoil is disappointing but hardly surprising: the external pressures upon it in a society fearful of the idiosyncratic are not to be underestimated. More, not a few of its members are zealots possessed by pantheistic feelings, forever declaiming their determination to defend the purity of an anthropomorphised nature, and lacking the hard-headed pragmatism and scientific nous that, when I worked in anti-nuclear campaigns of the Friends of the Earth, I found existed within the British organisation. Many commentators have remarked on the similarity of mood within the German movement and that of the 1920s *Jugendbewegung*, an idealistic anti-industrial youth movement inspired by romantic notions about nature and the simple life; but that movement, like the pre-war *Wanderbewegung* which had ancient predecessors, is less innocent; to the sensitive ear, pagan drums can be distantly heard among some sections of the German greens which have even attracted to it racialists declaring they want to preserve 'Aryan ecological purity'. And such eco-racism is being peddled not only on the fringe of the green movements but even within established parties. The Bavarian Minister for the Environment, Peter Gauweiler, does not hesitate to link immigration with pollution. To the concept of environmental protection as an expression of love of the homeland, a corollary is being added: that of hatred of foreigners. I noted in the spring of 1993 that, much to their credit, some greens were unfurling banners in the shopping malls of Frankfurt expressing hostility to this abuse of their idealism.

Many dedicated and highly intelligent young within the green movement are impatient with such trends, as they are with the fundamentalism of some of the devotees, and have distanced themselves from many of the extravagances; but consequently, inevitably, splits have taken place. The danger now appears to be that those who wish to free themselves from the charge that they are more concerned with trees than people is that they dilute their principles, and become 'respectable' pragmatists. Already, by October 1993, there were those in the ruling Christian Democratic Party who were canvassing the view that the present Green Party could, in the coming elections, become their coalition allies, hardly an augury to justify a hope that the Greens will be exemplars leading Germany away from its obsessional concerns with propriety and order.

It may well be that the next challenge to Germany's law and order syndrome will come when a breaking point arises in former East Germany as its peoples find their treatment intolerable, and a reaction takes place against West Germany's arrogant condescensions and its inept attempt to reduce the task of national reconstruction to a purely brutal economic affair. For the present, the challenges from East Germany have been contained within the bounds of legitimacy; but the lawful strikes in the steel industries in May 1993, and the startling election results achieved in December of that year by the ex-Communist group, the PDS, in Brandenburg, may be intimations of worse to come, for conditions in bewildered East Germany are a particular breeding-ground for mischief. A glance at some of the graffiti on display there tells us that many youngsters are looking for targets to displace the hatred felt against fathers who imposed upon them the rules of a strict authoritarian regime. Wolfgang Brück of the Leipzig central institute for youth study has made the cogent observation: 'In all the trials I have witnessed involving anti-Semitic incidents, the juvenile offenders respond in the negative when asked whether they personally knew any Jews.' In many cases, it turned out that the authors of anti-Semitic graffiti were children of high Party officials or Stasi officers. Upon closer questioning, Brück has explained, they confessed that they really weren't aiming at the Jews at all, but at their fathers. Finding no Jews, these unemployed youngsters may yet find their real targets, and attack the upholders of law and order whom they will regard as their fathers in disguise.

A squeamish regime

It may well be asked what purpose is served in this essay, possessed with a conceit that it is making a small contribution to the European cause, in focusing attention upon the negative aspects of one particular German trait. Is it not inflammatory, likely to provoke not soothe national susceptibilities, to harp upon what John Ardagh has described as 'an abiding flaw in the German social character'? If, it may well be urged, we concentrate upon the quirks in the national characters of British, French and Italians, as we well could, are we not making the already difficult task of uniting Europeans into a common citizenship impossible of achievement? In any event, are we knocking the trait out of envy since from it flow organisational skills and disciplines which have brought such success to the German manufacturing industry? And who can dispute that the quality of life found in the trim and clean West German cities gives every appearance of superiority to that within our dishevelled towns? While certainly no one who has travelled on the underground systems of Hamburg or Munich could not wish that the cleanliness, space, and punctuality to be found there were features of London's tube network. Besides, it could be argued, if the Germans are comfortable within the rigid framework they have set themselves, is it not sheer officiousness on our part to lament a predisposition which we dislike, but which does not impinge upon us?

Such a tolerant response is unfortunately not open to us; inexorably, as man's insights in this century have increased, quirks, eccentricities and idiosyncrasies have long since lost their naïveté: yesterday's oddities have become today's neuroses. We cannot retreat into unselfconscious ignorance; an armoury has been provided that shatters beyond repair the outer casements of our whimsies. Presented with individual behaviour that lays such stress on regulation, order, duty and cleanliness, we know today that we have before us a catalogue of traits long since associated with a particular phase in a young child's development as he journeys to adulthood; at a particular period of time his self can receive a rebuff, can be almost derailed, and from then on, such are the consequences of that near-fatal lurch, the journey onwards towards and throughout adulthood is never again undertaken with the original confidence. Care, order and a strict timetable must be adhered to, lest worse befalls. And always accompanying and heightening the anxiety, there will be the fear that the ticket for the voyage will be lost and that, when the inspector arrives, there will no money to purchase another.

These traits tell of the struggles fought during the period of our toilet training; the paediatricians and the psychoanalysts have taught us that the central position occupied by the training of our excretory functions during our early years may be modified but can never be excluded from the rest of our lives. The shit created by us, which in turn has created sensations for us, is a plastic source of fantasy and the very first object in which our relationship to others is concretised: to expel or to hold back, to give or not to give, to submit or to disobey, the seemingly trivial contest of wills forges a link, a meaningful nexus, between those involved. As one distinguished Italian psychoanalyst has emphasised:

> Within the nexus, a significant relationship of mutual tension and desire is gradually developed between the child and its mother.

Moved by love for her and by the fear of losing her, by the pleasure of gratifying its desire or the pleasures of being compensated for not doing so, the child slowly renounces total control of its new-found power and agrees to produce the golden eggs only when and where she demands. But in order to re-exert some authority over her in turn, to win her recognition in some revenge for all the wrongs inflicted on it, it learns at the same time to postpone, to disappoint her, to make her wait.

With sensitivity and love, a happy armistice can be achieved. The baby gives his great gift, the precursor of all gifts, and the mother's formal prohibitions are now felt as wondrous approvals.

But such happy peace treaties are not always signed. The child, lacking the blessing of an empathic mother, and brought up within a strict and rigid family system, already suffering from a brusque mother who has denied the infant at the breast the satisfaction of its sucking impulses, now desperately aims at compensatory satisfaction during the phase when anus and defecation are the major sources of sensual pleasure and form the centre of the infant's self-awareness. It is a goal it is unlikely to attain, for a mother who is peremptory when the child wants satisfaction at the breast is the same severe unemphatic mother who denies her child the pride in its own first creation, its faeces. The child who is prematurely and strictly toilet-trained will all its life unconsciously deploy stratagems to cope with the parental imperatives which far too abruptly compelled it to relinquish the phase which offered so many delights.

A particular price has to be paid by an infant if it is doomed to have a mother whose own self is poorly consolidated and who, therefore, reacts by focusing excessive and indeed sometimes exclusive attention to the faeces and the anal region than to the total proudly assertive anal-phase self of her child. Without sufficient compensation available to the child to make up for the parsimony of the grudging breast, those traits which the psychoanalysts have taught us belong to the clinical phenomena of the anal character are built up on the ruins of an oral eroticism whose development has miscarried.

And one of the most obvious traits of those who have been so curmudgeonly treated is an excessive concern with order and cleanliness. In households where tidiness and scrupulous cleanliness are imposed, it is almost inevitable that the child suffers negative reactions as it passes through what, in a more benign environment, would be a confident assertive anal phase. When excessive prohibitions are imposed, the outlawing of any coprophiliac impulses – of the pleasures of a proud infant looking at and touching its creations – leave their mark on the adult disposition. These are the adults who in their league table of values place cleanliness next to godliness, and order and regulation above spontaneity and warmth. Such extravagant promotion of attributes indicates the continued need for a defence against a nostalgia that the adult feels may pull him back to his unspent coprophilia. The hypertrophy – the magnification of the opposing tendency – is the reaction-formation which forms a bulwark against the unacceptable impulses, too abruptly forbidden, which still endure.

But there are consequences, other than an obsessional concern for order and cleanliness, which stem from a childhood which has been lived under a squeamish regime where compulsive and regular relinquishment of faeces is strictly enforced. The dissonance between mother and child, destroying the elementary rhythm which can come from a more mothering mother, means the child is never reconciled to its loss of its golden eggs. That infant, as an adult, will often passionately seek out the equivalences of the prized shit to which it had attached magical values. All the esteem which it had felt in its creations and which it was so cruelly compelled to suppress, is transferred to that most ancient equivalent – to gold, to money. In dreams, as in folklore, as Freud has told us, gold and money are seen in the most unambiguous and magic way to be a symbol of faeces.

Few of us could claim that we can totally regulate our relationship to money according to the demands of reality. In all of us an interest in money can in part be traced to the early excretory pleasures of defecation; but for those who endured an acute deprivation of the early excretory pleasures of defecation, those early libidinal influences can be so overwhelming that their relationship to money is leached away from rationality.

In Germany, the passionate relationship between its citizens and the Deutschmark, reveals such a pathological nature, and the note of hysteria that enters into any discussion which queries the Deutschmark's status is soon sensed by an outside observer. 'Nothing,' *The Times'* correspondent Anne McElvoy has acutely commented, 'moves the modern German soul, east or west, to such flights of emotion as the Deutschmark.' She is not guilty of exaggeration. The *Guardian*'s economic editor, Will Hutton, noting how irrational the German man in the street becomes when the Deutschmark is discussed has ironically remarked: 'The *Bild*, Germany's mass circulation tabloid, talks of "our beloved Mark" the way the *Sun* might talk about the beloved

Lady Di.' The Bundesbank indeed is the Defender of the Faith, of the Deutschmark, and is certainly accorded as much popular support in Germany as the royal family, until recently, received in Britain.

There are those naïve enough to insist that this German preoccupation with the sanctity of the Deutschmark can be explained simply by the continuing memory of the disastrous inflation Germany experienced in the 1920s. Such a recollection may well play a part, but those events took place 70 years ago, and one would need to be credulous to believe that recall is the major factor operating today when we are faced with German assertions that no policy is too tight to curb the risks of inflation, whatever national or international economic disruption may follow. A scrutiny of the German penchant for regulation and order therefore is no mere exacerbating tease: it leads us, as we examine its ætiology, to canvass the view that it is a defence against coprophilia, against the direct expression of undisguised anality.

But it is a defence that is only partially successful; denied the right to admire the treasured shit, the admiration is transferred to its socially approved equivalent, the Deutschmark, upon which worshipful praise and sanctity is lavished. The Deutschmark becomes a totem; and all Europe is called upon to attend its shrine and submit masochistically to its economic demands. Those who resist are heretics against whom a religious war must be waged; and in the battles now raging in the chancelleries of Western Europe around the significance in valuation to be placed upon the Deutschmark, the European ideal can founder as the Bundesbank imposes its anally fixated economic policies.

The anal character

It is surely no accident that the brilliant breakthrough made, in 1921, by the psychoanalyst Karl Abraham when he correlated certain characterological features with persisting fixation by the adult on particular early infantile drives, took place in Berlin: there he would have found, not only in his consulting rooms, distortions of the spirit telling of the consequences of an arrest of a man's libido at the anal phase; in Germany, then even more than now, such distortions embedded in institutional as well as personal life were not necessarily seen as such, for they were regarded by many as societal norms, for the pre-Hitler social system, labelled by the Mitscherlichs the 'patriarchal-bourgeois social system' was, in their view, 'anally determined'.

The disruption caused by the Nazis when they made an official break with the 'patriarchal-bourgeois' values that were held by nations belonging to Western culture does not appear, in many respects, to have stopped continuity between the conservative society the Mitscherlichs labelled, and within which Karl Abraham developed his ontogenetic approach to human personality, and present-day Germany. The relationship between father and son, between authority and citizen, may have, as a consequence of the Nazis, suffered more than a hiccup; but what of the relationship between mother and child, the factor so determining the impress the anal phase makes upon adult behaviour?

Nazism devalued the father; it set up the fiction of an omnipotent and infallible leader, and a variety of techniques were used to make it easy for the youngster to identify with this leader as father, and all this usually took place with the blind agreement of the real parents. When the crash came, the father had already, in large measure, lost all authority, and an overview of the development of post-war German society and politics seems to suggest that it took a considerable time for the father to regain it. The optimists would indeed claim that the rigid obedience, formerly part of the patriarchal family regime, has gone forever, and that relinquishment is reflected in the more relaxed and questioning attitudes within today's democratic state where the diktat no longer rules; others, more pessimistic, as I am, cite the hierarchical structures in many of Germany's institutions, as in its industry and political parties, as mirror images received from a heavy-handed patriarchal family system that has by no means been dismantled. We would claim that the shadow of the intimidating father, after the Hitler and immediate post-war years, is once again falling heavily upon many sectors of German society.

But, one suspects, beneath all the man-made turmoils that Germany has endured in this century, whatever modifications may or may not have come about in father-son relationships, that the pattern of early mother-child relations has remained substantially unchanged. It is difficult, in the absence of evidence to the contrary, not to make that inference, for, without it, we would be left with no adequate explanation to account for the continuing envelopment of German society in legalism, and for its irrational and passionate love affair with the Deutschmark, which is putting at risk all Europe's economies. Mother of yesteryear, in the Wilhelminian and Hitlerian periods, as the mother of today, rejecting, or indifferent to, the faecal gifts proudly presented by a child, is not only responding to a libidinal drive: she is also responding to the child's self during the early stage of its consolidation.

The psychoanalyst Heinz Kohut, whose emendations to classical psychoanalytical theory have proved so influential, has demonstrated how important is the nature of the mother's response, and how it influences a set of inner experience that plays a crucial role in the child's further development. If a mother rejects the child's tentatively established self – a still vulnerable creative-productive self – then the mother, possessed of an 'inability to respond to the child's total self, leads her to a fragmentation-producing preoccupation with his faeces . . . The child's self will be depleted and he will abandon the attempt to obtain the joys of self-assertion and will, for reassurance, turn to the pleasures he can derive from the fragments of his body-self.'

Lacking the encouragement, the praise and admiration, that the child's efforts on the pot deserve, he feels his self crumbling or empty and tries to obtain comforting pleasures from the stimulation of the anal zone: the child makes a quasi-addictive use of a body fragment. No wonder that later, as an adult, he has to establish massive defences to protect him from returning to his illicit infantile delights and becoming a total druggy; and he devises more socially acceptable stratagems to cope with the fixations prompted by the over-investment of libidinal energy that took place at his anal stage. His insistence upon law, order and regulation, and over-valuation of the significance of money, are part of the bundle of boring repetitive syndromes of the anal character.

The eighteen anal-retentive male members of the governing council of the Bundesbank, whose decisions on interest rates, the status of the Deutschmark, and the European Monetary Union, can reverberate, often disastrously, through our and other European domestic economies, pretentiously affect that their conclusions are reached wholly objectively; that the determining influences in the Bank's statistics and national economy department which tracks every monetary movement in Germany with microscopic intensity, assessing how trends in productivity, growth and unemployment, are likely to affect inflation and thus the beloved Deutschmark. For my part, however, I believe that unacknowledged morbid coprophiliac displacements are as determinant as any statistic in the Bundesbank's decision-making. The German *hausfrau*'s imperious injunctions, given when the Bundesbank members, as children, sat upon their pots, are playing a significant and malevolent part in Europe's struggles with economic recession.

Visiting the spotless home of today's young German *hausfrau*, one remarks how she still runs a house that is as painfully tidy as, no doubt, was her mother's; and one notes how any children who create the slightest disorder are admonished for creating a mess. Mess is the operative word: that is to be confined to the lavatory where one is likely to find, as American guidebooks often complain, a toilet bowl so shaped that the sight of shit is kept well in view, and one is almost compelled to view one's own faeces before flushing takes place. It is difficult not to infer from such obviously unspent coprophilia that rigid toilet training of children remains of the old order. A 1948 study of the Germans by the anthropologist Rodnick contains a corroborative report of this inference:

> Since toilet training habits are important in the emotional experiences of the child, it was interesting to note how early the child is conditioned in German family life. Among all classes, toilet training begins when the infant is about five months old. There is a belief among German mothers that the child should be completely 'housebroken' by the time it is a year old.

A later study in 1964 of a south-west German village confirmed the continued concern with early toilet training: babies were delivered to a kindergarten-nursery at a fixed hour, and collective toilet training was immediately commenced upon their arrival. There is considerable variation and difference of opinion as to precisely when a child should be deemed to be toilet-trainable, but in view of the comparative data emerging from cross-cultural studies, it seems that a cross-cultural norm for the beginning of toilet training is roughly 24 months with a lower minimum in American culture of 18 months. In Germany it is generally taking place very much earlier.

Hints abound of some of the consequences of such a training. The violent heavy metal music integral to the male neo-Nazi skinheads of Düsseldorf has a popular libretto emphasising the cleanliness which makes them true defenders of the Fatherland:

> We fight shaved, our fists are hard as steel,
> Our heart beats true for our Fatherland.
> . . .
> We will stand true for our Germany,
> Because we are the strength for Germany,
> That makes Germany clean.
> Germany awake!

Predictably, after Neo-Nazi skinheads had burned to death Turkish women in Mölln in November 1992, skinhead youngsters in the area, when questioned, stressed their 'clean' credentials and replied: 'We just like the idea of a clean Germany for Germans.' Punks they hated: they were left-wing and dirty.

There are less sinister intimations of premature toilet-training. When I am enduring German meals, I see how my hospitable hosts love their stuffed intestines and their innumerable types of sausages; and I note their enormous consumption of bananas, a fruit which is exported far more to Germany than to any other country in the Europe. King-size bananas indeed are of enormous importance to Germans. Adenauer held up the signing of the Treaty of Rome to ensure the special protocol in defence of the Germans' right to bananas of their choice; and history repeated itself in 1993. Great passion has been aroused over the threat from the Community that in future the huge bananas from Latin America should be replaced by small bananas from Britain's and Spain's former tropical territories; the issue ended up in the European Court of Justice when, in June 1993, to the fury of the German government, that Court refused its demand for an injunction against the import system which favours the small banana-producers of Grenada and Guadeloupe. Intimations of such equivalences, and the pleasures associated with them, abound in Germany. When sitting in a beer garden with conversation enveloped by the farting wind instruments of the oompah brass bands, or when observing in a spa the Germans revelling in mud baths, I am often reminded of my time in the House of Commons where for so many years I sat in a Chamber passing Motions. And, as a wine-buff with little enthusiasm for most German wines, I am aware that my dislike comes from the German growers' obsession with acidity. Not for them the French concern for alcohol or the wonderful Piedmontese affirmation of a tannin conferring muscle but not roughness; acidity, however, is for the Germans a taste metaphor for cleanliness. Acidity sweeps the mouth clean, and acidity therefore is virtuous and, German wine-growers have told me, should be the ideal of any wine. This, however, is an appreciation unshared by most of their fellow-Europeans and explains, in part, the failure of German wine in the export market.

Sexual 'liberation' or oppression?

When I tease German friends with some such observations, they, not surprisingly, insist my conclusions are hopelessly impressionistic and that I am misleading myself. They claim old repressive attitudes are on the wane, and Germany is as permissive as any other Western European country, with a consequent home environment that would frequently discourage the training which I regret.

I am not convinced by their persuasions; indeed, research outside that of anthropologists and social scientists, also continues to invalidate their view. One distinguished American folklorist, Alan Dundes, examining the relationship between German national character and German folklore, found an enormous number of proverbs, folksongs and jokes dealing with anality:

> This penchant for *scheisse* is also observed in the writings of Luther and Mozart, not to mention Günter Grass and Heinrich Böll. From early toilet training (beginning as early as five months) and a long tradition of swaddling (in which infants were left immersed in their own faeces for periods up to 12 hours), one can see a consistent pattern.

I doubt if that pattern is now substantially disrupted.

I accept that there may be many children of parents who went through and identified with the student rebellion of 1968 who fortunately have had an upbringing that is far more relaxed; but I suspect these are a minority, and that what is being described to me as Germany's contemporary permissiveness does not necessarily improve the quality of a child's upbringing.

Popular sex education certainly arrived in Germany with the pill, but serious sex instruction books and films have, even more than elsewhere, been succeeded by hard-porn movies and commercial empires of sex shops and blue movie cinemas. The woman head of one of the large pornographic companies is not hyping her wares when she declares:

> Since 1975 pornography has in most respects been legal in Germany – and I am simply catering to a market as the law allows me to. Germany today is one of the most liberal countries in this field. And the Germans are a very sexually liberated people – more than the Americans who are somewhat inhibited except for some groups in California.

We should not, however, assume that such 'liberation' automatically produces mothers today free from the inhibitions imposed upon them by the martinet mothers of yesteryear. Indeed, there is an articulate opinion among some moderate women feminists in Germany that the considerable growth of promiscuity among young women is, like pornography, oppressive to women: that there is a shadow side to the emancipatory gains that have been made, that traditional German machismo is being served and women are being further depreciated and treated as sex objects. Such a view, if correct, does not encourage a belief that the young mother in the home will feel the increased self-esteem so necessary if the child too is to gain a confident self.

It has certainly been brought home to me that the legislation in Britain with which I have been associated – even though it brought some relief to those afflicted with appalling distortions of the spirit imposed upon them by former legal and societal taboos – has not brought freedoms which some of my over-enthusiastic supporters claimed would result. Legislation, and verbal disavowals of yesterday's repressive condemnations, should not deceive us: attitudes unconsciously held by many can be far different from those which they consciously affect. The seemingly emancipated can remain unconsciously subjugated to persistent childhood attitudes. Conscious investment in the ideals of sexual freedom can be accompanied by a savagely puritanical but unconscious conscience that operates unceasingly and relentlessly. As Schiller, the great German poet, commented: 'Not all are free who mock their chains.'

Those in bondage, bequeathed with anal fixations by unempathic disciplining mothers, will not in one bound be freed simply by society granting more sexual licence. The pornography now pouring into East Germany, like the newly opened sex shops, will do little to modify the adult behaviour of the infants who have been reared under the authoritarian regime. In the GDR, even babies in the crèche were at one time put to bed at a nationally stated time, and children's toilet habits were similarly regulated. In the child care centres, where the state provided generous, indeed often remarkable facilities, one would see infants sitting obediently in rows upon standard-issue potties: the curriculum was fixed, and this was defecation time. Out of such an ambience, it is unlikely that, as adults, they will be free from excessive concerns with order and correctness.

Nor is it a happy augury that so many of the women of East Germany now feel so defeated. East German feminists have told me that they lived in a different psychological reality from that of the women of the western half. They claim that reunification has created unemployment that forces women to stay at home; that day nurseries are closing or have raised their prices dramatically; that the role of the

man as the sole breadwinner is being reinstated; their work gave them
their identity, and now, losing their independence, they are defeated.
And as Kohut has stressed, it is particularly the depressed child of such
a dejected mother who, lacking the joyous corroboration of an
admiring mother of his creative efforts, is left with so enfeebled a self
that, in the attempt to assure itself that it is alive, even that it exists at
all, turns despairingly towards pleasure aims through the stimulus of
the erotogenic zone, and can thus become anally fixated. That child, as
an adult, will so often display the characterological attitudes revealing
he cannot forgo these initial delights which so assisted his survival; lest,
however, his nostalgia draw him back to undisguised infantile anality,
he encases it within a prison governed by a strict regime where law,
regulation and order ensure it does not escape. He becomes his own
gaoler and, suffering imprisonment, his adulthood can be severely
constrained.

Unwelcome insights

Such an arid adulthood is doubtless avoided by many in West
Germany, for the teachings of paediatrician Spock in the United States
and Donald Winnicott in Britain have spread throughout the Western
world; but the considerable changes in the manner of bringing up
children that have taken place in Britain are not apparent in Germany.
Paediatricians and child psychologists are not there held in high
esteem. West Germany is a country which has gained its self-esteem
through its material success and things can be more important than
people, and insights into the dynamics behind the economic success are
unwelcome.

Kohl setting, not unusually, a bad example, publicly depreciates
psychiatrists and their work. In May 1992, he showed his usual
ambivalence towards psychiatry when he denied there was even a trace
of a risk of the emergence of German nationalism, saying that those
who supported such a rise were 'unreasonable individuals'; and then he
gratuitously added, with heavy Teutonic humour: 'Psychiatrists say
that up to four per cent of the population really should receive
psychiatric treatment – maybe that includes the psychiatrists themselves.' His smouldering resentment may be prompted by the
psychiatrist's incapacity to transform his mentally handicapped son, a
child whom he will never mention when he speaks of his other son; in
Britain, hiding away the mentally sick and handicapped, and feeling

ashamed of them are attitudes that have been considerably altered. But in Germany where material success is so overvalued, handicap is too often interpreted as failure, and the blow to the narcissism of the parents of a handicapped child is severe. In such a social environment, the paediatrician and child psychiatrist are swimming against the tide; and it is not therefore surprising that their influence in modifying traditional methods of baby and infant care is much limited. Perhaps, too, their influence is limited because they are not free from unfortunate influences in their own childhood: visiting hospitals in Germany will bring you to psychiatrists who, decidedly unlike those in Britain, always wear white coats, and explain their garb by saying their patients expect this of them. But one wonders whether their spotless attire is being used to protect them from the murky thoughts that their patients dredge out from their unconscious and pour upon them.

It would be encouraging if we could find evidence that there was a widespread change in attitude; then we could hope that those who have more recently passed through their infancy are on the way to an adulthood free from the hang-ups, in the form of reaction-formations to anality, which invade contemporary German economic and political decision-making, often to the detriment of all the European Community. Unfortunately it seems that many German mothers are more resistant to accepting the counselling of the paediatricians; for they would encourage mothering to be patient, more giving, more time-consuming, more loving. They would wish for a tuning-in between mother and child. The establishment of such rhythms with a baby, however, requires perforce, some sacrifice of the material lifestyle which seems to be especially attractive to so many German women; and when choices have to be made, their living standards take precedence over motherhood, which is being widely rejected. West German nationals have had since the 1970s one of the lowest birthrates in the world, with six births for every seven deaths, and an average of 1.3 children per marriage.

Kohl has found such a situation threatening. Although, as I have indicated, I find a singularity in the persistent German passion for *Lebensraum*, the usual syndromes found in imperialist expansions are not absent in the German desire for bigness: phallic pride comes into play, and a visible display of population decline is felt as depreciatory, as an assault upon male potency, arousing unconscious castration fears. A male political leadership, more confident about the length of their penises, would not have become alarmed in an over-populated world at finding that they have a slightly declining population, particularly when the workforce is being effortlessly augmented by immigrant workers; the fact, however, of the contrasting high birthrate amongst the immigrants has aroused still further the unconscious fear that the German male could become the eunuch of Europe.

Kohl, in 1985, responded to his apprehension characteristically, using the only armoury with which he and his political allies appear to be comfortable. The problem was to be resolved by patriotism and money. For the sake of Germany, Kohl called for a target of 200,000 extra babies a year. Women would be bought into motherhood by cash incentives. Financially help would be offered to young hard-up pregnant women so that they would not turn to abortion, maternity benefits would be increased, maternity leave extended and subsidised, and escalating child allowances, increasing with each additional child, would be on offer. Through money, love would flourish. 'We must change this back into a child-loving country,' Kohl declared in tones that aroused the hackles of the feminists who believed the moves had little to do with loving, and much to do with a misogyny that wished to push back women into the home.

One distinguished woman sociologist, however, made a different comment on the incentives: the excessive punctiliousness and thoroughness upon which Germany insists could, she thought, tip the balance into women responding to the call for motherhood. 'Just as German women went over to the pill more thoroughly than others, so if they could but be convinced that baby-making is fun, they might again set themselves to it wholeheartedly.' One would like to think that the characteristic of unremitting thoroughness, despite its dubious roots, could be thus pressed into service; thoroughness, however, may lead to the manufacture of excellent and reliable cars but can splendid babies be similarly produced? If, as the German sociologist suggests, the German mother was able to give herself 'wholeheartedly', that is, with all her heart, to mothering, then we would all be in debt to her; for that she has in the past fallen short of being what the inspired paediatrician Winnicott called the 'good enough' mother means that now, when the pound is locked into the Deutschmark, her inadequacies were experienced in every high-interest mortgaged home in Britain.

The full financial consequences for Britain of the faulty mothering, which finds its expression in the dominant cloacal economic and political culture of Germany, was experienced on 1992's 'Black' Wednesday; then the Bundesbank, adamant that the beloved Deutschmark was to remain protected by high interest rates, humiliated Britain and forced sterling's devaluation. Fundamentally, it was Thatcher's own mothering, atypical for Britain but akin to that endured by so many in Germany, that had left Britain defenceless; for Thatcher had been brought up in an obsessively clean household where a living-in martinet of a grandmother shared the domain with Thatcher's obscenely greedy father, a man possessed of a classic anal character; and Thatcher's inadequate mother corroborated, rather than shielded her from, the inimical environment. Inevitably her unspent coprophilia found expression in overvaluing money, as I have sought to show in my psycho-biographical study of the woman; and, no less inevitably, displacing her frustrated love of her faeces on to sterling, she hopelessly overvalued it. To have entered the European Exchange Rate Mechanism (ERM) with an overvalued pound at DM2.95 was total folly, and to have attempted to defend it at that level, madness. It cost Britain billions as we ravaged our reserves in a vain bid to ward off the speculators; and although temporarily staved off, the long-term consequences, as the costs of our imports rise, have yet to be endured. The irrational assessment of Thatcher, her Chancellor and the Treasury, added to Britain's economic dilemmas; and these will be compounded, not resolved, if we immerse ourselves in yet another fairy-story, and pretend black has become white, and that by the wave of a magic wand 'Black Monday' must henceforth be regarded as 'White Monday'. The irrational follies surrounding the whole affair have left the mark triumphant and the pound unstable, a devaluation which creates a ratchet for overseas ownership; in February 1994 the Germans, through BMW, unsurpringly seized their opportunity and swallowed up Rover, the last British-owned mass car manufacturer.

Today, a hapless John Major, Treasury officials, economic editors, the 'six wise men', City analysts and Opposition politicians, vie with each other as they propose often contradictory remedies for our economic woes; as they sift through the statistics and trends, examining them even as in ancient times entrails were examined to predict and control the future, they would not deign to glance at the results of the mothering bestowed by the German *hausfrau*. Yet if they did, they might begin to understand the relevance of the 70-year-old warning, never more pertinent than today, of Freud's innovatory early follower, Sandor Ferenczi:

Whatever form may be assumed by money the enjoyment at possessing it has its deepest and amplest source in coprophilia. Every sociologist and national economist who examines the facts without prejudice has to reckon with this irrational element.

Social problems can be solved only by discovering the real psychology of human beings; speculations about economic conditions alone will never reach the goal.

But, as they blindly stagger on, will the bankers and politicians ever learn?

Expulsion and defecation

Anal eroticism is always associated by psychoanalysts with sadism; the early psychoanalysts indeed always described the developmental stage through which, as infants, we all must pass, as the sadistic-anal phase. This link between sadism and anal eroticism has demonstrated itself all too vividly in Germany in this century. In the concentration camps the guards displaced the fury they evidently felt against their over-controlling mothers by wreaking vengeance against their prisoners who had to obtain their permission when they wanted to defecate: great pleasure was obtained by the guards in granting or withholding permission to visit the latrines. Because of these extreme restrictions over excretory functions, the hapless prisoners were often covered with their own excrement, a fact that facilitated the guards' work because their prisoners then appeared less than human. The prisoners lost the morale to resist what one distinguished inmate – Bruno Bettelheim – has described as 'excremental assault', and they disintegrated, making themselves even more vulnerable to the Gestapo's manipulations.

Refined forms of this sadism persist in our treatment of prisoners in this country. The slopping-out system continues in many of our prisons and provides ample corroboration for any who may still doubt that expelling a man out of society to a prison can be treated by the community as an act of defecation. The primitive idea that removing an object is equivalent to defecating may be a remote notion to many grown-up people; but child psychiatrists know that according to the child's view the way to get rid of a person one no longer likes is by means of defecation. The prison authorities get the message from the outside world: the prisoner is shit, must be treated as shit and must live and sleep amongst shit.

When, after the escape of the spy Blake, I was appointed to a new small expert committee to advise the Home Secretary on security and other penal issues, one of the first recommendations we made was that in new prisons a screen flush lavatory should be attached to each cell together with a washbasin with running water; but officialdom proffered the most extraordinary rationalisations to persuade us not to make such a recommendation. And the insistence that prisoners could not be trusted to possess a toilet of their own was irrationally insisted upon despite our assurances that we had seen such facilities provided without difficulty to the most dangerous criminals of Europe and America. It would require a Swift, whose excremental vision long preceded Freud's exposition of the sadistic fantasies that accompany the anal stage of libidinal development, to savage adequately the elaborate defences of those resisting our proposed change. For years now prison officials have been engaged in a rearguard action, establishing electronic unlocking by which, at night, one prisoner at a time on each landing can be released to go to the lavatory. For the pretence of security a cunning control of the prisoners' motions has been gained by some authorities as a demanded price for giving up the stinking chamber pot in the cell. The redoubtable Judge Stephen Tumim, Chief Inspector of Prisons, is now continuing the fight to end slopping-out but, even as the Tories promise to build six new prisons in the future, recent public expenditure cuts continue to fall heavily on prisons; the implementation of Tumim's recommendation requiring civilised toilet facilities, coming some twenty years after my committee made the same recommendation, is likely to be further postponed.

To draw attention to the controlling powers exercised by concentration camp guards and some of our own prison officers is not, I believe, an irrelevance when we examine the events of September 1992: the gaolers' behaviour is but a slight caricature of the conduct of the sophisticated bankers of the Bundesbank when they brazenly demonstrated their power over Europe. They illustrated yet again that the libidinal excitations belonging to anal eroticism have close and manifold connections with sadism, and that, as Freud in his early works explicated, what 'we call sadism when we find it in the services of the sexual function' finds expression in other activities in 'an apparatus for obtaining mastery'. Our expectations are that a society enveloped in a cloacal culture will formulate economic and political policies embossed with sadistic and domineering displays of mastery.

Such expectations are unhappily often realised, and never more blatantly than when the Bundesbank successfully manoeuvred the dispatch of Britain from the ERM. Britain, in effect, was expelled, and the Bundesbank rejoiced, for its goal, as David Marsh in his recent informed work on the Bundesbank has made clear, is to sabotage indirectly European Monetary Union, for such a union is 'a fundamental challenge not only to its ethos and viability, but to its existence'. At present, the Bundesbank can well be described, as Marsh does, as the bank that rules Europe. It intends to retain its mastery and control, and will fight for survival.

Chancellor Kohl, full of conflicts reflecting the contradictions within his electorate, has political mood changes; he swings from assertiveness to actions designed to contain the smouldering German aggressive nationalism which, even as he publicly denies its existence, he fears could prove overwhelming. He therefore insists on the goal of European political and monetary union, for thus he assuages his own and his neighbours' fears that a strong united Germany will threaten European stability. In October 1992, at the annual congress of his party, he warned the sulking delegates, fearful that their Deutschmark under the Maastricht Treaty could be submerged within a common currency: 'If the Treaty does not come into force and we are set back on the path to Europe, then we will fail before history and run the risk that Europe and the Europeans will be caught up by their dreadful past.' He refrained from specifying the nation that, above all, had created that 'dreadful past', but he and all the delegates present understood the reference. The Bundesbank, however, will have none of this: the Deutschmark is theirs and is to be shared with no one. Sitting on its throne at Frankfurt, the Bundesbank fights against the Maastricht pledge to have by 1999 a common currency. It is determined stubbornly to maintain its monetary predominance.

The tumult that this determination occasioned in September 1992, with Italy and Britain dispatched from the ERM, did not arise from a clash of objectively made rivalling economic assessments in the chancelleries of Europe. What we witnessed was an anally-determined psychodrama where a cast of immature protagonists acted out the unresolved dilemmas of their infancy. Indeed, Britain's expulsion by the Machiavellian directors of the Bundesbank could well have been expressed in the language used by German students when, for some misdemeanour, one of their number is excluded from their gatherings: '*Er gerät Vershiss.*' And even as the expulsion of such a student is thus quite openly compared to the physical expulsion of a stool, so could be Britain's exclusion, manipulated by the Bundesbank, from the ERM.

The control that the Bundesbank exercised over the event was what Ernest Jones, Freud's biographer, would have described, in other contexts, as 'sphincter control'; the clinical material available to the psychoanalysts has long since convinced them that co-related with the development of muscular control, there is a strengthening of sadism.

The Bundesbank's exercise of its muscle in the days preceding Black Wednesday is a textbook example of the way all the components associated with the phase of infantile sexuality, when it is centred and organised around its anal zone, can come into play as adult men, whose psychosexual development had been arrested at the anal level, show off their mastery: when those men had sat upon the pot they wished for applause as they displayed their faeces; but instead they had received only tacit or overt disapproval from their poorly consolidated, squeamish mothers, and now they worked out those early frustrations.

Their mood was one of spite and anger for recent frustrations had reactivated older ones. The Bundesbank had suffered a rare defeat when the passion for German reunification had overwhelmed it and compelled it to give away its precious Deutschmarks to East Germany when the politicians had successfully insisted parity of esteem should be extended to the almost worthless currency of the GDR. Now the Bundesbank was determined Europe should pay the cost of that reunification, and their Deutschmark was not to be further diluted. The then Bundesbank president, Helmut Schlesinger, his sadism barely masked, 'inadvertently' told the newspapers *Handelsblatt* and the *Wall Street Journal* that sterling was overvalued: the wound thus inflicted, the markets did the rest, the pound was killed, and a European common currency postponed, perhaps for ever.

By such action the Bundesbank recovered its poise; now it was able again to bask in its illusions of omnipotence, and to infuriate Europe with the accompanying arrogance. When, in the infant, delusions of power that mastery of the body, and particularly of the sphincter, bring are too brutally demolished by the insensitive mother, unable or unwilling with love and patience to woo the child away from fantasy to acceptance of reality, that child as an adult may seek to recover the delusions snatched away too abruptly from him. As the psychoanalyst Otto Fenichel found from his neurotic patients: 'Fantasies of omnipotence connected with thoughts and words turn out to be repetitions of the infantile narcissistic overvaluation of the excretory functions.' The Bundesbank's policies are hallmarked by such compulsive repetitions. The paediatrician Donald Winnicott has told us that one of the main tasks of a mother is to pinpoint the moments when the infant displays the potential to move out of his omnipotence; then she can introduce a moment of frustration, a lack of satisfaction at the right moment and the right time. But if the child has not a 'good enough mother', the transition from the infantile omnipotence to a more accurate grasp of reality fails, because the needed momentary and mild confrontations between mother and child are made too early and too brutally; and the child then suffers the experience which Winnicott has termed 'impingement'.

It is these impingement experiences which appear to determine much of the Bundesbank policy-making; irrationally, they seek within their policies to regain the absolute power which their earlier hallucinatory omnipotence had bestowed upon them, and which was so prematurely wrested from them. The bankers who boast of their realism should not be taken at their word: their economic policies often can be products of the most regressive of dreams. And they are dreams they will not easily relinquish. Helmut Schlesinger, in November 1992, criticising the Maastricht Treaty when addressing the Euro-MPs in Strasbourg warned: 'You can only offer the Germans a new European currency if you can guarantee it will be just as stable as the Deutschmark.' It was a warning repeated by the Constitutional Court in October 1993. When legitimating Germany's adherence to the Maastricht Treaty, the Court made clear that there was to be no question of Germany's membership of a European currency union being automatic; only the Bundestag had the right to decide whether the criteria for abolishing the mark had been met, a condition which undoubtedly comforted the Bundesbank that it could not be sidestepped by Euro-enthusiast ministers favouring monetary union, and thus lose its present power.

No one understood better this nostalgia for absolute power which possesses the acquisitive than the economist John Maynard Keynes. In the Thatcherite years his theories were mocked but now, amidst the wreckage that an insane adherence to monetarism has brought upon us, once again his economic views are being treated with a renewed respect; but they need to be comprehended and applied, with a recognition of Keynes's profound understanding of the psychology of the capitalist, and the psychodynamics of the capitalist financial system. It is evident that Keynes's escape from the flawed utilitarian assumptions of classical economics was facilitated by an extensive reading of Freud in which, in 1925, he immersed himself. A revelatory bibliographic footnote in his *Treatise on Money* makes it clear that he was well acquainted with all the major psychoanalytical literature then available dealing with anal sadism; and there continued to be a correspondence between his account of the nature and operation of the motivations behind the upholders of finance capitalism and that provided by psychoanalysis. By the time Keynes published his *General Theory of Employment, Interest and Money*, he was adding to his view that

the two motivations behind contemporary capitalism were love of
money and a money-making 'instinct' by emphasising a third
motivation – a sadistic love of power. He saw, as clearly as any
psychoanalyst, how love of money and money-making can take on a
sadistic coloration, and he wrote:

> Dangerous human proclivities can be canalised into compara-
> tively harmless channels by the existence of opportunities for
> money-making and private wealth, which, if they cannot be
> satisfied in this way, may find their outlet in cruelty, the reckless
> pursuit of personal power and authority, and other forms of self-
> aggrandisement. It is better that a man should tyrannise over his
> bank balance than over his fellow citizens; and whilst the former
> is sometimes denounced as being but a means to the latter,
> sometimes at least it is an alternative.

Sometimes it is indeed an alternative, but not always. It can arise, as
the Bundesbank's conduct chasteningly shows, that a bank, not the
depositor, can use a command of bank deposits and credit to tyrannise
all of us. Bankers may try to mask this desire for domination behind an
anally-determined compulsive orderliness; but a rigid and pedantic
administrative or economic system does not only leave them in control
of things. It can make people themselves enter into the system they
create. All systems with authoritarian rules, Karl Abraham remarked,
'not only testify to an obsession for order in its inventor, but also to his
love of power which is of sadistic origin'.

Keynes was coy about acknowledging his intellectual debt to Freud.
When he took up his cudgels on Freud's behalf, in a debate raging in
the letter columns of the *Nation* over the merits of psychoanalysis,
taking pains to mask himself behind a pen-name, he wrote:

> Professor Freud seems to me to be endowed, to the degree of
> genius, with a scientific imagination which can body forth an
> abundance of innovating ideas, shattering possibilities, working
> hypotheses, which have sufficient foundation in intuition and
> common experience to deserve the most patient and unprejudiced
> examination, and which contain, in all probability, both theories
> which will have to be discarded or altered out of recognition and
> also theories of great and permanent significance.

There were good reasons why Keynes wished to keep his enthusiasm
for Freud's work under wraps. His reading had led him to a paper by
Ernest Jones which he cites in a footnote: it was an article in which

Jones affirmed that of all the 'resistances' which arise when psychoanalytical interpretations are given, none produce greater storms of resistance than the interpretation of anal-erotic traits. Keynes, attracting enough controversy by his own innovatory and unorthodox economic works, evidently thought circumspection was needed, and avoided making explicit that his work was in any way based on psychoanalytical psychological premises. The resistances Keynes feared still exist, and those interpreting in psychoanalytical terms our present economic dilemmas will face, as the least of the ensuing criticism, the charge of reductionism. But this is no time for pussy-footing, and I believe it to be healthier to focus attention on the fundamentally obscene motivation of the Bundesbank and its allies since it is unlikely that tempering legal reforms that took place in 1992, which led to some changes in the numbers and composition of the Bundesbank's central council, will materially alter the bank's conduct.

The Bundesbank believes itself to be the proud possessor of independence unmatched by any other national bank, freely able to make its decisions untrammelled by governments or electorates; in fact, fundamentally, it lacks freedom, for it acts under a repetition-compulsion which determines its conduct however disastrous may be the consequence. The scenario of September 1992 was repeated unchanged in August 1993. All Europe, and in particular France, in the light of the mounting international currency crisis, pleaded that the Bundesbank reduce its discount rate; the cajolings were of no avail. Kohl failed in his attempts to get the interest rate cut in order to protect his relations with Paris; inexorably, rigidly, the Bundesbank continued to sit tight. Like a stubborn child retaining its stools, no persuasions persuaded the bank to relax and when the inevitable disaster fell, the bank revelled in its triumph; the Bundesbank had succeeded yet again in slowing down European unity moves and in preventing any dilution of German control of the mark. German bankers barely concealed their delight at France, with its reserves almost wiped out, paying the price of its hubris in daring to believe the franc had won the same stature as the mark, and was left deeply in debt to the Bundesbank. There was to be no shit like German shit.

There was almost no criticism of the Bundesbank's conduct in the German press nor, as I found when in Germany during August 1993, did the man in the street doubt the decision of the Bundesbank; the unemployed of Europe may suffer but the mark was the totem that must be worshipped. It was ironic that even while the currency crisis was raging, I found myself being told by local trade union leaders that they despaired of rallying effective resistance to government plans to de-regulate the labour market, cut social security benefits and paid leave, and impose longer working hours. Once persuaded that all this was being done to save the mark, the workers, they feared, would capitulate; this view was also put to me by management consultants who smugly informed me that resistance would lapse as soon as the workers realised that unless the government's plans were substantially implemented, the mark could be devalued. When Britain devalued in November 1967, Harold Wilson, with characteristic insouciance, could persuade the worker that his pound was unaffected; and now the French premier, Edouard Balladur, could likewise, not without some impact, bemuse the French worker. But there is no possibility of German workers reacting tepidly to a threat to the mark; too many of them share with bankers the same childhood potty experiences and, because of them, share too the irrational prejudices and anxieties of the Bundesbank bankers.

We must hope that the implementation of the Maastricht Treaty will give Europe the opportunity to emancipate itself from the present thraldom to the Bundesbank. It is envisaged that the proposed European Central Bank should have an executive board of six members and governing council comprised of the governors of all the national central banks within the Community. This will mean that policy will be determined by men and, it is hoped, women, drawn from many countries with different cultures. If the governors can be made sufficiently democratically accountable, then out of such an amalgam it is possible that the ethos of Europe's present economic life will be, at least in part, free from the suffocating cloacal culture which the German Bundesbank now imposes upon the citizens of Western Europe.

Longings for the calculable

The search for an explanation of the German need for order and certainty has led us to the child-rearing practices of the German mother; but can we acquit the German father of all responsibility for these traits, and for all the bundle of anxieties that find expression in German social and political life whenever the encompassing framework of propriety and legalism is assailed? One is driven to ask are there particular historical circumstances which lead, in Germany, to a desperate wish to have and maintain a family system where an

assertive authoritarian father will ensure that there will be no disorder
or questioning at home; where a controlled family life, as a controlled
public life, will keep chaos at bay?

No German commentator, whatever his political prejudices, ever
appears to dispute the reality of this German condition, where a
disproportionately distraught response is prompted by any display of
scepticism, and where to stifle any doubt there is a continuing response
of assertive dogmatism, a response which has earned the Germans the
reputation for arrogance. Michael Stürmer, Chancellor Kohl's guru,
asserting that a deep sense of insecurity is embedded in the German
psyche, has searched for an historical starting-point of German *Angst*,
that characteristic uncertainty and dread which fears that just around
the corner lurks disaster and which, as a consequence has engendered a
profound German desire that the future be known, seen and calculable.
'We yearn,' says Stürmer, 'for the calculable. We need to know, to be
able to measure. To be as far as it is humanly possible certain of the
direction that events will take.' Stürmer would persuade us that this
desire to keep in control, to hold the maintenance of order as a
supreme value, stems from the chaos inflicted upon the Germans when
the Germanic territories were the battleground of the Thirty Years War
of 1618–48. Given the horrifying cannibalism that raged in Germany
during those years, it is unsurprising that Stürmer concludes that the
desolation and destruction of those wars was nothing less than the
'existential catastrophe of modern Germany' which it is essential to
understand if one is to make any sense out of the subsequent history of
the Germans.

It may indeed well be that the collective traumas suffered by
Germans three centuries ago continue to play their part in determining
the structure of Germany's family system; that the stern father
maintaining strict order is a protection against the chaos which befell
the Germans and which remains within the collective memory.
Stürmer is a dangerous conservative historian, ever complaining that
the importance of the Third Reich is over-emphasised; and proposing,
as he takes a longer view of the country's history, that events like the
Thirty Years War, when other countries made Germany their battleground, illustrate his constant thesis that because encircled Germany
was under threat on two fronts, national security required it to be
governed by anti-democratic authoritarian governments under Bismarck and, later, Wilhelm II. He would be unlikely to draw my
conclusion that insight into the significance of the Thirty Years War
illuminates some of the sources of the still extant father-authoritarian

family system within which Germans of today have received their upbringing.

Stürmer is playing quite another game, trying to minimise Germany's responsibility for the First World War, and guilt for Hitler's Reich. But his distasteful motivation in emphasising the significance of the Thirty Years War to contemporary Germany should not lead us to dismiss as extravagant his view that the traumas of 1648 continue to reverberate throughout the body politic of Germany. His time-span of three centuries is brief compared with Jung's divinations of the linkage between paganism and Germany's twentieth century psyche; and Freud, in his *Moses and Monotheism*, boldly insisted that traumas that endured for millennia, not centuries, shaped the Jew.

What is clear is that, whatever may be the ultimate source of the authoritarian traits that appear to be endemic to the family system and institutions of Germany, there are certain significant and identifiable historical events which have played their part in ensuring their persistence; and those events have been occasioned not only by social forces but also by personages whose ghosts still stalk contemporary Germany. In 1946 the psychoanalyst R. Money-Kyrle chose a different historical starting-point from Stürmer when endeavouring to trace the development of these striking German authoritarian traits. He directed attention to the shaping influences of Frederick the Great and his father, a perspective which Money-Kyrle had gained as a result of his extensive fieldwork in the personnel branch of the Allied Control Commission. He has told us that many of the most intelligent of the Germans he was probing:

> believed that the Prussian monarchy, and the philosophy that supported the Prussian state ideal, had helped to form an authoritarian character which was well adapted to the autocratic system of the Hohenzollerns. And they believed that an inability to adjust this character to the liberalism of the Weimar Republic was the predisposing – though not the precipitating – cause of the rapid spread of Nazism.

Money-Kyrle qualifies such an interpretation by eschewing the temptation of making the Hohenzollerns the sole scapegoats for the authoritarian attitudes which he found so chronic and still prevailing in 1946; he shifts a great deal of the responsibility for Germany's vulnerability to authoritarianism, and for its discomfort when asked to shoulder the responsibilities of a democracy, to the meticulous bureaucrats, with their heavy sense of duty, who served the

Hohenzollerns so well. They, as supreme administrators, were, it is suggested, the carriers of attitudes which can enable a sense of duty to authority to outweigh moral counterbalances.

That Money-Kyrle should come to a conclusion that culpability lay with the official classes was because he discovered such attitudes firmly prevailing in the high-ranking civil servants whom he was scrutinising in 1946. They were men who had achieved their ascendancy in their profession before the Nazis achieved power, and had continued during the Nazi regime, with few qualms, to serve their new masters. Forty years on we can feel little confidence that such a bureaucratic class, with all the authoritarian attitudes it carries, is not still in place in Germany.

The authoritarian members of the German bureaucracy at the close of the last war are not to be regarded as 'milder' versions of Nazi extremists, and we should not so regard Germany's present state and city civil servants. The civil servants Money-Kyrle encountered were drawn from patriarchal homes: the typical Nazi had an entirely different background. He was:

> more often the product of a disturbed or broken than that of a patriarchal home. He was born just before, or during, the First World War and brought up by a mother who had become neurotic in the absence of her husband who, as often as not, never would return. So he developed the kind of instability that in another culture might have made him a delinquent – especially in the then prevalent conditions of widespread unemployment.

Not surprisingly, he fitted well into the Nazi state, for it institution-alised delinquency in pursuit of their political 'ideals'; but the civil servant products of a patriarchal family system are not unstable transitory men. They have more stamina and, within the confines of the strict parameters laid down by their background, they can function well.

We see the continuity of this class of civil servant in the governance of many of today's German cities whose affairs are managed in so different a manner from those of our own local authorities. Here in Britain, although under Thatcherite governments they have been lamentably stripped by Whitehall of many of their powers, our councils, as I well know from my own experience as a councillor, are possessed of a vitality which springs from an intimate contact with the voters: and the blemishes and cacophonies and triumphs of our councillors reflect the opinionated and often wilful views and priorities of the local inhabitants. But in the well-ordered cities of Germany, so often the highly-paid *Oberburgermeister*, the chief mayor, a chief executive elected for at least eight years and flanked by five *Burgermeisters*, full-time salaried specialists, is the head of an oligarchy of technocrats who rule with a high-handed paternalism. Their tidy paternalistic professionalism may lead to efficient management but it guts any democratic participation in the rule of a city. They fit well, however, into a long tradition catalogued by the American historian Gordon Craig who has written:

> It is not too much to talk of a progressive bureaucratisation of Germany in the seventeenth and eighteenth centuries and a concomitant growth among the inhabitants of the German states of habits of deference towards authority that seemed excessive to foreign observers. These last may have had ancient roots – it was a mediæval Pope who called Germany the *terra obedientiae* . . .

The present authoritarian city governance would be unlikely to have been chosen, and to have been administratively successful, if it was not mirroring, corroborating and accommodating an electorate matured within a severely paternalistic family system. There are protests by 'greens' and some younger critics against the powers possessed by the technocratic oligarchs, but the overwhelming majority of citizens willingly and passively accept the decision-makings of the managers. An awareness of the past role of the official classes in Germany leaves one with an unease when noting the character of some of the institutions which these present-day bureaucrats operate: it raises doubts over the strength of Germany's present attachment to democracy which some Germanophiles so confidently assert is now inviolable.

Within a democratic family system, freedom is the essential ingredient; within the authoritarian family, liberty is quenched; and national and local institutions can reflect these differences. The general acceptance of forms of governance having, by British standards, tenuous criteria of accountability is a reminder to us that the permanency of democracy, as we understand it, cannot in Germany be taken for granted; and I believe too it indicates to us that Germany's emancipation from the thraldom of the authoritarian and paternalistic family system is far from complete. In a modern state with a universal suffrage there is a fundamental incompatibility between authoritarian national and local institutions and a democratic family system: one or the other must be renounced, and I doubt if Germany has yet come to terms with this necessity. Meantime, we observe the resultant tensions, and see, on the one hand, some German politicians expressing concerns about the fragility of Germany's democracy and, on the other, so many years after Hitler's end, constant reaffirmations by leading German politicians of allegiance to democracy, affirmations that are so strident that they ring with tones of over-compensated doubt.

Angst and the heavy-handed father

The proliferation in 1992 of violent attacks on minority groups increased my misgivings that once again the heavy-handed father is continuing to exert a malignant influence upon German affairs. I recall when the time came in 1946 to search for the precipitates which caused the Germans to need scapegoats upon whom, under the Nazis, they could unleash pent-up violence, that an accusatory finger was pointed at the German father. No one illuminated to me more this contribution of the domineering German father to the Nazi persecutions than Henry Dicks, the one-time professor of psychiatry at Leeds who, in 1942, was appointed by the government to lead a team of psychiatrists and anthropologists charged with the task of making an objective description of the character of our enemies. I first met Dicks in 1973 after he had written an over-generous review of the book I published in that year, but I do not think that my gratitude to him causes me to overvalue his profound understanding of the German disposition. His findings in the immediate post-war years stemmed first from his considerable work among German prisoners-of-war and then later in his fieldwork as head of the personnel branch of the occupying Control Commission; and those findings have a disturbing relevance today as German mobs rampage in the Turkish ghettos of German cities.

Dicks spelled out in his clinical findings the grave injury to character arising from the emphases on dominance and submission in the authoritarian state and the authoritarian family:

> There is a residue of unexpressed rage or hate which has to be disposed of in the economy of the personality, because energy is indestructible. Deflected by custom and taboo from its primary object – the father and all his symbols in the nation – this hate manifests itself in other ways . . . it provides the urge to bully all those who are weaker – this was the standard approved way, the 'done thing' among Germans . . . Never far below the surface of

the German character is the tendency to psychological projection. Germans have great difficulty in accepting in themselves considerable charges of smouldering hatred against the paternal authority. Therefore, at a time when economic and social conditions had produced a general feeling of dissatisfaction with authorities – now felt to be bad – a revolution was averted by the widest possible use of these projective mechanisms; guilt tension was relieved by being directed on to outside scapegoats who were regarded as the only disturbers of the peace ... This paranoid behaviour could be interpreted in terms of psychopathology as being founded on the stifled wish to be the favoured and irresponsible baby, and on the unconscious rejection of paternal authority and order which they had so overwhelmingly to accept in their own society. The resultant unconscious frustration-rage and its attendant guilt feelings were projected on to the many scapegoat symbols, and led ... to all the heresy hunting.

The scapegoating of non-Germans in the riots of 1992 and 1993 is not simple copycat misconduct of 60 years ago; but there are too many congruences for us to exclude the factor which Dicks identified as of major significance. Identifying the cause of these riots requires us to note the operation of a displaced rage coming from a younger generation feeling, but not daring to acknowledge, a terrible anger against fathers perceived, at least unconsciously, as tyrannical. And the fathers themselves, as the much-criticised tardy response to the rioting by the federal government revealed, are frozen into indecision when witnessing the revolt, for they sense it is directed against them, perhaps even more than against the immigrants: deep down they know the young are repeating what they or their fathers did, and their buried guilts for their past excesses inhibit their present responses.

However, the most inimical consequence of a fatherhood widely felt as oppressive, although not necessarily acknowledged as such, is that it engenders, I believe, the sickness which wracks Germany: it is a disease which presents itself in that peculiar tension, that singular inner agitation, symptoms which are all subsumed under the label *Angst*. No one doubts the ubiquity of *Angst*: it pervades the German culture. Its continued existence is recognised by Germanophobe and Germanophile alike, and in recent years its disturbing presence has again been addressed in essays by Germany's president, by conservative historians like Stürmer, and it has been portrayed by innumerable radical novelists and film-makers. I do not think I am fanciful when I say that these days, whenever I am in Germany, I find myself consciously warding off the infection: one senses so frequently, whether talking to politicians, writers, management consultants or lawyers, the surfacing of an awesome anxiety which oozes into the discourse. In Britain the increasing atomisation of our society, a legacy of the Thatcher ideas, has induced a feeling of isolation and despair among many; and it is fashionable in France to speak of a current nervous condition variously labelled as *morosité*, *désarroi* (helplessness), *chagrin* and *ennui*. With a severe economic recession and more than three million unemployed in both countries, it is not surprising that there should be in Britain and France a loss of national self-esteem which has expression in melancholy. But the panic I found in 1993 in the prosperous city of Munich in response to the belated and first intimations of a recession possessed another quality; and I found that same quality in disconsolate Berlin where the wall of suspicion increasingly divided those from the West and the East. A glance at the shelves of bookshops in both cities could persuade one that Germany's economy was suffering from some terrible terminal illness. Titles like *Can the Germans Still be Saved?* proliferate. Suddenly fearsome apprehensions were abroad. Crises abounded. The German president, Richard von Weizsäcker, articulated the mood: 'Industry and the economy are stuck in a cost and innovation crisis, labour in an employment crisis, the political class in a credibility crisis and society in an orientation crisis.' His comment showed that yet again Germany's *Angst* had been provoked, revealing itself to be no new or transitory phenomenon but one deep-seated and with a long history. It is of a different order to the current reality-based anxieties in France and Britain.

Many and various have been the attempts to explain both the ætiology of the condition, and the responses to it. Stürmer suggests it stems from the insecurities of the Thirty Years War. Others, like Joachim Fest, author of the standard German biography of Hitler, ascribes what he calls *die grosse Angst* (the great fear) to anxiety induced by modernity. The technical-economic process of modernisation came later to Germany than to other countries and was then much faster and more radical in its realisation and as a result, Fest suggests, it aroused more irrational fears and more violent movements of reaction. Again, there are those who attribute the anxiety to the traumas Germans have suffered from their defeats in the twentieth century. I doubt if such external events, terrible as they often were, explain its source; more likely they activated a pre-existing condition which flared up when Germany was being laid to waste, or when it was being subjected to other strains which led the Germans to find confirmed their worst fears that disasters always loom on the horizon.

How strongly the politicians, lawyers and administrators fear being overwhelmed by this *Angst* is shown as they defend the necessity of the myriad laws and regulations which permeate German society: they believe rights and freedoms are at risk unless entrenched in laws, laws that are now, in post-unification Germany, being extended in every detail to the five new *Bundesländer*. We look quizzically at the German network of laws covering broadcasting and banking, education and the health service, the public service and all its ramifications, the multiple relationships between central and regional government, the responsibilities of trade unions and of employers, the armed forces and the rights of the citizen in uniform. No area is excluded and the purpose is to omit nothing. Unapologetically, it has been explained to me that this elaborate framework is an effective antidote to *Angst*; but I am sceptical of these desperate Sisyphean attempts to seal off the *Angst* which so demonstrably continues to seep into the German culture.

And now, if a weighty thesis advanced by Alan Watson is accepted, we are witnessing a new and massive attempt to overcome *Angst* by Germany's committing itself to the European Community. Kohl, Watson rightly points out, has in recent speeches made clear that the German government's Euro-enthusiasm can be seen as an explicit attempt to banish *Angst* from the German psyche. In Edinburgh in 1991 Kohl made clear his belief that Germany's need for European integration was greater than that of any other country. He declared that its geographical position, and its past failed policies of vacillating between East and West, meant that *Das Land der Mitte* can only feel secure if the nation-state itself becomes integrated into a European union. 'In a fundamental strategic sense,' Watson writes, 'the European Community is thus the antidote to her own *Angst*.'

Watson is surely correct in his assertion that the motivation behind the eagerness of the Germans for greater European integration is flight from *Angst*; but, although we and continental Europe are the temporary beneficiaries of this German commitment, Germans are in my view misdiagnosing their own condition. Encirclement may indeed have exacerbated the condition but I doubt if it is the cause of *Angst*. Indeed, as Kohl's speeches reveal, despite the collapse of the Soviet Union which has dramatically diminished external threats, still the *Angst* remains. And that, I believe, is because the threats causing this all-pervading anxiety come primarily from an inner not an external world: it is a world which the Germans appear to fear exploring. Even as in

elaborate protest marches and candlelit vigils, Germany affirms its
anti-racism but will not dare to peer into the abyss where the cauldron
of racism unceasingly simmers, so similarly it seems ready to cling to
European institutions rather than turn round and squarely face the
pursuing *Angst*.

The collective behaviour of the Germans, blessed with economic
success and freed by the end of the Cold War from the possibility of
serious external attack, yet still engulfed in these deeply felt anxieties,
demonstrably not reality-based, appears to be akin to that of an
individual enduring an anxiety neurosis. The clinical picture of such a
sufferer often reveals that his illness – his overwhelming feelings of
undefined vague anxieties that appear to have no objective cause –
comes from his attempt to ward off the threat of unacceptable
instinctual demands whose existence he is desperately seeking to deny:
he is attempting to keep these instinctual demands out of consciousness, to repress them.

Freud throughout his whole lifetime was engaged in exploring the
sources of the *Angst* which he found in so many complex forms in his
patients; and since he concluded that repression was the most
significant operant in producing neurotic anxiety, we are entitled to
ask, when we see its envelopment of German culture, what are the
libidinal demands which the Germans are so desperately anxious to
repress. If *Angst* follows upon repression, and if, as Freud explains,
'The essence of repression lies simply in turning something away and
keeping it at a distance from the conscious', from what is Germany
fleeing as it rushes into the European Community? What is it that it is
so strenuously attempting to distance?

Freud provides us with a signpost to the answers to our questions.
Having placed the responsibility for *Angst* upon the process of
repression, he elaborates: 'It is the idea which is subjected to repression
and which may be distorted to the point of being unrecognisable: but
its quota of affect is regularly transformed into anxiety – and this is so
whatever the nature of the affect may be, whether it is aggressiveness or
love.'

Taking Freud's hint, we are thus bound to ask what prohibited idea
have the Germans to repress, and what massive quota of emotional
energy, aggressive and sexual, is then so transformed that it becomes
this clinging incubus of *Angst* which Germany cannot dislodge.

The answers to our questions are, I believe, to be found within the
turmoil of our earliest childhood. Freud has taught us that very early in
our lives the time comes when we must outlaw our desires, and

suppress our aggression. The Oedipal wish to possess the mother and supplant the rival father is the impossible desire which, in some way, we must relinquish. The incestuous choice must be forfeited for, if pursued, we fear there will be a terrible retaliation. Every boy has to pass through this Oedipal phase when he concentrates his sexual wishes upon his mother and develops hostile impulses against his rival father; but how we live through and later emerge from this rite of passage depends very substantially upon the structure of the family system within which the drama is enacted. The emphases in classical psychoanalysis have left us with an impression that this is a dramatic and conflict-ridden phase, a time when the aspiration of the child crumbles under the impact of retaliatory castration fears; but this may only be part of the story. It may well be, as Heinz Kohut has postulated, that if parents respond positively to the primary affectionate and competitive assertiveness of the child, then the Oedipal phase need not be wholly dominated by unassimilated lust and hostility. Contrariwise, what is certain, however, is that if the household is ruled by a domineering unempathic father, then it is inevitable that all the child's smouldering hostility, stirred by the father's provocations, will flare up.

The extent of those provocations in Germany is awesome; we have in recent years become acutely aware of the extent of sexual abuse in Britain by fathers upon their own children. But the widespread brutality within the German family is on a different scale. In January 1994 *The Times* reported that each year in Germany some 300,000 children are sexually abused and 20,000–30,000 are taken to hospital after being beaten up by members of the family. Few of these cases are referred to the police. The indifference of the general public to the behaviour of brutal fathers to their children was demonstrated in 1993 when the Child Protection League in Hamburg carried out an experiment playing a tape recorded of a screaming child and a shouting father through an open widow; 989 people passed by but only four telephoned the police.

The Justice Ministry are now responding in turn to the scandalous problems by, in effect, acting as punitive surrogate fathers; punishment is to be heaped upon punishment. Draft regulations were drawn up in February 1994 enabling parents to be gaoled for physical punishment if it is administered above a certain level; children can be hit on the bottom but not on the face, although smacking children to alert them to 'potential danger to body or limb' – such as crossing the road at the wrong time – will be permitted. The notion that the deep-seated familial problems of so many Germans can be contained by prison sentences is, of course, psychologically naive; but the very nature of the authoritarian reponse to the problems reveals how the bureaucrats of the Justice Ministry, like the beaten children they affect to protect, are victims of the domineering and often brutal father who is still presiding over so many of the family units within Germany.

It is, of course, within such an authoritarian family that the hostility of the child will be more intense, and consequently his fear of punishment will be greater; and it is that specific anxiety, the fear of his own hostility which will attract terrible retaliation, that has, by such a child, to be massively repressed. But that specific anxiety, although banished from consciousness, can and does emerge in other disguises: and although the hostility may lie buried and the threat of retaliatory punishment may long since have become obsolescent, still in an adult who has suffered a terrorist childhood it may emerge as free-floating general apprehensiveness, ready to attach itself in the form of what Freud called 'expectant anxiety' to any possibility that may freshly arise; and such expectant anxiety is often a guarantee it will arise. If we fearfully wait for ever for the lightning to strike, be assured it will. For, as Kierkegaard has taught us, in a psychological sense, what a man most dreads he yearns for, and what one fears one desires. Fear of death itself, the unbearable tension of expectation, can become a motive for suicide, and fear of pregnancy can become a motive for conception. And when the realisation of the feared event occurs, so often there is an over-reaction. In many ways we can interpret the extraordinary panic-stricken reaction of Germany to the tragic distribution of HIV-infected blood in November 1993 in Kierkegaard's terms. The lightning had struck and the old fear that pure German *βlut* could become tainted was now realised, and with that realisation came an extraordinary, wildly undirected panic. The Germans so often are ready to misinterpret the warning signals of anxiety which reach them as coming wholly from the external world, whereas in truth they often emanate too from their own buried internalised drives; this is akin to what happens to an individual afflicted with a typical anxiety neurosis. And this surely is the quality of the *Angst* which is so pervasive in Germany.

When external events prompt reality-based anxieties, irrational anxieties also flare up and wild panic can result. Germany at present is facing no transitory recession; its pride in its economic success is being punctured as increasingly it appreciates that there are serious structural problems shaping its manufacturing base, problems that are unlikely to be resolved without creating huge unemployment. The political response to this threat shows distinct signs of panic: there is much talk of the creation, after the coming elections, of a Grand Alliance of the main political parties to put through painful measures; but I have found among Germans whose judgement I respect a view that such an alliance could result in fierce extra-parliamentary opposition that, denied voice in the Reichstag, would be heard on the streets. Those Germanophiles who present a picture of contemporary Germany as a remarkably stable land underestimate the force of the underlying *Angst*. When difficult political decisions have to be made, as they have to be to deal with Germany's economic problems, *Angst* can become a bad adviser.

Some possibilities are, I believe, open to Germany to master and control its *Angst*. If there are those who would mock at the possibility of a substantial modification in the German family system, which would accord more rights to women and children, and within which love not fear would yield discipline, then I would stress the extraordinary changes, in my lifetime, in Britain's family structure which have brought about democratisation of the family, with all its benefits and travails. Germany is an open society with informed minority groups potentially able to create a more relaxed ethos, making it more likely that the homestead provides emotional security, not *Angst*; but this will never come about if the cause of the prevailing anxiety is sought only in external, not inner, circumstance.

To hope that Germany should cease to be so ill at ease with itself is not an unselfish aspiration. It bodes ill for the future of the European Community if our most significant partner is riddled with anxiety. The anxious nation, like a neurotically anxious individual, can become almost paranoiac, as dangers are perceived which do not exist or when minor hazards are regarded as formidable and menacing. Unreal anxiety can prompt unnecessary aggression; it can also sometimes inhibit decision-making, as choices are seen as threats, not options. More, it can be extraordinarily infectious, disturbing others and subverting their confidence. One anxious company director can unnerve a whole board; and one neurotically anxious individual in a family can often throw a whole family into disarrray. The integration of Europe is a complex task: it will require continued negotiation and innumerable consensus decisions, and there is no certainty that the task will be completed. If Germany cannot quench its *Angst*, it will export it; then indeed the Community may be lost, for all Europe could suffer an untreatable nervous breakdown.

PART VII

Private Travail, Public Faces

Temperament and decision-making

During my years in the Commons I had no serious disputes with my spirited and often opinionated constituency party members, excepting one. My decision to defy the party whips and vote in 1972 for entry into Europe stirred up emotions which led the constituency members to threaten me with de-selection at the next election. In vain I pleaded with them to remember the internationalism of the founding fathers of the Labour movements, and fruitlessly I adumbrated the advantages that entry would bring to almost all the industries sited within the constituency; the more foolproof my arguments, the more infuriated did they become at my stubborn insistence that my decision was irrevocable. With mixed feelings, they had tolerated many of what were then considered as my eccentric crusading campaigns, but this was too much for them: evidently buggery was one matter, Krauts and wops another.

Twenty years later, in 1992, I attended a reunion dinner of those, in all parties, who, by their historic vote, had taken Britain into Europe. There were not a few absentees, death or disablement barred their presence; and some of the Labour MPs who had been in the fateful lobby had the sulks, not wishing now to consort with their party political opponents. It was difficult on that occasion not to muse upon the unhappy tensions my vote had caused in my constituency, and not to reflect, then, as now in the renewed European debate, how temperament plays as great a part in determining our attitude to Europe as any assembly of facts and statistics claimed to favour our particular viewpoint.

More determinant than all the logical arguments presented by Edward Heath to the Commons and the nation to persuade us to permit him to lead us into Europe was his own temperament. At that reunion dinner this was yet again brought home to me. As I stood at the pre-dinner reception, reminiscing with some of my erstwhile colleagues, I became aware that Heath, who had entered the room, was staring at me evidently waiting to catch my eye. He was standing alone having as he has a rare talent for creating an empty space around himself. His diffidence is notorious but on this commemoration evening he advanced towards me, effusively and warmly greeting me. It may be he was conveying to me his approval of my hostile psychobiography of Margaret Thatcher, his arch enemy, over whom, with stamina and courage, he had eventually triumphed; but rather, I think, he was engagingly buoyant because he recalled his great battles when some of his most fierce political opponents, like myself, came to his aid, enabling him to recapture some of the joy which only fulfilment of deepest needs can bring; and when he took us into Europe it was such a personal need that was being met.

In the 1970s, when political battles raged around the issue of our entry into Europe, I then commented how individual temperaments, like those of Heath and Enoch Powell, not objective assessments, were playing a dangerous part in our decision-making. That caveat remains in place today and the debate about the Maastricht Treaty has again revealed how politicians can use public events as a screen upon which to project private travail; and how the irrational anxiety of a handful of leading politicians can shape a nation's major political choice. Provoked now by the growth of Germany's economic power and by the all too visible negative aspects of contemporary Germany, those anxieties swirl around their public pronouncements. Thatcher and Tebbit light up the worst prejudices, while Heath seeks to quench any apprehensions by extravagant denials of any of Germany's ills.

All of us to some extent mix up external reality with our own internal world: we unwisely assume our reactions and attitudes at any one time are proper and trustworthy indicators of what is actually happening in the external world. But, in my political experience, no debate has revealed more the distortions of politicians' inner life than the arguments frequently offered by the protagonists as, according to temperament, highly selected facts are advanced to justify their differing points of view; and it follows, therefore, that too often their conclusions are not reality-based. Indeed, few issues in my lifetime have precipitated such regressive adjustments to reality than the call to leave our Motherland and take the journey into Europe. The external facts upon which Euro-sceptics and Euro-enthusiasts make their judgements are immutable; it is to their inner lives that I believe we must address ourselves if we are to understand what causes them to hold such passionate views, and to form such differing judgements that they are ready to divide their own parties, to desert their usual well-determined allegiances, and to form alliances with their political opponents.

Since one presumes to insist that a prerequisite for a successful

European Community is a Germany prepared to have insights into its own predicaments, we cannot, without being humbugs, shirk a self-examination of our own concern which expresses itself in this long drawn out anguish over our own identity, and causes us continuously to vacillate between the belief that we lose it or rediscover it within a European community. And, as in Germany, faced with neurotic immobilisation inhibiting decision-making, a search for external reasons is made to explain our waverings. Even as Germany would seek to avoid probing the German psyche by attempting to explain its hesitations in historical and geographical terms as the 'land in the middle', so some attempts have been made to explain our hesitations and stumblings in terms of our history as an island people. One of the most persuasive exponents of this thesis is Giles Radice, the title of whose recent work *Offshore* tells us succinctly of his diagnosis. Radice, a Euro-enthusiast, was a good colleague whose essential probity I always respected; his fault, I found, was to be too trusting towards undeserving fellow MPs, and here again, in accordance with his habit, he warns us against being prisoners of our recent past and urges us to believe that we can now have a well-founded confidence in the new thriving democratic Germany.

No one can dispute his view that Britain's geographical position on the periphery of Europe, and its history, unlike that of the other eleven members of the European Community, of never having experienced serious military defeat, occupation, civil war or revolution for at least two hundred years, contribute towards an insular culture and a disdain for the continental, a disdain springing from still-prevailing delusions of imperialist grandeur. But this is only part of the story. It leaves unanswered why so many sophisticated protagonists, well able to take into account the dangers of nostalgia, and often too keenly aware of recent British history to permit themselves the indulgences of an old-fashioned jingoism, nevertheless have so little enthusiasm for the European cause. Radice's view may suffice to explain the reactions of gutter politicians like Tebbit, or vulgar populists like Teddy Taylor; it does not explain the responses of men like Michael Foot and Tony Benn or the elegantly crafted intellectual criticisms of John Biffen. Nor does it explain the emphatic Europeanism to be found among many Conservative MPs who on other issues, like immigration policy or capital punishment, would be ready to take up near-Neanderthal stances.

Margaret Thatcher fell because her anti-Europeanism could not be tolerated by her pro-European ministers. The Tory MPs in the leadership contest which led to her fall split down the middle; and the main cause of the division was their differing responses to Europe. All these men and women had been subject to the same heritage culture of which Radice writes, and that shaping, and their interpretation of the past and present had hitherto brought them all together within a broad political consensus. But on Europe that agreement could not be maintained. All that has occurred in the Maastricht debate is, for me, just additional corroboration of my expressed written opinion made twenty years ago that the European debate had, from its commencement, been enveloped in a miasma of very personal prejudice; predilections, formed by unconscious needs reflecting the distortions of individual inner life of the participants, govern the debate. And much of the continued parliamentary tensions continue because whips have sought to drive members into lobbies quite alien to their temperaments. To ensure that our judgements be less clouded, we need to seek the source of these differing temperaments; and that means going back, to begin at our beginnings.

Ocnophils and philobats

Once upon a time, for all of us, when first we were born, we had the bliss of what some psychoanalysts describe as 'primary love'. Primary love is the relationship in which only one partner, the babe, may have demands and claims; the other partners, the mother and, through her, the whole environment, must have no interests, no wishes, no demands of their own. There is a complete identity of wishes and satisfactions; the environment must be in complete harmony with the demands and enjoyments of the babe. Such a paradisiacal condition does not last for long; only too soon the discovery that firm and independent objects exist destroys the babe's illusory world. From then on, the existence of external objects, resistant, aggressive and with ambivalent qualities, must be painfully accepted. No longer can the babe have the primitive relationship with the world which he had experienced as structure-less, friendly expanses. Now he has to acknowledge that vitally important parts of his world are both independent and inscrutable, creating a structure; from now on, the world will consist of firm, resistant objects and of spaces separating them.

Thirty-five years ago a distinguished president of the British Psycho-Analytic Society, Michael Balint, claimed that, although there are many gradations and shades, there are two basic ways in which people

respond to this traumatic discovery. One is to create a world based on
the fantasy that firm objects are reliable and kind, that they will always
be there when one needs them and that they never will mind, and
never resent, being used for support. Those who so clingingly respond
he described as 'ocnophilic' types. But there is, too, another possible
basic reaction to the discovery that the world does not belong to me. It
is to attempt to re-create the lost world which goes back to life prior to
the traumatic experience when objects emerge and destroy the primal
harmony of the limitless, contour-less expanses. For these people,
described by Balint as 'philobats', objects are felt as dangerous and
unpredictable hazards. A philobatic world consists of friendly expanses
dotted with these menacing objects. Safety lies among the expanses;
and objects, above all people, are hazardous, to be vigilantly observed
and decidedly kept at a distance.

The attitude of our politicians displayed in the European debate
adds a surfeit of supportive clinical material to Balint's shrewd and
important contribution to the typology of character. The two extreme
types, ocnophil and philobat, I have seen for decades locked at
Westminster in an unselfconscious struggle as they plead for or against
entry into Europe. The first group, possessed of ocnophil bias, the
virulent Euro-sceptics, clings to objects and cannot feel safe except
when at home or in familiar surroundings; the second group resents
ties and is thrilled and excited while journeying from place to place,
and finds pleasure and pride in the skills which enable it to do so.
Despite all the purportedly balanced views, the arguments so often are
but reflections of the distortions of these inner lives of the participants.
For, of course, the original object to which both ocnophil and philobat
are relating is the mother, or part of her. The ocnophil clings, the
philobat distances; each in his way is attempting to deal with the loved
and hated mother, adjusting himself to his first anguishing discovery
that she and her attributes are separate, independent of him.

Those who may be sceptical of the existence of these early infantile
adjustments to reality, and their ultimate invasion into adult political
thinking, should glance at the games their children play. Rounders,
musical chairs, hide-and-seek, oranges and lemons, and many of the
computer games, all show the same design reminiscent of our earliest
strivings to cope with the discovery of the external world, all revealing
our earlier hesitant advances and retreats in and out of the primary
safe but illusory bliss. In the playground the child creates a zone of
security, the 'home', the 'house'; outside the home is a catcher, a
chaser, a seeker. The other players, leaving the zone of security, the

'home', accepting exposure to danger voluntarily in the confident hope that somehow or other they will reach security again. And when we are, seemingly, grown up, it is not only vicariously, watching cricket at Lords, when runs can usually only be scored by leaving the safe zone within the significantly named crease, that we re-enact our earlier humbling to master our environment.

Some adults show their philobatic dispositions more obviously than may be revealed by a politician with the same bias. There are those, like pilots, who feel safer in the skies than clinging to home, those who ski with death on the slopes or drive fast with great stimulation on the road. For these men, danger and fear are felt only when an object has to be negotiated; the pilot has to take off or land, the skier negotiates trees and crevasses, the driver to mind other cars. Their philobatic world is literally one of search for the friendly expanses and wariness towards all firm objects. It is in fact the world of the acrobat; his swivels and feelings of security come when he is not bound to land, not tied to mother earth. Up he goes, mastering the fixed and flying trapeze, the unsupported ladder. And all of us, calling up our feelings from our earliest beginnings, become yet more excited or fearful as we observe the distance from the ground increasing, and as the precariousness of his attachment to some firm structure – which in the last analysis means the earth – becomes even greater.

But it is to be noted that there is a marked ambivalence to mother earth. Always, extravagantly, the acrobat must assert his independence, always display flagrantly the symbol of a never-flagging, erect, potent penis. Narcissistically holding on to his pole, magically reinforcing his own potency and confidence, the acrobat tightrope walker performs his feats, defying desperately the attraction, the gravity pull of the earth. The skier leaps from the slopes, holding quite close his phallic stick. The pilot rides high up with his joy-stick. The earth will, they hope, be forgiving and receive them back in the end, but she is dangerous and destructive and an irresistible attraction which, if yielded to, will mean, to them, destruction.

Extreme philobats, no doubt, can in sports, climbing mountains or in speed-boats, harmlessly indulge themselves, and milder ones can make good pilots although there are hazards – for passengers clearly cannot afford to have a pilot wrestling with too compulsive an attraction to the ground. The philobats may behave like those dare-devil motorists, happy and accident-free on the highway, who repeatedly scrape their cars as they enter their own garages. But in politics such men need to be checked; those who have in adulthood worked through insufficiently their earlier problems of adjustment to the external world, and often show it by their incapacity to relate appropriately to their mothers, and thus to all womankind, may be unable to conduct their reality-testing with the needed objectivity to which an electorate is entitled.

Heath and the friendly expanses

Edward Heath, who can legitimately claim primary responsibility for taking Britain into Europe, presents a rare catalogue of the traits which Balint attributed to the extreme philobat; and Enoch Powell, the most fierce and eloquent opponent of our entry, no less richly illustrates the clinical picture of the extreme ocnophil as delineated by the psychoanalyst. Warned by the traits of both these men, we may temper many of the extravagances with which, according to our own typology, we, as Euro-sceptics or Euro-enthusiasts, lace our arguments; and, in particular, it may cause us to modify the assessment, over-optimistic or pessimistic, that we make of joining hands with Germany in the project of re-shaping Europe and its institutions.

As Powell prophesies the doom awaiting us if we become increasingly integrated with Europe, so Heath, the unremitting propagandist, never flags as he urges us to quit home waters and sail into areas which are, necessarily, unknown; for he has a complete assurance that we shall arrive, and return when we wish, safely. Indeed, it is his certainty on the complex European issues that is most disturbing, even to those of us who have favoured entry. It is the self-same certainty which has enabled him to stand up to his critics in the Commons, swatting like flies the puny, empty-headed young Tory MPs who presume to interrupt him, and who, when rebuffed by his ripostes, seem to fade away into the distance, for Heath is a master of distancing all who cross his path.

He keeps his distance from women and, indeed, from men. When he was younger he escaped from land to sea and sailed his well-publicised yacht, demonstrating his masculine prowess; he conducts his choir, or an orchestra, wielding the phallic baton, even as he enjoyed himself as Chief Whip. In negotiation with foreign bodies, he shows great skill, a particular capacity that appears to give yet greater correspondence between his personality and the disposition of the philobat delineated by Balint. Such a display of skills is to be expected; for those who, as babies, react in an extreme philobatic manner to the discovery that the harmonious mix-up of the primitive attitude to the world has ended, do so, as Balint describes, 'by developing exaggerated egocathexes leading to an undue preoccupation with the functions of ego, the personal skills, and neglecting the development of proper, intimate and lasting object relationships'. That his relationships lack intimacy is not only testified by his evident celibacy but in the complaints that I have heard from more than one socially fluent former Tory minister who have told me how, outside the political matter in hand, they are reduced to silence in their attempts to conduct a lengthy conversation with him. My short conversations with him, as after a shared radio interview or in the Hansard room correcting the draft typescripts of speeches which we had just delivered, have always been directed to the subject which momentarily brought us together; he is courteous and careful not to permit any small talk that may lead to the personal.

In a rare glimpse of his fantasy life, Heath has revealed how incapable he is of moving towards any real relationship with others. 'I've always had a hidden wish, a frustrated desire, to run a hotel,' he once said. It is a sad dream, corroborating his evident incapacity to enjoy developed personal relations. The hotel-keeper greets his guest with the ever-present and meaningless smile, like Heath's fixed smile, which is charming, pleasant and correct, but distant; and, of course, all who come, soon go; ships that pass in the night. Not for Heath the dream of an anchored home, wife and children; only the impersonal hotel over which he presides and where undemanding transitory acquaintances, but not relationships, are formed. The ever-perceptive Anthony Howard has recently pointed out what he regards as the 'most singular factor about Heath is that not until the age of 47, when he had already been earning a cabinet minister's salary for four years, did he betray the slightest desire to have a home of his own. Until then, he had been quite content to live in a "broom cupboard" to which few, if any, of his friends were ever invited.' Heath's fate is indeed not to embrace a lover in a home; rather, his destiny is to hug himself, as he often does on the front bench below the gangway, and then at piano or organ it is his pleasure to play all alone.

Heath evidently distances himself from others in order to avoid the specific danger of narcissistic injury. When, however, he is wounded, his narcissistic rage is boundless and never-ending; against all the odds, and often battling against a tide of vituperation and calumny, he was unmoved as for years he maintained his vendetta against Thatcher until, in the end, he contemptuously saw her off to the Lords while he remained authoritatively in place in the Commons. It is impossible to withhold admiration from him for this courage, which demonstrated how his philobatic traits can, functionally, sometimes work for the benefit of the nation.

Now, more recently, he has scorned John Major's two-feet-on-the-earth 'back to basics' policy. Nothing was more likely to arouse Heath's ire than a call to go back rather than soar forward. Angrily he has asked: '. . . who on earth could have landed us with a cry of "Back to basics"? . . . No one has ever captained an advance by shouting to his troops "Back, boys, back". There is nothing for the future in that.' His criticism of Major was well-founded on facts; but Heath, in making his onslaught, was also being propelled by his temperament which compels him to regard as menacing any policy which he interprets as mundane, as earth-bound.

However, extreme philobatism does not always work benignly; nor, as in Heath's case, is the philobatism necessarily confined to the quirks and idiosyncrasies of a remote social life or personal leisure hobbies and interests. The political danger lies in the philobat's supreme and unjustifiable confidence which stems from his determination to believe in his 'friendly expanses'. He can regress in his thinking to the primitive state where the world lacked unpredictable outside objects and consisted only of kindly substances which constituted these friendly expanses; and in his fantasy life, he believes those friendly expanses will encompass his safety as a yacht in a kind sea, as a mother holds her babe, as perhaps our ancestors in phylogenesis were safely held by the ocean, or as we ourselves were held by the amniotic fluid in our mothers' wombs. Thus he is always in danger of not making objective assessments on the basis of the realities of a situation, but on the denial of the evidence of any untrustworthy, unreliable and treacherous objects. The philobat can lapse into the firm, but often unjustifiable, belief that his skills will be sufficient to cope with all dangers, that it is up to him to conquer the world and, indeed, that the world will not mind being conquered. The philobatic world is not the world of the potent; it is the world of the omnipotent.

It must be acknowledged that the philobat can develop considerable skills; he needs them to get away from his undesirable objects. He sometimes achieves a consummate aptitude in his attempts to re-create something of the harmony that existed before the discovery of separate objects. But along with his often impressive skills, shown in his sustained efforts and his painstaking attention to detail, there is the self-abandonment to a fantasy, presuming friendliness where none exists and imposing optimistic views when none are justified. He expects the world to 'click in' with him; he does not make the needed realistic adjustment to the world.

In the House, Heath's attitudes have often been interpreted as rigid and arrogant; these are, however, but symptoms of his philobatic bias leading him to believe in his omnipotent capacity to command the world to come to heel. But the world is not so pliant. His philobatic skills certainly helped us to go into Europe; but his excursions into China and his meetings with Saddam, although leading to the release of hostages, can hardly be regarded as great triumphs, and his bland assumptions when he was Prime Minister that his industrial relations policy would not be resisted by the then powerful unions, despite warnings to the contrary, led to disastrous strikes, and cost him his premiership. His real yearning, however, was not to regain the premiership and to preside over domestic policies; his deepest wish became abundantly clear when in 1990 he spoke enviously to the Queen of James Baker, the then US Secretary of State: 'Lots of people would like to be Secretary of State,' he said. He wished to be like Baker, away from home, roving around the world armed with the seeming omnipotence of an all-powerful State.

It was, however, in his participation in the Brandt Report, that his strengths and weaknesses as an extreme philobat were well revealed. His readiness to serve on that multinational Commission, which was charged with the task of creating a programme for world survival on the basis of North-South collaboration, sprang from his temperament as much as from his concerns for the future. The text of the report that emerged was largely drafted under the supervision of Heath. It was replete with noble aspirations, facing global challenges with global responses; but the real world is cruel, and Heath's belief in his 'friendly expanses' misled him as he optimistically minimised the many obstacles preventing the fulfilment of his idealistic programming. Heath's philobatic traits can leave him unable to acknowledge what is tractable and what is not; and he carries this self-same attitude into the European debate where, predictably sanguine, he denies contemporary Germany has any special characteristic that threatens the success of the European Community.

Powell and the spiritual motherland

Even as Heath reveals himself in the European debate as the most extravagant of philobats, so, of all the anti-European British politicians, Enoch Powell shows himself as the most persuasive of ocnophils. The charge of reductionism could well be sustained if we wish to explain their respective attitudes simply in terms of a typology, however sophisticated. But how overriding this tug of temperament can be is particularly seen in Powell's history, for the presently tenacious patriot, as a young man, was wholly seduced by a non-English culture. Indeed, in his teens and early twenties the intellectually precocious young man was a displaced person: he lived his spiritual life at Cambridge as a German.

Powell is five years older than I am; but as a provincial lad in my very early teens, I was profoundly conscious, even if I was attracted to German literature, of the increasing menace of the rise of Nazism in Germany, and held on to my hopes that the other Germany would still assert itself. The rise of Nazism, however, passed over Powell's head as he became increasingly intoxicated with German *Kultur*; and this despite the fact that the scholarships he gained enabled him, as an undergraduate, to make numerous forays into Germany which, one of his biographers tells us, had become his 'beloved country'.

Powell's awakening only came when the Nazi regime was already well ensconced; then, when the Nazi gangsters fell out, and Röhm and other homosexual Brownshirt leaders were slaughtered, suddenly he woke up, too late in the day, to the naked brutality of the regime. Why this particular assault upon the homosexual leadership acted as the catalyst could lead to not a few speculative musings; but what is certain is that for Powell the event was shattering. He has, in characteristically histrionic tones, told of his dismay:

> I can still remember today how I sat for hours in a state of shock, shock which you experience when, around you, you see the debris of a beautiful building in which you have lived for a long time . . . so it had all been illusion, all fantasy, all a self-created myth. Music, philosophy, poetry, science and the language itself – everything was demolished, broken to bits on the cliffs of a monstrous reality. The spiritual homeland had not been a spiritual homeland after all . . . Overnight my spiritual homeland had disappeared and I was left only with my geographical homeland.

And from then, having clung so passionately to Germany, his choice of object changed; and he was to cling, no less passionately, during all his lifetime to his 'geographical homeland' but, although his Damascus conversion, demonstrated by his determination to don uniform and fight the Germans the moment war broke out, seems complete, it is not so. An ocnophil does not easily release his hold; and from his Germany he tore away, holding on to it firmly, so much of German philosophical extravagances that they pervade all his forceful speechmaking. There, one will always hear apocalyptic warnings, fraught with nervous overtones, calls for regeneration, and demands for recognition of race. The language may be English, the format may be classical, but the idiom is German. The House would listen to him, fascinated but unconvinced by his eloquence: this man, professing more than any other member the quiddity of his Englishness, was felt to be an alien intruder; and although the members may not have understood the reasons for their disquiet, it surely stemmed from the German metaphysics which envelop his persuasions. And so he has continued into his old age: at 80, he was revelling in a nostalgic address telling of his early love for German philosophy in a address to the Wagner Society. It was inevitable in the excessively pragmatic English House of Commons that he was marked out as an outsider; early in my parliamentary life I realised Powell was far more an outsider in the House than I was as a Welsh Jew.

His flight, in his prolonged adolescence, into German metaphysics, was perhaps his alternative to flight to excessive religiosity which so often marks out young men yet to come to terms with their own sexuality; for he declared himself a committed atheist, and doubtless affirmed his disbelief with his customary display of logic. God, the Father, he had to repudiate, for Powell could not accept he was born into a Kingdom but, as one of his admiring biographers tells us, he was born into a family which was 'a republic of free persons'. His upbringing left him unable to tolerate any father surrogate. God was relegated even as within the family's republic father had been demoted to a decidedly minimal role while Enoch's mother shaped the child into a mental athlete, and to that task she gave up her school-teaching and made the child her single pupil. All Powell's biographers agree there was an intense alliance between the young Enoch and his mother. It is a legitimate inference to believe that from the earliest beginnings mother and child clung to each other: the ocnophilic habits of mind thus established were to endure for ever.

His temporary turning away, during his adolescent years, from his motherland to the 'spiritual' land of Germany reveals how hard was his battle – singularly tied as he was to his mother – to overcome the unconscious incestuous tugs that often operate when, with the onset of puberty, the patterns of our first years, our Oedipal years, are reactivated. Long before Freud, Byron in his *Don Juan* noted how the young Juan, stirred by the sexuality assailing him, turned for protection to metaphysics:

> And turned, without perceiving his condition
> . . . and concluded into a metaphysician.
> In thoughts like these true wisdom may discern
> Longing sublime, and aspirations high,
> Which some are born with, but the most part learn
> To plague themselves withal, they know not why:
> 'Twas strange that one so young should thus concern
> His brain about the action of the sky;
> If *you* think 'twas philosophy that this did,
> I can't help thinking puberty assisted.

For Don Juan, metaphysics was an inadequate shield against his unconscious incestuous desires; he ran away from them into a frantic promiscuity. Powell has resolved his dilemma in an alternative mode, by a distaste for the flesh expressed in his publicly yearning to be a monk. His fear of sexuality leads him to be frightened of an imagined potency of blacks; and he is forever citing the statistics which reveal population increases telling of the copulation practices of the immigrant community. For twenty years in the Commons, although, in debates, addressing each other through the Speaker when we agreed or disagreed, outside the Chamber we passed each other by, never speaking to each other. He could never forgive me for the laughter I caused in the House when, after his notorious race speech I said that if there were less eunuchs in the land, there would be less Enochs.

But neither his austerity, nor his hold on remnants of German metaphysics, could in themselves be enough to leave him feeling unthreatened by his dangerous ocnophil tendencies: somehow his attachment to his mother had to be mortified even as it was acknowledged. His struggle to resolve that conundrum has left him the most articulate of anti-Europeans; for heroically, his mother-love has been displaced, with a passion telling of its source, to the motherland which must remain undefiled by foreign influences.

Under this compulsion to hold tight to mother surrogates, felt by him to be replicas of Britain, his political judgement deserts him. His romantic imperialism was part of this behavioural pattern. His language when he wrote of India was of a lovesick swain: 'India claimed me almost from the first moment there. I started to love and learn thirstily. I bought and read omnivorously anything about India I could lay hands on.' There are more than shades of the instructing teacher-mother as he learns from India and practises Urdu among Indian villagers. His love, of course, was blind. His failure to see the realities of the situation is clearly revealed in the crazy plan which he put to Churchill in 1946 to take and hold tightly India with ten divisions. Some of his biographers suggest that the tale of this desperate plan is a canard, but Rab Butler, not given to such fantasising, always insisted on its existence, and his affirmations have the ring of truth. Powell could not bear to see his loved one wrenched from him, and fumed against the granting of Independence, but when he had mourned his loss, he saw it as it was. He was helped by psychoanalytical insight to free himself from his fixation to Empire and India, for he has written: 'So the psychoanalysis through which lies the cure for Britain's sickness has to be twofold: first, we must identify and overcome the mythology of the late Victorian Empire; then, we must penetrate to deeper levels and eradicate the fixation with India from our subconscious.' But this attempt, at one remove, to examine his own motivation, is incomplete. It gave him the intellectual courage to discard his whole concept of a world role for Britain but then, when he began to re-think Britain's national status, he still remained locked into his compelling need: to cling to some mother surrogate. The boundless passion he had bestowed on the British Empire was now concentrated upon Britain itself, and from then on he was to devote a lifetime to defending his motherland with a xenophobic fervour.

The bonds between him and his motherland must never be slackened; only when he was so held could he feel safe. No political sacrifice, therefore, would be too great to ensure that the ties remain in place; and no one is better instructed in the necessary sacrificial rites than Powell. His oft expressed personal regret that, unlike some of his comrades, he was not killed during the war, have a true Germanic ring resonant of a belief that only death brings victory and redemption; but Powell's attraction to sacrifice does not lie in pagan myth but in Christian theology. God the Father had not proved tolerable to Powell as a young man and in his atheism he denied Him priority, as his own father had been denied. But God the Son was to prove another matter entirely. The isolation of the only child growing up in a literary, non-gregarious family, overvaluing the word and seemingly deficient in human relationships outside the books, could not be sustained. The atheist must walk and die in his own footsteps, his eternity limited to his work and his children; Powell lacked the resource to maintain that position. He turned to, and identified himself with, his Saviour, ready to emulate his Redeemer and, in 1974, to sacrifice himself for what he believed to be the true word.

The political sophisticates who were astonished by Powell's renunciation of his safe seat and power base at Wolverhampton, rather than fight under what he believed to be Heath's false banner of the European Community, did not understand their man. He was acting out his needs; and lacking, as ever, subtlety or pretence, he made this explicit to those attuned to listen. After briefly announcing his decision not to participate in what he described as 'a fraudulent election', he remained silent for two weeks except for one public intervention, and that was his little-noticed sermon entitled The Meaning of Christian Sacrifice: the Road to Calvary. Powell was indeed, with masochistic relish, on his way, enjoying every moment at the stations of his cross. To those who accused him of being a Judas he retorted, with full justification, that he received no reward for his services. His critics misunderstood his role; his mimesis was no fringe part in the drama. His grandiosity, always teetering on the edge of omnipotence, insisted he was the central figure and as such he endured his political crucifixion.

He did not, however, suffer his martyrdom in silence. He saw Britain's marriage to the European Community as hideous miscegenation, a fate worse than death. From his political death-bed he taunted the British with having enjoyed the 'rape of their national and parliamentary independence'. His anguish sprang from the sight of seeing the Mother of Parliaments, which he has always absurdly idealised, devalued by an association with foreign breeds. From his attachment to Parliament came his confidence and mastery; now Brussels was to snatch from him his sustaining Commons. And, with rage, he quivered with every ocnophil strand of his being.

His has been a noble rage. Only John Biffen who, in gesture and presentation, so strongly identifies with him, has in the 1993 Maastricht debates, matched his eloquent anger. Most of the rest of the nit-picking crew opposing the Treaty are mean men, timid and provincial, ever-fearful of venturing from home, unworthy heirs of Britain's greatest ocnophil politician. They are like the comic, not the tragic, characters often depicted in innumerable scenes in plays, novels and films, turning desperately to something felt to be very precious, who save it from all sorts of perils; finally they arrive in comparative safety, examine it at close quarters and discover that the precious object which was to give them security for ever is really worthless. We do not respect such characters for their foolishness, for we sense the infantilism which has prompted them; they had never forsworn the dream that our environment should meet our wishes for security without our even asking for it. However, to insist upon security, to use force to obtain it by clinging to it, is always humiliating. And even as we witness the political antics of the anti-Maastricht politicians we hear the whines of the humiliated; the extreme agoraphobic ocnophil can, in politics, be a poor creature.

Warding off our prejudices

If all Euro-sceptics and Euro-enthusiasts were as exotic as Powell and Heath, there would be a temptation to squeeze all the protagonists in the European debate into a Procrustean typological system, for Balint's typology is of a different and more persuasive order than those of Jung's extrovert and introvert or Kretchmer's schizoid and cycloid personalities, or, indeed, of Freud's erotic, narcissistic and obsessional types; all these theories of types offer descriptive rather than dynamic classifications, and, as analysts tell us, unlike Balint's types, are not really helpful in their clinical work.

The validity of Balint's theory, however, should not mislead us into believing that all can be slipped into ocnophil or philobat slots, for no one is an absolute ocnophil or philobat and few are so tyrannically governed by these traits as Heath or Powell. Nevertheless in politics, as in other walks of life, we find constant reflections of these temperamental attitudes; we speak of the ocnophilic tendency when we say someone has a sluggish mind, whose thinking is bogged down, and who clings to words, phrases, habits or ideas, and cannot let go of his particular thinking, pastime or occupation; another, with a philobatic bias, has a free flight of ideas, flits from one thing to another, is a lone wolf. In our adaptation to reality those less fixated in their attitudes may, however, glide from ocnophilic to philobatic attitudes and if the prejudice of either attitude, at a particular point, overcomes them, then, for a while, their reality-testing may become seriously deficient; for neither the fitful absolute philobat nor the ocnophil is fully justified in his picture of the world. Both are relying on faults and omissions in their testing of reality.

The perception of the European Community and, in particular, of Germany, can be extraordinarily distorted by such lapses into ocnophilic or philobatic prejudices. Too often, fear is the dominant emotion, sometimes unconscious, sometimes explicit, which prompts responses to Germany; and those responses can, according to temperament, be either phobic or counter-phobic. The phobic deals with the anxiety prompted by fear like an agoraphobic afraid to leave his homeland, while the counter-phobic, in philobatic manner, uses a manic defence to deal with his anxiety, denies the existence of any danger or, if sensing that some exists, will avoid any threatening confrontation. Obviously the typology Balint has depicted is not exclusive to the English; but just as the geography and history of *Mitteleuropa* teases out and exaggerates a pre-existing *Angst*, so Britain's history and insular geography encourage adult ways of thinking more appropriate to the primitive responses of babies first discovering the existence of a world outside themselves. When, as in this essay, we tell of the dilemmas of the Germans which make it difficult for us to live with them, so too we should explain to ourselves prejudices which we must overcome. To enjoy a genuine liaison with the Germans, we must ceaselessly monitor our own psyche as well as theirs; it takes two to tango.

PART VIII

Conclusion:
The European Community
and National Character

Two dusty professors

As we conclude our explorations, again and again the questions pursue us. Do our doubts about a living-in relationship with Germany spring from prejudices – our own and the Germans' – formed in times that are past and are now dangerously subverting the reality-based political judgements? Should we expect to experience within a cohabitation with a modern Germany quarrels that are little different in kind to those we may have with France over fishing and farming, or with Italy over failure to enforce sufficiently Community-based regulations, or will disputes, far more profound and sinister, test the relationship? Are those, like America's well-known German historian Gordon Craig, being excessively sanguine, or are they realistic when they insist that 1945 represents a caesura in German history so much sharper and more conclusive than any previous break in modern times that too much has changed in Germany ever to permit a return by the Germans to their 1930s' mental attitudes?

It is often said that the answers to these questions depend upon the weight we place upon historical memory and cultural tradition in contemporary Germany; but I do not think that the answers depend on what is usually understood as the continuities that link a people with its past. Certainly that would not apply to Germany, for what we have to assess is not only the persistence of its memories but also of its amnesias, its dreams, and its denials of the here and now. Nietzsche, with his customary piercing insight, when identifying the malady within Wagner's music, told us what he thought of the Germans: 'They are of the day before yesterday, and the day after tomorrow – they have no today.' And one is left querying whether even the cataclysmic events that have fallen upon Germany since Nietzsche's time now invalidate his judgement.

The unease and suspicion felt towards a people believed to be possessed of dangerous dreams of 'the day after tomorrow' are not confined to the insular British and to Jews still mourning their terrible losses. Those fears grip not a few of the Germans themselves. In October 1993 Günter Grass bluntly warned: 'I understand the Germans. They'll always jump from one leg to the other, weak one

249

minute, strong the next. . . . Unity has always been a disaster. . . . German unity, from Bismarck to Hitler, was the basis for Auschwitz.' And throughout continental Europe, many, in their several ways, tell of their disquietude. The author and leading journalist Giorgio Bocca spoke for a considerable body of Italian opinion when he was recently asked his view on what effect German power will have on individual European countries. He told of his feelings as he moves out of Italy and approaches the Germanic lands; he is overtaken by a mood only a little dissimilar from the one that can envelop me as, regularly, I leave my home in Tuscany and drive north to my home in Britain.

> An Italian who arrives in South Tyrol understands that behind that scenery, behind the perfect lawns, behind those stylised villages, there lies not only a different urban and rural civilisation but also a different geometry of thought, the German aspiration, the German presumption of formalised perfection, the German faith in the collective, in the *Volk*, in the condition that is the opposite of the approximate, individualistic, Catholicly pessimistic Latin concept.
>
> Since the time of the Lombards, the German world has believed that it can create Europe by dominating her militarily and economically. And today the 'march south' is repeating itself with the same directives. The impossible military domination has been replaced with a domination of currency; it is the strong German currency that will make European policy. And, as in the times of the central empires and of Nazism, the encircling of the Latin world begins with the conquest of the East of the Balkans.
>
> Should I conclude, then, that it is better that the European project fails and that 'Western' alliances be reconstructed against Germany *über Alles*? I respond, No, a little paradoxically.
>
> There is only one way to prevent the German mania for perfection from going towards other apocalyptic clashes, the last of which made Europe run the risk of disappearing. Accept the German hegemony, and try to curb it. Hell, yes, let's let them command for a while without the *Wehrmacht*. And let's hope for the best.

I doubt if a Britain, possessed of a more confident sense of nationhood than Italy, would be prepared, or should be prepared, to acquiesce in such a German hegemony and leave the rest to hope. But although our responses may be less passive, and the precipitating causes ought to be distinguished, nevertheless the different 'geometry of thought' of Germany jars no less upon British and French sensibilities than on Italian. Why this should be has been best explained by Germans themselves, sometimes in a spirit of reconciliation and sometimes in defiance. Gordon Craig has helpfully directed attention to a lecture in 1922 of the German philosopher Ernst Troeltsch who faced up to the estrangement between the German system of ideas – in politics, history and ethics – and that of the rest of Western Europe and the USA. His lecture stemmed from his view that it was an estrangement that had led to the First World War, and his analysis reminds us yet again of the German rejection of the Enlightenment, a rejection which contributed so much to the outbreak of Second World War; Troeltsch's lecture of half a century ago has a contemporary significance for it warns us against the fallacy that the differences we have with Germany are akin to those we have with our other ten partners.

Troeltsch argues that the basis of Western political thinking was the view of all men forming a single society, which Dante has called *humana civilitas*, and being governed by a common *jus naturale*; but this had never in modern times been congenial to the German mind. In England and America, the idea of Natural Law had inspired the demand for personal liberty and for the right of the people to control the leader they had themselves chosen; in France, it had become a theory of direct self-government, equality, and full participation in the control of the State. Such ideas had never taken root in Germany, largely because of the failure of the Enlightenment, and the mainstream of German philosophic thought had subsequently rejected 'the universal egalitarian ethic . . . the whole of the mathematico-mechanical spirit of science of Western Europe, and a conception of Natural Law that sought to blend utility with morality . . .'

Troeltsch was challenging a dominant German tradition, one that had emphasised the inner development of the individual and of the German nation as a unique cultural expression: he was asking the Germans to relinquish this obsession which he believed made them indifferent to the Western view that human beings and nations should seek: 'on the basis of equality and by a mere process of incessant climbing to increase the range of reason, well-being, liberty and compulsive organisation, until they attain the goal of the unity of mankind.' Because of their indifference to the Western view, they had indulged their inner world-directedness which induced them to leave the practical realities of existence, and the decisions affecting the life and well-being of ordinary people, in the control of the State.

Certainly in 1922, as subsequent events only too chasteningly revealed, Troeltsch was asking the impossible. Troeltsch, and those Germans sympathetic to his views, were playing on an uneven playing-field. Only intermittently in recent centuries has Romanticism, the *malaise allemande*, as the French label this enveloping mood, been quiescent in Germany. Romantic Germany was deaf to Troeltsch's pleas to desist from its antipathy to the Enlightenment. The Romantic movement of the eighteenth and nineteenth centuries was part of Germany's twentieth century treasury; the rationalism and systematic thinking of the eighteenth century and the Enlightenment's apotheosis of the intellect, its utilitarian prejudices, which rejected the claims of tradition and prescription in favour of efficiency and relevance, and its optimistic belief in progress – all this was alien dross. As Craig has explicated: 'The Romantics preferred the fullness and incoherence of life to the mathematical order of the *philosophes*; they turned from the prim elegance of the French garden to the tangled mysteries of the German forest.'

And in the twentieth century political romanticism endured. Contemporaneously with Troeltsch's lecture, another professor was, with far greater success, luring academic Germany still deeper into the 'tangled mysteries of the German forest'. That professor, Richard Müller-Freienfelf, was affirming that those holding Troeltsch's views should be placed in the category of thieves who would plunder Germany's heritage: 'Whoever should strive to transform Germany . . . in the sense of the West, would be trying to rob her of her best and weightiest quality, of her problematical endowment, which is the essence of her nationality.' The question must be put as to whether all such sentiments have been extirpated, or beneath the declarations of fealty to the European Community by German politicians, and among their electorates, do other passions smoulder?

Even as Craig dusts off the lecture containing Troeltsch's admonitions of three-quarters of a century ago, to explain today's Germany to his readers, so, no less in this exploration, to answer our question, I believe one must turn to the formidable and distasteful work of scholarship by that conservative and eloquent professor of æsthetics. Müller-Freienfelf's 1921 book, *The German, His Psychology and Culture*, is perhaps the most revelatory work on the German psyche published in this century. From him came no apologies for Germany's antagonisms to the Enlightenment; he went further, as he marshals his case to prove Germany's uniqueness and creativity come not only from a rejection of rationalism but from its essential opposition to the Judaeo-Christian and classical ethos of the West:

> The true German religious feelings . . . exist everywhere in Catholics as well as in Protestants. It is necessary only to strip off the foreign mask of the dogmas. . . . for in the past as well as in the present, the true German does not see his god in Jerusalem or in stone temples but rather in dark forests and beneath the infinite starry firmament.

Müller-Freienfelf's work found immediate resonances: the large first edition circulated widely throughout the 1920s and was republished in 1929. His teachings are today most 'politically incorrect' and this no doubt explains why, as in other awkward works written during the Weimar Republic, it rarely surfaces in today's Germany. But I believe we ignore him at our peril, for long before Jung was identifying the source of Germany's élan, and almost two decades before Freud was emphasising the consequences of Germany's late conversion to Christianity, Müller-Freienfelf wrote:

> The most essential fact to remember about the historical situation of Germany is that the Germans appeared on the historical scene comparatively late in the development of European culture. This has in the past exerted such a strong influence (and continues to exert it), that its importance must not be underestimated. At a time when the Mediterranean nations could look back upon a thousand years of great culture, the Germanic nations had attained a level of civilisation no higher than that of Kaffirs or other Bantu tribes when Europeans began to colonise Africa. The Germanic nations, to be sure, were a race of unbroken, youthful vitality, when they began to play a role in the history of the world; but they were, nevertheless, 'barbarians', and as a nation of primitive civilisation they collided with the strongest, most highly developed culture which the world at that time had brought forth, with Rome, the heiress of all the Mediterranean civilisations of the pre-Christian era.

Then Müller-Freienfelf mourns how this in the end meant that the Church of Rome 'supplanted the German religion'.

> In Germany itself the old gods were degraded to hobgoblins, and an oriental religion crossed with a late antique spirit was forced upon the Germans. No one has yet laid bare the tragedy resulting

from this; it has always been one-sidedly proclaimed that the achievement of forcing the youthful German nation into cloisters and churches, into confession and the stool of repentance, was great cultural progress. Unfortunately no one will ever be able to disclose the tremendous schism, which came into the German soul. No one will ever be able to portray the torments which of necessity arose when a foreign religion wrested the holy relics from the German people ... After all, what has the so-called Christendom of the Middle Ages, this bastardisation of Roman dogmatics, to do with the Nordic belief in spirits?

What purpose, it may be impatiently asked, is there in Craig today bringing out of the academic lumber of the 1920s a pompous lecture alleging fateful consequences to the hostility of Germany to the Enlightenment? And, surely, even more irrelevant, if not absurd, is my recalling an opinionated professor carrying on about Wotan and the old German gods. This is the post-*Wirtschaftswunder* world; a hard-nosed Germany where people have cultivated an extraordinary work ethic, a nation concerned with the acquisition of more and more consumer goods, a nation governed by bankers, technocrats, managers and management consultants, whose preoccupations are to maintain its standards of living in the face of recession and the need to overcome the economic and industrial problems of its eastern regions, a practical nation who restored the world of money and materialism, a nation with its feet on the ground leaving to an ineffectual minority of intellectual scholars with no political influence the asking of the question *Wohin?* – what's it all about?

Curiously, it is Müller-Freienfelf who alerts us to the consequence of the discontents which can lie behind, and indeed explain, the frenetic achievement of Germany's economic power. He asserted:

The German may be understood only if it is realised that he is dissatisfied with his own nature and that he thus concentrates all available energy on the counterbalancing of these shortcomings. The battle against oneself, the inner dissension, and the tendency resulting therefrom to develop oneself above and away from one's own disposition are essential features in the portrait of the German.

In his own vocabulary Müller-Freienfelf is describing a phenomenon which the psychoanalyst would describe as over-determination: the attempt to resist the passions which may prove overwhelming by a psychic defence mechanism which we may see in the puritan, as by work and primness he keeps at bay his deepest needs and desires. It is a brittle mechanism and in an individual it can often crack and lead to collapse. We should not take Germany's remarkable economic success at its face value, simply as a heroic and sustainable accomplishment untainted by other yearnings. The energy of present-day Germany is not fully consumed in its material triumphs; that would be to demean the potential of the German spirituality. A German without *Sehnsucht* – an almost untranslatable word, longing, yearning – would be no German at all. Only an obtuse foreigner with no personal relationship with Germans and locked into his own mind-set could challenge Müller-Freienfelf when he tells us:

> ... only those emotions may be considered typically German as are not inseparably associated with definite objects of the external world, but which refer simply to imagined vague recondite states. *Sehnsucht* is characteristically German. Yearning for home and yearning for far-off places, formless blissfulness and formless awe, indefinite bitterness, an indeterminate tenderness and enthusiasm – these are the feelings which predominate in the spiritual life of the German.

It is from these yearnings that we have the wondrous contributions of the German composers, Bach and Beethoven, Brahms and Schubert and Bruckner, all moved by a titanic opposition to a cruel fate, all conquering inner sadness by opposition to it, all the scherzos in which we may still note the dark underlying substratum from which the happy mood has wrested itself away, and which so often appear to be ghastly dances of life and death; all absolute music, permitting freedom for the love of the indefinite, the intangible, the infinite. But this *Sehnsucht* may also be expressed in a most destructive political romanticism, a yearning for the impossible and a readiness to smash to smithereens any institution or person felt to challenge or obstruct the irrational quest.

The debate that is being avoided

In the nineteenth century this romanticism ebbed and flowed. Sociologists suggest it seems to have run its course in the years 1830–48 when bourgeois self-confidence was at its height, and when the German middle class had every expectation of seizing political power as the middle classes in France had done in 1830 and as they had succeeded in doing in Britain in 1832. The failure of the Revolution of 1848 destroyed these hopes and did serious, and perhaps permanent, damage to middle-class *amour propre* and self-confidence and, in the subsequent period romantic escapism and regressive behaviour became again the order of the day. Wagner's sultry combination of eroticism and religiosity, and Karl May's exotic novels of impossible adventures, provided dream-worlds where the frustrations of the present could be overcome in the fantasy of a return to a lost world of childhood. Such escapism was relatively, but certainly not wholly, innocuous; it cleared the way for the darker aspects of romanticism when the post-First World War economic difficulties made many in the middle class fear that the bourgeois epoch and its values had ended; and Germany returned to its old resource – the forces of irrationality, violence and death which then provided a terrible ideological imperative.

Now in Western Germany, economic consideration seems, as in the 1830s, to have substantially contained the inimitable aspects of German romanticism. It has only presented itself violently in the 1970s, in the growth of terrorism and the activities of the Red Army Faction, as it had, less intemperately, in the anarchist groups within the student movements of the late sixties. But, given the history of German romanticism, we would indeed be gullible to accept that it is now permanently banished from German political life. It is a potential which must always be taken into account in our political negotiations with Germany. We know from experience, as the IRA has continued for decades to bomb our cities, how unyielding violent political romanticism can be; and how persistently an extravagant but gentler romanticism can smother all political realism. When, in 1979, I forced a referendum upon the government upon the devolution issue, and then in Wales, in rebellion against my party, successfully led the anti-devolution campaign, it was because I knew I was not then fighting over a mere administrative issue, but against the romantic nationalist movement that had become an ugly and regressive phenomenon. Politics without romanticism would indeed be impoverished, for from the political romantic often comes the vision which more practical men can fulfil. But the singular nature and history of German romanticism tells us too how misshapen some dreams can be.

To make such assertions and, indeed, to write in the mood which tempers this essay, is to invite an accusation of racialism. To present any idea of national character has become so associated with the concerted effort of Nazi Germany to adduce spurious evidence to demonstrate German superiority that there remains a fear of asserting the notions of differential group identities; and, in Britain, yielding to paranoiac reactions of many within its large black population, there has emerged a particular apprehension, resulting in an avoidance of discussion of the profound differences that exist between any peoples, including the peoples of Europe. Endless debates continue on our economic and institutional compatibility with our European partners; but usually the question of national character is dodged. It is a question not to be left to Thatcher whose affirmed beliefs, in her memoirs, about national character are but an outcrop of her vulgar chauvinism; for what remains central to the success or failure of the European Community is our capacity to acknowledge and, if necessary, to overcome the deleterious national character traits which each nation possesses. We must break the taboo which prohibits, as 'politically incorrect', the opening of a debate which alone could lead to modifications of responses that otherwise will sabotage all hopes for a more united Europe.

This is the debate that is being avoided. We camouflage our suspicions and fears of our foreign neighbours, particularly of Germany, affecting that the prolonged Maastricht debate comes from concern about the small print of the Treaty. Like vacillating and coy lovers, attracted and repelled, fearful of matrimony, we drown our deeper emotions under a torrent of words and forever postpone consummation. This dissimulation will undo us; pompous declarations of future intentions, embodied in treaties, are vain denials of the turbulent feelings which presently assail us. Our betrothal rites with our European partners are being conducted by politicians too prim to dare to be in touch with real feelings. Absurdly, dowries and financial arrangements are being endlessly discussed; but the nature of the person with whom we are to live, and our own feelings towards that person, are too embarrassing to be mentioned.

Those of us who wish to see a genuine European citizenship must not regard the national cultures of Western Europe, and particularly that of Germany, as varieties of ethnic cuisine, innocuous relics of human diversity; such a depreciation of their vigour and underestimation of their sicknesses will cheat us of our goal. Nor, as the furore over Maastricht demonstrates, should we deceive ourselves that the embarrassments that a scrutiny of national traits brings can be avoided by clamping down upon Europe an excessively rigid and comprehensive framework. Not only is there much justification in the taunts of the critics of Maastricht that the Treaty was obsolete even before it was

ratified, but, more, peeping through all the many ambiguities within
the Treaty are the embarrassments it was seeking to avoid.

Maastricht has surely taught us that we need to eschew further
grandiose architectural plans for a new European order; they are
unlikely to leave the drawing-board. If we retain our ultimate vision of
an integrated Europe, a haven of civilisation in a much-troubled world,
then modesty will become us; we are more likely to make progress if we
are ready to engage in a series of *ad hoc* and largely pragmatic, but
psychologically informed, responses to specific crises, problems and
challenges. Responses tend to evolve organically on an incremental
basis. Provided such unostentatious responses are not governed only by
national self-interest, but always steadfastly express our desire for a
Europe that is a genuine community, we will not fear to be frank with
those who are our Community partners – above all, with Germany; for
then, unlike now, continental Europe may trust us. But there can be no
trust between Germany and ourselves, as there can be no trust in
human relations, if large areas of communication are forbidden
territory.

Into that territory this essay has deliberately trespassed. Some will
regard it as an odd contribution to the European cause, believing that
such contributions can only exacerbate Anglo-German relations; but I
suspect that many young Germans whose fathers and grandfathers
failed them would think otherwise. Euro-enthusiasts may in any event
regard this essay as less than two cheers for Europe, and Euro-sceptics
regard its conclusions as equivocations. But whatever the resistances, I
believe we should not concede that the European debate should be
dominated by professional politicians who demean politics by treating
it as a branch of economics. By endeavouring to explore the German
psyche, and a little of our own, we remind our desiccated politicians
that although they are dead, we are still alive.

List of sources

Abraham, Karl, *Contributions to the Theory of Anal Character*, Hogarth Press, 1954

——, *A Short Study of the Development of the Libido*, Hogarth Press, 1954

Abse, D. W., 'The group psychology of mass madness', *Political Pyschology*, vol. 4, no. 4, 1983

——, *The Depressive Character in Depressive States and their Treatment*, ed. Vamik D. Volken, Jason Aronson, 1985

——, 'Charisma, Anomie and the Psychic Personality', address to International Congress on Social Psychiatry, August 1964

——, and Reckrey, Ruth, 'Politics and Personality', *British Journal of Social Psychiatry*, vol. 4, no. 1, 1970

Abse, L., *Private Member*, Macdonald, 1973

——, *Margaret, Daughter of Beatrice*, Jonathan Cape, 1989

Alexander, Franz, *Psychoanalysis and Social Disorganisation: the Scope of Psychoanalysis*, Basic Books, New York, 1971

Ardagh, John, *Germany and the Germans*, Penguin Books, 1991

Azrin, Nathan H., and Foxx, Richard M., *Toilet Training in Less than a Day*, Pocket Books, New York, 1974

Balint, Michael, *Thrills and Regressions*, Hogarth Press, 1959

Bankier, David, *The Germans and the Final Solution: Public Opinion under Nazism*, Blackwell, 1992

Benson, Ross, *Charles: the Untold Story*, Gollancz, 1993

Berke, Joseph H., *The Tyranny of Malice*, Summit Books, 1992

Bettelheim, Bruno, 'Individual and Mass Behaviour in Extreme Situations', *Journal of Abnormal & Social Psychology*, vol. 38, 1943

Borchardt, Knut, *Wachstum, Krisen Handlungsspielraume der Wirtschaftspolitik*, Gottingen, 1982

Brunik, Micha, *Die Tages Zeitung*, February 1993

Bullock, Alan, *Hitler – a Study in Tyranny*, Penguin Books, 1962

Burleigh, Michael and Wippermann, Wolfgang, *The Racial State – Germany 1933–1945*, Cambridge University Press, 1991

Castles, Stephen, *Here for Good: Western Europe's Ethnic Minorities*, Pluto Press, London, 1984

Chasseguet-Smirgel, Janine, 'Time's White Hair we Ruffle', *International Review of PsychoAnalysis*, p. 14,433, 1987

——, 'Reflections of a Psychoanalyst upon the Nazi Biocracy and Genocide', *International Review of Psychoanalysis*, p. 17,167, 1990

——, *The Ego Ideal*, Free Association Books, 1985

Childs, David, *Germany in the Twentieth Century*, Batsford Books, 1991

Cosgrave, Patrick, *The Lives of Enoch Powell*, Bodley Head, 1989

Craig, Gordon, *The Germans*, Penguin, 1991

Davies, A. F., *The Human Element: Three Essays in Political Psychology*, Penguin Books, Australia, 1988

Dicks, R. H. V., *The Concept of National Character*, Hutchinson, 1950

Dickinson, John K., *German and Jew – the Life and Death of Sigmund Stein*, Quadrangle Books, Chicago, 1967

Dove, Richard, *He was a German: a Biography of Ernst Toller*, Libris, 1990 (paperback ed. 1994)

Dundes, Alan, *Passing Through Customs*, University Wisconsin Press, 1987

——, *Life is like a Chicken Coop Ladder*, Columbia University Press, 1984

Eckstaedt, Anita, 'Two Complementary Cases of Identification Involving Third Reich Fathers', *International Journal of Psychoanalysis*, p. 67,317, 1986

Eickhoff, F W, 'Identification and its Vicissitudes in the Context of the Nazi Phenomenon', *International Journal of Psychoanalysis*, p. 67,33, 1986

——, 'On the Borrowed Unconscious Sense of Guilt', *International Review of Psychoanalysis*, p. 16,323, 1989

Eksteins, Modris, *Rites of Spring: the Great War and the Birth of the Modern Age*, Bantam Press, 1989

Enzensberger, Hans Magnus, 'The Great Migration', in *Krauts!*, ed. Bill Buford, Granta Publications, Winter 1992

Evans, Richard J., *In Hitler's Shadow*, I.B. Tauris, 1989

——, 'Myth of the German Psyche', the *Guardian*, 19.7.90

Frankland, Mark, in the *Observer*, 7.11.93

Freud, Sigmund, *Three Essays on the Theory of Sexuality*, Selected Edition, VII

——, *The disposition to obsessional neurosis*, SE, XII

——, *Totem and Taboo*, SE, XIII

——, *The Ego and the Id*, SE, IXX

——, *Moses and Monotheism*, New SE, XXIII

——, *Anxiety and Instinctual Life: Introductory Lectures*, SE, XXII

——, *Inhibition Symptoms and Anxiety*, SE, XX

Freud, Sigmund, and Zweig, Arnold, *The Letters of Sigmund Freud and Arnold Zweig*, Harcourt Brace & World, New York, 1970

Garton Ash, Timothy, *In Europe's Name*, Cape, 1993

Geiss, Imanuel, *The Weimar Republic between the Second and Third Reich*, Methuen, 1988

Hahn, Kurt, *The Young and the Outcome of War*, Lindsay Press, 1965

Hatch, Alden, *The Mountbattens*, W. H. Allen, 1966

Heath, Edward, in the *Sunday Times*, 1.10.90; the *Guardian*, 18.11.93

Heine, H., *The Poetry and Prose of Heinrich Heine*, Citadel Press, 1948

Hilton, James, *The Duke of Edinburgh*, Frederick Muller, 1956

Hinshelwood, R. D., *A Dictionary of Kleinian Thoughts*, Free Association Books, 1989

Hitler, Adolf, *Table Talk, 1941–1944*, Oxford University Press, 1988

Hoffman, Peter, *The War, German Society and Internal Resistance*, Methuen, 1988

Howard, Anthony, 'To the lighthouse', in the *Sunday Times*, 4.7.93

Huschka, Mabel, 'The Child's Response to Coercive Bowel Training', *Psychosomatic Medicine*, vol. 4, 1942

Jackel, Eberhard, *Germany's Way into the Second World War*, Methuen, 1988

James, Harold, *The German Slump*, Clarendon Press, 1986

Jefford, Andrew, 'Wine and National Character', in *Wine Magazine*, February 1993

Jung, Carl, *Wotan*, Neue Schweitzer Rundschau Zurich, BS 111, March 1936

——, *Essays on Contemporary Events: Reflections on Nazi Germany*, Ark Paperbacks, 1988

Kahn, Charlotte, 'The Different Ways of Being a German', *Journal of Psychohistory*, vol. 20, no. 4, 1993

Kahr, Brett, 'Sexual Molestation of Children: Historical Perspectives', *Journal of Psychohistory*, vol. 19, no. 2, 1991

Kershaw, Ian, 'Germany's Present, Germany's Past', Bithell memorial lecture, Institute of Germanic Studies, University of London, 1992

Klee, Ernst, *Persilscheine und falsche passe: wie die Kirchen den Nazis halfen*, Fischer, 1992

Knowlton, James & Cotes, Janet, (trans.), *Forever in the Shadow of Hitler*, Humanities Press, USA, 1993.

Koonz, Claudia, *Mothers in the Fatherland. Women, the Family and Nazi Politics*, Jonathan Cape, 1987

Labanyi, Peter, *Images of Fascism: a Visualisation and Æstheticisation in the Third Reich*, Methuen, 1989

Langer, Walter C., *The Mind of Adolf Hitler*, Secker & Warburg, 1973

Laplanche, J., and Pontalis, J. B., *The Language of Psychoanalysis*, Hogarth Press, 1973

Lee, Joseph J., *Policy and Performance in the German Economy, 1925–1935*, Methuen, 1989

Maccoby, Hyam, *Judas Iscariot and the Myth of Jewish Evil*, Peter Halban, 1992

Mann, Golo, *Reminiscences and Reflections*, Faber & Faber, 1990

Marsh, David, *The Bundesbank: the Bank that Rules Europe*, Heinemann, 1992

Millar, Peter, *Tomorrow Belongs to Me*, Bloomsbury, 1992

Mitscherlich, Alexander and Margarete, *The Inability to Mourn*, Grove Press Inc, New York, 1975

Mommsen, Hans, *The Breakthrough of the National Socialists as a Mass Movement in the Late Weimar Republic*, Methuen, 1989

Money-Kyrle, R., *Some Aspects of State and Character in Germany*, IUP, New York, 1951

Müller-Freienfels, Richard, *The German, his Psychology and Culture*, New Symposium Press, USA, 1936

Ostow, Mortimer, 'On Identification and the Nazi Phenomenon', *International Journal of Psychoanalysis*, p. 67,277, 1986

Overy, Richard, 'Mustered to Master the Past', in the *Observer*, 30.5.93

Payne, Robert, *Chungking Diary*, Heinemann, 1945

Peukert, Detlev J. K., *The Weimar Republic*, Allen Lane Penguin, 1991

Powell, Charles, 'Minute quo', the *Independent on Sunday*, 15.7.90

Prawer, S. S., *Heine's Jewish Comedy*, Oxford University Press, 1983

Radice, Giles, *Offshore, Britain and the European Idea*, I.B. Tauris, 1992

Raushning, Hermann, *Gespraeche mit Hitler*, Europa Verlag, New York, 1940

Rees-Mogg, William, in *The Times*, 11.11.93

Robertson, Edwin, 'The German Psyche', in *International Minds*, vol. 2, no. 2, 1990–1991

Roth, Andrew, *Enoch Powell: Tory Tribune*, London, 1970

Sagarra, Eda, *Blut und Boden: Fiction and the Tradition of Popular Reading Culture in Germany*, Methuen, 1988

Schneider, Peter, *The German Comedy*, I.B. Taurus, 1992

Schrader, Barbel, and Schebera, Jurgen, *The 'Golden' Twenties*, Yale University Press, 1990

Shawcross, William, 'Fear and Hatred in the New Germany', *Vanity Fair*, May 1993

Sontheimer, Kurt, *Weimar Culture*, Methuen, 1988

Steiner, George, *In Bluebeard's Castle*, Faber & Faber, 1971

Stern, Carola, *Ulbricht: a Political Biography*, Pall Mall Press, 1965

Stern, J. P., *Hitler, the Fuehrer and the People*, Fontana Press, 1990

Stone, Norman, in the *Sunday Times*, 2.12.90, 29.11.92; the *Guardian*, 27.6.91, 10.7.91, 9.9.91, 11.11.93; *The Times*, editorial, 2.6.93, 9.12.93

Stüdemann, Frederick, in *The European*, 14–20.1.94.

van der Vat, Dan, *Freedom Was Never Like This*, Hodder & Stoughton, 1991

Volken, Vanik D., *The Need to Have Enemies and Allies*, Jason Aronson, 1988

Warren, Richard L., *Education in Rebhausen: a German Village*, Rinehard & Winston, New York, 1967

Wasserman, Jakob, *My life as German and Jew*, Allen & Unwin, 1934

Watson, Alan, *Germans – Who are They Now?*, Thames-Methuen, 1992

Wehr, Gerhard, *Jung – a Biography*, Shambhala, 1988

Whiting, John W. M., and Child, Irvin, *Child Training and Personality: a Cross-Cultural Study*, Yale University Press, 1953

Winnicott, Donald, *The Maturation Processes and the Facilitating Environment: Studies in the Theory of Emotional Development*, Hogarth Press and The Institute of Psycho-Analysis, 1965

——, *Through Pædiatrics to Psychoanalysis*, Collected Papers, Tavistock Institute, 1958

Winslow, E. G., 'Keynes and Freud', *Social Research*, vol. 53, no. 4, Winter 1986

Yerushalmi, Yosef Hayim, 'Freud on the "historical novel"', *International Journal of Psychoanalysis*, vol. 70, pt. 3, 1989

——, *Freud's Moses – Judaism Terminable and Interminable*, Yale University Press, 1991

Index